Land Lords of the World

Land Lords of the World

JUSTICE AND PROSPERITY VS.
INJUSTICE AND POVERTY

Joseph Adam Gondek

VANTAGE PRESS
New York

Published by Vantage Press, Inc.
516 West 34th Street, New York, New York 10001

Manufactured in the United States of America
ISBN: 0-533-11957-X

Library of Congress Catalog Card No.: 96-90211

0 9 8 7 6 5 4 3 2 1

I dedicate this book to the Holy Spirit, whom I constantly invoked to guide me and give me the courage to undertake and pursue this most difficult task of trying to explain the issues underlying economic injustice and poverty and finding a solution to the problems they bring.

And to the Immaculate Heart of Mary, ever open to those who are poor, and to Saint Joseph, the patron of the ordinary citizen seeking justice and honesty in the world.

Acknowledgements and Thanks

To Anthony and Leo Frigo for graciously consenting to have me build a whole chapter on their family's microeconomics.

To Robin Stachowicz Mehrens, for the orginal, symbolic drawing for the title page and cover.

To Mr. and Mrs. Peter and Denise Paramski Maloney, for the candid photo of their firstborn son, Maxwell John.

To the many friends who "encouraged" me for five years to get it done.

To the countless "sources" recognized at the end of each chapter, including the West Iron District Library which provided me with those out-of-print.

To Vantage Press for producing a fine book.

To the Encyclopedia Britannica Corporation for their permission to use their Annals of American History and quote extensively from a masterly satire on debt.

Contents

Foreword

This book has the potential to change the world and there aren't many books about which one can make that claim.

The author, Father Joseph Gondek, my friend for the last twenty-eight years, has spent a lifetime serving the poor and needy of our society.

He knows how to work within the existing structures to make things happen. In our county he initiated a County Housing Commission, serving as its chairman for fourteen years. In that role he succeeded in bringing in $6 million of housing for low-income and elderly people. He pushed for and supported a St. Vincent De Paul center in town, to which I send all those who come looking for short-term help. He inspired his parish to sponsor both Vietnamese and Cuban families. His rectory was the first place that anyone looking for help went.

But even as he gave his life to serving, he was driven by a feeling that there was something wrong that could not ever be corrected by doing business as usual. So he studied. Not just a book or two on economics but a mountain of books. His prolonged study led him to a vision of how things might be corrected and this book is the result of that vision.

The book itself is not a condemnation of economic systems but a well-thought-out description of a very real problem and a practical, possible solution.

Everyone, even those who disagree with the conclusions or who have a different vision, ought to read it.

—Rev. Dr. John Linna
Crystal Falls, MI, April 3, 1996

Author's Note

This book is for all, yet especially for those who love their children and grandchildren, whose future is threatened with debt, taxes, and unemployment.[1]

Its primary focus is on unjust structures, not on the people who at any given moment in history may be the exponents or functionaries of the structures that have been identified by the encyclicals of the popes as the root causes of poverty. The book is a veritable and complete education in the realities of economics, not just the language and theories. It is solidly based on scholarship but presented for the general public in simple, understandable terms.

It leads to the conclusion that changing names of people occupying responsible positions in our society, be they land lords, plutocrats, elitists, democrats, republicans, or whatever else one may wish to call them, will not change anything meaningful unless the unjust structures within which they operate are permanently eliminated and replaced by ones that are honest and just. The consequences of that change contemplated in the final chapter present an unparalleled vision for the future. They follow logically from premises that are honest and just and are achievable by citizens with political will, courage, and commitment to the ideals of love for God, country, and family.

The Title: The creative use of *Land Lords* as two separate words covers a much wider range of applications than the word *landlords*, which is limited in scope.

Note

1. See Endnote for chapter 13.

Preface

Why This Book?

After reading books on economic matters for sixty years, I have still not found what I have been looking for. That book would:

1. Survey history, at least from the beginnings of industrialism, in a search for the genesis of the imperialism of money identified by the popes as the root cause of economic injustice and poverty in the world.
2. Show the continuity and growth through the centuries of international banking, as it promoted imperialism throughout the world but especially in the United States.
3. Define in a way understandable to the average person the economic terms used by the media when they report and comment on economic issues and problems.
4. Identify the cause-and-effect relationships between economic activities and structures and the principles or premises on which they are based.
5. Provide a logical, scientific, practical, and well-integrated plan for a solution of the problems spawned by the current financial and political environment.
6. Motivate and inspire well-meaning citizens to take the action necessary to make the changes required to implement the solutions.
7. Do all the above in clear, nonabrasive language within the confines of a single book.
8. **Be written in a genuine spirit of love and emphasize love, cooperation, and unity as the basis for the solution of the world's problems instead of constantly appealing to selfish national interests and dwelling on the shortcomings of nations and people.**

Over the years I have been involved in many social issues and projects and have given hundreds of talks. Those who listened have responded repeatedly that I have a way of coming to the core of the issues and foreseeing long-range consequences of current actions or plans that others do not see. Undoubtedly, my studies in the humanities and in philosophy, especially logic (the science of correct reasoning), criteriology (discernment of truth), and ontology (the study of being and reality) have helped me to recognize the cause-and-effect relationships that eventually become evident to all.

With the encouragement of others, I decided to write the book I had been searching for. Four more years of intensive reading and study produced *Land Lords of the World*. With this book I enter a highly complex territory where the acknowledged "angels of economics" fear to tread, and I offer insights and logical solutions that only a few of them have dared to suggest. I have also been encouraged by this quotation from Robert T. Kennedy:

> Each time a man stands up for an ideal, or acts to improve the lot of others, or strikes out against injustice, he sends forth a tiny ripple of hope. Those ripples build a current that can sweep down the mightiest wall of oppression and resistance.

Who Am I, the Author?

My name is Joseph Adam Gondek. I was born of immigrant Polish parents, Albert and Zofia Palka Gondek, on July 28, 1911. With our parents raising a family of eleven children on a farm during the Great Depression of 1929–33, when all they could get for potatoes was five cents a bushel and a cow sold for ten dollars, I learned what it is to be poor and hungry. Nevertheless, we were all proud and paid our taxes, trying to make it without public assistance, of which there was very little. I have seen abject poverty in countries like Mexico and Egypt and have myself not known where I would find shelter for the night.

During fifty-eight years of ministry as a Catholic priest, I have dealt with the needs, problems, and suffering of thousands of people. In my concern for social issues, I have worked with the government bureaucracy of HUD for fourteen years as chairman of the local housing commission and have witnessed the utter waste and infighting that goes on when government tries to run things that belong in the private sector or on the local level.

This work is an act of love for God, our country, and all humankind, especially the billions in need of love and compassion throughout the world. May this tiny ripple of love be multiplied millions of times with your assistance and added to that torrent of hope Kennedy wished to see.

Introduction

The Roots of Violence

On August 13, 1993, Pope John Paul II addressed a record-breaking crowd of young people and the political and business leaders of Colorado. At exactly the same time Pres. Bill Clinton, the United States Justice Department, and members of Congress were in conference in Washington, D.C. At both gatherings the concern was over the seriousness of the problems of violence and how to curb it.

The pope reaffirmed what he had been saying repeatedly in different ways throughout his stay in the city. More pointedly, he said that violence is "rooted in the human heart." There can be no solution to violence without changing human hearts. That is the biggest challenge of all. Nobody can change what is in other people's hearts but the people themselves.

There are always reasons, not excuses, for the emotions that lead people to act violently: anger at injustices and discrimination, real or imagined, political and economic oppression, fears of all kinds, feelings of hopelessness and despair.

Throughout the world unemployment is an issue that causes anxiety among nations. Other critical issues are population, immigration, emigrations, discrimination, ecology, and more. All create problems that arouse emotions in human hearts that may lead to violence.

There is an economic base at the root of all these issues. People want to live. They want to earn money to provide for themselves and their families. There are also moral factors and false perceptions involved, but these are greatly influenced by economic issues.

The Handicap of Ignorance

The first president of the United States belonged to the moneyed class. Yet George Washington admitted he did not understand finances and banking, and he appointed Alexander Hamilton to be the first secretary of the Treasury. The most unfortunate thing about that appointment was that the brilliant and clever Secretary Hamilton used his knowledge to serve his own selfish interests and those of his friends in the financial community. Still, he did not succeed in gaining much personally and eventually discovered that he had been used by financiers smarter than himself.

Other presidents have been outwitted by powerful financial interests. Woodrow Wilson was maneuvered into signing the Federal Reserve Act; toward the end of his life, he admitted that he had been deceived by the financiers. Another highly intelligent president who admitted openly at an interview that he didn't understand money was Richard Nixon.

There also have been presidents who did understand finance and used it with honesty and integrity: Thomas Jefferson, Andrew Jackson, Abraham Lincoln. They accomplished great things. Other leaders, and ordinary citizens as well, have grasped the simple truths about the functions of money; it is not the arcane subject that we are led to believe by those with vested interests in reserving that knowledge and the control of money for themselves.

Economics Is Not an Exact Science

The fact that the author is not an economist is an advantage to readers because it will allow them to become participants in the reasoning. Everything the author has to say must stand on its own evidence and on the merits and validity of his arguments and logic. The conclusions readers arrive at will be their own, and hopefully will motivate them to action.

Economics is not an exact science; there really are no definitive authorities with the "last word." There are, however, some good thinkers and writers who merit our respect. But there is also a lot of confusion. Nobody's thinking is any better than the premises it is based upon. If the premises are not sound, the thinking of the best writers cannot lead to good conclusions. Economists write mostly for other economists in technical language that average citizens seldom understand. Very few people, including our legislators and chief executives, have any clear concepts about the workings of our national economy. They rely on "experts," who vary widely among themselves, presenting a confusing picture for their employer-followers. The work and theories of major economists are respected here but not necessarily accepted, particularly when found to be based on bad premises, developed illogically, or based on erroneous scientific data or reading of history.

The Profile of This Book

We shall be looking primarily at the major economic problems that we are faced with in our country. Most of us already know what these problems are, though not all of us are fully aware of their seriousness and their implications for our society. We shall look at those aspects, but our interest will be primarily on the causes of these problems. We must identify the causes and remove them before thinking of solutions. Healing cannot begin before the bleeding stops.

A Preview of Our Method

To develop a clear understanding of economic matters, I invite readers to follow the steps we take, chapter by chapter. These truths are not at all that difficult to understand. Our method is inspired by a story and supplemented by the findings of educational psychology and of good communications practices.

The story is about an old black pastor in the early history of the southern states. He had a great reputation for effectively getting the gospel message across to people in a way that motivated them to change their lives. Asked for the secret of his success, he said: "First, I read myself full and tell 'em what I am gonna tell 'em. Next, I pray myself hot and really tell it to them like it is in every way I can. Then, I tell 'em what I done told 'em."

You may notice that the media use pretty much the same formula when they want their message to take hold. First, they will make the announcements and run previews; then they repeat the full story over and over in different ways, and finally they take polls to see how effective they have been and what points they need to reinforce. I will follow roughly the same approach in presenting my message. It will be particularly important for us to remember these procedures when we make plans to implement our citizen agendas as we travel the road to honesty and economic justice in the final chapters of this book.

A Special Personal Message to You, Dear Reader

You have gotten this far upon opening this book. Few people are interested at all in even picking up a book on economic or political issues. I congratulate you as a citizen who can make a difference for our country by becoming involved, once you have read the whole book. As you read the following *preview*, you will recognize this as an effort to follow the *method* described above. It is a look ahead at the kind of questions you will find answered here. All aboard then! for the adventure, the journey of exploration and discovery.

You Will Discover

- **How to close the gap between the rich and poor and provide a level field for both on which to play the game of our economic life.**
- **How to approach the problem of violence in our society, recognize its principle causes, and remove them.**
- **Where, how, and by whom money is created for use by the government and the country's citizens.**
- **What sovereign nation was the first to legalize the creation of money by private banks based on government debt; when, and how it happened.**
- **How the debt-based money system came to the United States.**
- **Why our sovereign nation is $5 trillion in debt and to whom.**
- **Why it is physically impossible for our government to get out of debt and eliminate deficits under our present debt-based money system without ruining the nation's economy, infrastructure, and social programs, no matter how sincere the efforts of Congress and the president.**
- **Who the Land Lords of the world are.**
- **How some nations prospered for centuries without debt.**
- **How the imperialism of money keeps nations in debt and poverty.**
- **How the same conditionalities imposed by the International Monetary Fund and World Bank on many nations are now imposed on our nation, with the same consequences.**

You Will Discover Further

- How to institute an honest, nonusurious money system first in our country and then in the world to neutralize the imperialism of money before the year 2000.
- How to balance the nation's budget, eventually amortize the nation's debt, and update its infrastructure without destroying essential social programs or raising taxes.

Land Lords of the World

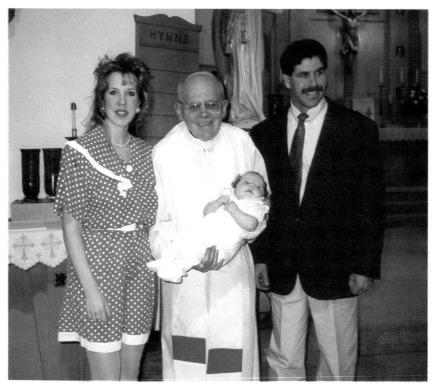

Author's human touch for Maxwell John and parents, Pete and Denise
Paramski Maloney (their first-born)

Chapter 1

Injustice, Poverty, and Associated Problems

For thousands of years, people have been oppressed by injustice and poverty. The Hebrew and Christian Scriptures and the teachings of the popes of the Roman Catholic Church witness that truth and have repeated over and over again the cries of the poor and oppressed for justice. Where there is injustice, there are people who are unjust toward others. Injustice does not exist in the abstract. It subsists in human beings who take advantage of other human beings. Clearly they do not consider themselves brothers and sisters of all in the human family. Rather, they look upon other people as objects to be used in the pursuit of their own selfish aims. The thought that we are meant to be our "brother's keeper" never seems to occur to them.

Likewise, poverty does not exist in the abstract. There is poverty because there are poor people. Jesus said, "The poor you will always have with you." That gives compassionate people an opportunity to identify with people in need and help them. But certainly the poverty that degrades the human dignity of billions on a worldwide scale, which is caused by unjust human structures in our society, is not the poverty Jesus spoke about.

Removing Unjust Structures

There are personal misfortunes that require compassion and love on the personal level and are greatly alleviated by individual effort. **But the massive and heart-rending poverty and injustices reported in the media every day can never be resolved by individuals working alone. The unjust and oppressive structures that are the primary causes of that poverty are so entrenched in our society and in its economic institutions that they must be**

1

confronted and addressed by an enormous and cooperative community effort.

Clearly and repeatedly identified by papal documents as the unjust structures preventing the development of healthy economies in most nations of the world are debt, the money system, and the international banking system, which is based and thrives upon debt. Not only do these structures prevent the development of industry and infrastructures in many nations, but they effectively choke off all indigenous efforts in that direction. Subsequent chapters will define more fully what these financial structures are and how they relate to poverty.

Churches and relief organizations repeatedly have called for cooperative efforts to remove the causes of institutionalized and widespread injustice and poverty by teaching and promoting respect for the dignity of every human being. They keep calling for the justice that would enable every person to live a life in keeping with that dignity. They have helped to educate and civilize whole nations. The generosity of all the members of these great institutions, which have helped in crises and in removing pockets of poverty around the world, are well-recognized and outstanding. But all this effort and compassion are nowhere close to a solution to worldwide poverty and injustice.

The Power of the Citizens

The best the churches can do, besides localized charitable work, is to continue keeping society aware of the seriousness of the problems associated with poverty and of their impact on the moral and spiritual life of people, and to keep reminding us of our responsibility to cooperate on a wider community level to remove the causes of poverty. Pope John Paul II speaks at length and with great emphasis about the need for such cooperation in the encyclical *Centesimus Annus (One Hundredth Year)*, issued May 1, 1991.

United and organized in a giant cooperative effort, the citizens of every nation have the power to change unjust and oppressive economic principles and structures. Some nations may need a little help with infrastructures and education from the larger industrial nations at the beginning. But, in general, based on the experiences of many nations, people prefer to provide for themselves and their families within their own nation, given honest financial structures. How this difficult task may be accomplished is discussed in the final chapters of this book.

Implications of Poverty

There is no one simple definition of poverty that serves all purposes, conditions, and circumstances. There are many problems associated with economic poverty. The decline of moral and spiritual values in our family life and in society at large, while caused to a large extent by affluence and materialism, is also exacerbated by abject poverty. Poor education and the inadequate knowledge citizens have of economic issues are other forms of poverty.

Hopelessness and the frustrations that result from people's inability to find adequate employment in order to support their families and a reasonable future are especially dangerous forms of poverty. As Pope John Paul II noted in Denver, they lead to violence or inertia. Poverty of values both contributes to material poverty and is in turn affected adversely by it.

The Principal Root Cause of poverty and oppression is pointed out by Pope Pius XI in the encyclical *Quadragesimo Anno* (*On Reconstructing the Social Order*) as the international imperialism of money. That is the ultimate rejection of love in the economic life of nations.[1]

Government Help

The government could tax its citizens for poverty programs to the point of plunder and still only temporarily address people's material needs. Infusing more money into poverty programs and thus adding to the national debt would only further institutionalize poverty and dependence. The government's true function is not so much to take care of people's needs in a paternalistic and bureaucratic fashion as to provide the honest and just financial structures that serve the common good rather than just privileged institutions. It can go a long way toward virtually eliminating poverty by removing the structures that prevent able-bodied citizens from obtaining gainful employment and themselves rising from poverty with a sense of personal pride and accomplishment.

A Call for Change

There are millions of people in our country who recognize that "something has to change." But not many, including our most well-intentioned leaders, know exactly what needs to be changed. Significant changes that will make the difference between poverty and adequate self-support for all citizens call for radical changes in our economic structures. Those changes will be as radical as honesty and justice are radical to our current economic environment.

The Answer to Poverty and Injustice

The more that intelligent people capable of thinking beyond material values and self-interest reflect on it with open minds, the more likely they are to conclude that the only power that will bring an end to injustice and poverty in the world is presented in Scripture:

> If I give everything I have to feed the poor . . . but have not love, I gain nothing. . . . Love never fails (1 Cor. 13:3, 8).

It is love that will help us to see the dignity of every human being. Love will help us see hunger, homelessness, destitution, and poverty as unworthy of that dignity. Love will free our minds of prejudice and open them to truth and knowledge wherever we find it. Love will spur us to look for the root causes of poverty, and love will make us learn all we can about them. Love will change our own attitudes toward material possessions and wasteful lifestyles. Love, if they permit it to enter their lives, will change the hearts of the greedy. Love, if they permit it, will change the hearts of the wealthy and powerful and dispose them to use their power and wealth for the common good. Love will motivate those in whose minds and hearts it dwells to take the actions necessary to change the dishonest structures. Love will not permit us to remain ignorant about the meaning of money and the way it encourages imperialism and becomes a root cause of poverty. Love will help alleviate other poverty than the material. Love will not fear criticism, opposition, and ridicule. Love will reverse our international relations and policies that promote genocide and plunder of nations by the imperialism of money, and change them to those that promote development that will bring peace and prosperity to nations. Indeed, love *can* prevail over all other forces lesser than itself, and it *will*, if put into action.

Love That Surpasses Human Love

The Letter to the Corinthians tells us that the love powerful enough to accomplish in us all we ask of it is a gift. We need to ask the Creator, who is supreme Love, for this gift. That statement presupposes we have a relationship with the Creator. If we do not, we live with a serious poverty, one that leaves us at a great disadvantage, unable to make full use of the power of love.

Summary

The great Russian novelist Fyodor Dostoyevski provides the closing summary for this chapter:

At the sight of human sin, you stand perplexed: should you combat it by force or by humble love? Always decide, "I will combat it with humble love." If you make up your mind about that once and for all, you can conquer the whole world. Loving humility is an awesome force; it is the strongest of all things and there is nothing like it.

Note

1. For a detailed discussion of this subject, see Appendix I, where you will find a summary of the encyclical *Progressio Populorum* (*On the Development of Nations*). There Pope Paul VI defines and explains *imperialism* more fully.

Chapter 2
The Gap between the Rich and the Poor

There *are* on the world scene people who are openly called "the elite" by the media. They are the big bankers, industrialists, monopolists, shapers and shakers of society and world events. Most, if not all, are millionaires or billionaires. Some of them, like the Rothschilds, trace their family roots back several hundred years.

Many of these people actually believe that they are destined to redesign society. There is no question but that some of them have goals that are praiseworthy, but they all have this in common: they want the privilege of creating and controlling the money systems of the nations, because that gives them the power to control and dictate politics and policies and tailor the world to their own pattern.

Second, the elite have no misgivings about their own importance. As secretary of state under the Ford administration Henry A. Kissinger said, quite seriously: "It's an awful feeling to get up in the morning and know that the destiny of the whole world rests on your shoulders and the decisions you make."

Third, while at times there may be disagreement among the elite, in general they come to each other's support when their privileged position is threatened; then as during their campaign to get the Federal Reserve Act passed during and prior to the Wilson administration, apparent disagreement is contrived for the purpose of deceiving the ignorant public. Wall Street bankers feigned opposition to the Act, whereas they were the ones who helped design the Act in the first place. Their supposed opposition moved people who opposed "Wall Street" to encourage their congressmen to vote for the Act.

The fourth area in which the elite agree is that the end justifies the means. It doesn't matter how we get what we want, so long as we get it. Did we see something like this in action when President Clinton got NAFTA approved?

The elite, then, are the land lords of the world. That is what they want to be forever, and they will do their utmost, no holds barred, to keep anybody from taking that privilege from them. The best estimates available place the number of the elite at about three thousand families worldwide. Naturally, they have many followers, people whom they may reward generously for their support or just use and discard.

We citizens, the tenants of the elite, don't wish any kind of personal harm. But with over two billion people of this world going to bed hungry every night, many believe the time has come for the land lords of the world to relinquish their hold on our economic destinies and for us to help them do it.

We must recognize that the above statement is innocuous and meaningless unless we are ready to flex the muscles of our wills and restore the power over the economies of nations to legislative bodies that will use it for the common good instead of for the profits of the privileged few. We must do that honestly and charitably. We cannot subscribe to the statement that our worthy end can justify injustice, deceit, or violence on our part as a means to the attainment of our goal.

Just what power do we have, what muscle must we flex? The power of the many is not the almost unlimited power of money that the land lords have. Yet that is the power that we must eventually restore to the government of the nations. Otherwise, the land lords will continue to use it to draw all wealth that we create to their own use. The following chapters on money will show how they do this.

The only powers citizens really have are those of numbers and knowledge. And the power of prayer. Prayer will assist us and strengthen us, but it alone will not do the job. We need to use the natural powers Providence has given us, our intelligence and knowledge and our numbers, and to organize into a new political party. Prayer alone cannot be a substitute for involvement. Specifics for that involvement will be found in the concluding chapters.

Papal Insights

Pope Leo XIII called attention to the gap between the elite and the many for the first time in his papacy in the encyclical *Rerum Novarum* ("On the Condition of the Working Class"), published May 15, 1891. He identified the part played by money and banking in the impoverishment of the working classes:

7

The mischief has been increased by rapacious usury, which, although more than once condemned by the Church, is nevertheless, under a different guise, but with the like injustice, still practiced by covetous and grasping men. To this must be added . . . the concentration of so many branches of trade in the hands of a few individuals; so that a small number of very rich men have been able to lay upon the teeming masses of the laboring poor a yoke a little better than that of slavery itself (no. 2).

Pope Pius XI, in the 1931 encyclical *Quadragesimo Anno* (*On Reconstructing the Social Order*), noted that even though some improvements had been made in other ways, the gap between the elite and the many had not narrowed in the forty years since *Rerum Novarum*; in fact, the gap had continued to widen.

The continuing growth of the gap is an indisputable fact. It is featured in headlines and news stories. The popes have been teaching us that to remove economic injustice and the ever-widening gap between the rich and the poor, we have the obligation to remove the unjust structures that cause that gap. In a political structure like the United States, this means that the people must organize and cooperate for effective political action.

The Root Causes of the Gap

Why is wealth increasingly concentrated in the hands of the few while poverty and deprivation extend to ever-increasing numbers of people throughout the world? What is that mysterious factor or evil structure that seems to have eluded our leaders for over a hundred years? Pope John Paul II, in the 1991 encyclical *Centesimus Annus* (*One Hundredth Year*), speaks of the need for a stable currency as a condition necessary for healthy economic growth. The major evil structure he identifies is our money and debt systems. He leaves the subject for others to explore and examine in greater detail.

We saw in the previous chapter that Pope Pius XI pointed out the root cause of poverty and oppression as the "international imperialism of money." In the encyclical *Populorum Progressio* (*On the Development of Nations*), published March 26, 1967, Paul VI explained that the new industrialism, while good in itself, provided the occasion for certain "pernicious economic concepts to grow up along with it" and provided the environment for that imperialism (no. 26).

The Secret of the Elite

From the megabankers' point of view, the combination of debt-based money, fractional reserves, and usurious interest is the key to immense riches and power. But this key to untold wealth by the few opens the door to exploiting the great masses of people and channeling the wealth they create into the hands of the few almost as fast as it is produced. Money is a claim on wealth, as we shall see in chapter 5. If we have the privilege or power to create money, we have the power to claim and channel the wealth of the world to ourselves. That is how the few have been able to become the land lords of the world. Economists accepting this three-pronged key as a legitimate tool for use in banking and money creation will never find a just solution to our economic problems; it is used, rather, to create them.

The economic power this key gives the elite is so great and so extensive that they are virtually in control of all governments throughout the world. Therefore any government edict will inevitably favor their interests. The history of the United States from colonial times provides abundant proof for that statement. Sometimes the elite have had to fight to maintain their privileged position, but with their power over the creation of money, they have always won in the end.

Chapter 3
Microeconomics

Production, wealth, exchange economy, money, banking, fractional reserve, honest money, dishonest money, usury, interest, inflation, taxes, debits, credits, and legitimate sources of money and credit —how much does the average citizen know about those concepts commonly used in a discussion of economics? The term *macro*economics refers to the total economy of a nation or of the world. *Micro*economics is the economy we practice in our own home, company, or community.

Before we can identify and understand the forces, structures, and principles that affect the total economy, we must try to identify them and understand how they function on a local or micro level. To do so, we will explore the fortunes of one company and how they affect the community where it does business. Then we can apply what we learn to the wider macroeconomy of the nation.

It is logical and valid to conclude that whatever effects we find coming from a particular cause on the local level, the same causes will have identical effects on the national level, multiplied many times both as to degree and extent, with much greater implications for the total economy. This will be true whether the effects are positive or negative, whether they are conducive to a healthy and prosperous economy or contribute to injustice and impoverishment of both individuals and communities. In chapter 5 we will see examples in practice of how the consequences of certain causes as presented here are greatly expanded and intensified as the size of the economy increases.

The Frigo Brothers Corporation

Years ago I had the good fortune of being a friend of an Italian immigrant who started a family business making specialty cheeses. Frigo Brothers cheeses were well known throughout the country all the way from New York to Iron Mountain, Michigan, where the head office was located, and beyond. Pasquale Frigo, the entrepreneur, came from Italy with a good education in business and economics and was very eloquent when speaking about these two subjects.

One day when speaking about the causes of depression and business failures, he said to me, "We are not worried about depression in our family. We have a million pounds of cheese in our warehouses. We take care of the cheese, and the cheese will take care of us."

The cheese factories, the whole business, the stock of cheese in its warehouses, the good will created in the marketplace, the investment in the enterprise, all represent the total *capital and assets* of the Frigo family enterprise doing business with the public.

Let's say that I am a dairy farmer, a producer of the original raw product used by the cheese factory. It has taken a lot of work and management on my part and that of my employees to build up an efficient and productive herd of dairy cattle. Every night and morning, we have to feed and milk the herd, then cool and store the milk in a regulation stainless steel tank until the Frigo Brothers truck picks it up to bring to the factory. Daily production is about 625 gallons (five thousands pounds) a day. The cheese factory will use this to make five hundred pounds of cheese and other byproducts. But Frigo Brothers will give me *credit* on their books for what amounts to four hundred pounds of cheese as my return on my investment in the farm and herd and to offset my *costs of production*—labor, feed, taxes, insurance, and so on.

But what would I do with four hundred pounds of cheese for each delivery of milk? So I ask the company, and it gladly obliges, to give me that credit in ten-pound *receipts, certificates, or bills of credit*, forty such receipts for each shipment, redeemable by bearer. This means that I can use these receipts in exchange for other goods I need. Any other holder of any number of these certificates can do likewise until they are finally honored by the cheese plant, no matter who presents them for redemption, by the actual delivery of ten pounds of cheese for each certificate.

In other words, my original *earned credit* has become money, *a medium of exchange*. I can use these bills for trading within the community, or I can save them, knowing that they are always redeemable at the plant for ten pounds of cheese each. I'll have cheese for my family to last a lifetime. Here, then, we have a rudimentary but sound and stable money system backed by honest productive labor and business. I need not be afraid that this money will lose its value so long as the corporation is conducting an honest business. There will be no inflation to depreciate the value of this money because no bills of credit

11

are issued unless there are ten pounds of cheese in stock for each bill. No bearer of these bills will receive any less value in cheese than ten pounds. This is stable, honest money. Besides being receipts for value received, the bills are also *claims* on the same value. They are all in units of ten pounds of cheese. Production and services of value have been *divided into practical units*. This is what money is supposed to be.

If I have enough of these certificates I can lend them to some *entrepreneur* who may want to start a pizza place or some other enterprise using cheese, or any other business for that matter, because at least in this community they can be exchanged for any other goods or services. This could be either a *loan* for an agreed-upon *interest* or an *investment* in the new business, sharing in the risks and hoped-for profits, maybe also in the management.

I get 40 bills of credit for each day's production. So does each of the other 499 dairy farmers in the community served by this factory. To keep the analogy simple, let us assume that each produces an equal amount of milk and each receives 40 of the same kind of bills of credit, each entitling the bearer to ten pounds of cheese at the Frigo Brothers plant. This means that every day the corporation issues 20,000 bills of credit, or 600,000 every month. They represent the *liability* of the corporation to honor each bill with the delivery of ten pounds of cheese when presented by the bearer.

But man cannot live on cheese alone. These farmers have many other needs. They use the bills of credit freely in the community as a *medium of exchange* for other goods and services. The bills are accepted because the corporation is part of the community, provides employment for many of its residents, and honors its commitments. So whether every person cares for cheese or not, everybody knows that eventually there will be bearers of the bills who use cheese and will redeem them at the corporation plant. So everybody in the community accepts these bills as money in an *exchange economy*. Even outside of the community there are people who accept these bills as money, especially if they like cheese. They know that this is *honest money* because it is backed up by *value* produced by the corporation and farmers. This is money, based on a *commodity* produced within this community of farmers, namely cheese. It is one step above a *barter economy*.

Other peoples around the world, including early American colonists, used other commodities as a base for their money as they moved into exchange economies. The merchants who entered international trade in the centuries of what Adam Smith in *Wealth of the Nations* called "mercantilism," settled upon and promoted the commodities of gold and silver as money. The trouble with using any commodity as a base for money, especially gold and silver, is that it is easy for shrewd and clever people to gain a *monopoly ownership and control* of that commodity and therefore of the money system based on it. Having control of such a money system gives them the power to control the economy of the whole nation.

Thus far in this analogy we have presented the concept of money as an honest medium of exchange and a stable storage of wealth, as a receipt for value given and a claim on the same value to be called for in the future. It is honest money because there is real and honest value backing it. These are the ABCs of good and honest economics.

But this is *not* the kind of money we have in our society today, with few exceptions. Our current money system has many new ideas in it, some of them advantageous, making it easier for people to use money. Unfortunately other ideas make it easier for a few people to become very wealthy at the expense of the rest of the citizens, many of whom end up in poverty. Subsequent chapters will develop these concepts further.

The Frigo Brothers Story Continues

Let us project the Frigo Brothers story into the future to see what else we can learn from the microeconomy of this small community. Let's say the family cheese business has been conducted honestly and in a businesslike way for several years. It has prospered and the community has thrived along with it, using the bills of credit as its money to move goods and services in trade. There were now twenty-five million bills in circulation.

It so happened, as it often does whenever money is involved, that a couple of persons who were less concerned with honesty than with getting rich contrived to find an easier way to cash in on the thriving economy of this community than by starting a productive business. They did not own a cheese factory to compete with Frigo Brothers, but they were very adept with a printing press. They decided to counterfeit the bills that were in circulation as money. They did such a good job that their receipts could not be distinguished from the original ones. Gradually they put this money into circulation. They did it by lending their "dishonest bills" to people in the community.

There was now more money in the community, and the economy started to heat up. Money was lent freely because there was plenty of it, so more people borrowed the bills of credit from these "bankers" to start new businesses. Services expanded. Everybody was happy. More and more people were coming to Frigo Brothers with their receipts. Each was a claim on ten pounds of cheese, as well as on anything else in the exchange economy of the community.

The company, as an honest operation, honored them all, not knowing that many of these bills were counterfeit, not backed up by production of value. They were claims, but they never were receipts. Soon the family realized that something strange was happening. It was rapidly depleting not only its current production of cheese but its inventory as well.

The company's board of directors was in a predicament, bordering on panic. This had never happened before. The board realized that if the company continued to redeem all the receipts coming in, the business would be ruined and it would have to close the plant. So the board decided to stave off that prospect as best it could. It leveled with the public by explaining that what was happening was an unusual situation that it did not fully understand. The board then announced that in order to save the business, the company must now ask for two bills for each delivery of ten pounds of cheese. This would be in effect until the situation cleared up or a better solution was found. This is *inflation*, first of all, of the *money supply*, which was expanded by people who created claims on what somebody else would produce. These people who *counterfeited* new claims did not bring any milk to be processed by the company into cheese with which to redeem them. Of course, this was stealing, depleting the warehouses without putting anything in them. It forced the company to ask for two claims for each ten pounds it tried to deliver.

This was *price inflation*, which soon spread to the rest of the economy. The issue of money unsupported by value is the principle cause of *inflation*. In a nation's macroeconomy, there can be other temporary shortages for other reasons. The people of the community, however, did not understand what was happening, and did not accept the company's explanation. Instead, they blamed the company for being greedy and raising prices. Fear took over and people redeemed their bills even at the higher price, making matters worse. So the company had to raise the price again and again. Eventually the business went *bankrupt*, of course, and the plant had to close.

Now the farmers had no market for their milk, and there was no one to redeem the remaining certificates. The group that was out for fast and easy money kept out of the public view. In the end, however, even they found their money had no value. The microeconomy of this community was now in a *depression*.

This is an authentic presentation of what happens in the macro-economy of a nation, but on a bigger scale. The causes today are more sophisticated, but the effects are the same. The results are more devastating when they affect a whole nation.

Principles of Economics the Story Helps Us Understand

1. The exchange of wealth, goods, and services is the basis of all economics.
2. Money is the medium of exchange in any economy that has developed beyond the barter stage.
3. Money is therefore a crucial element in the economy of any nation. The health of its economy is very much dependent on the honesty of its money. Anything a community chooses to use as a symbol of the value of its wealth, goods, and services that can be divided into convenient units for use in the exchange of those goods can be used as money.
4. As a symbol of the value of goods or services, money can serve several functions. It can be a receipt for value received, and in the hands of its bearer a claim on such value. It can provide a storage of value saved for future use *if the unit has a stable value maintained by the issuing authority*. It can also be a credit for future production of value.
5. Whatever other function money may have in a given case, it is always a claim on goods or other wealth. As such, the issue of money by an individual or corporation that does not add value to the economy will always loot the wealth created by others and result in impoverishing the producers and in enriching the issuers of the money.
6. An adequate amount of money in a nation promotes a prosperous economy.
7. Very important is the principle that the amount of money in circulation must be in balance with actual economic goods in existence or at least in committed and scheduled production, so that there may be stable value for all the money or bills of credit issued. An excess of money in proportion to the exchangeable goods and services available will cause inflation. Too little money in the economy will fail to move goods and make the economy sluggish or bring on

15

a recession. In any nation this balance must be maintained in a professional manner. (How this can be done is treated in chapter 21.)

8. Money and credit should never be created by private individuals who have no economic goods to give it value. In our example we saw that this amounts to stealing, causes cycles of inflation and depression, and distorts the economy.

9. The difference between honest money and dishonest money is not obvious; looking at it doesn't reveal which is which. We know money is honest or not by knowing how we got it.

Chapter 4
Honest! This Is Money

Most people have no idea what money really is, how it comes into being, how it affects problems, where it comes from, what it's supposed to do in a nation's economy, how it happens that government debt becomes the nation's money, why the government has to borrow, or where the people it borrows from get it.

Knowledge of Money Is Indispensable

Because money is of such paramount importance in an exchange economy and involved in all our economic and social problems, we will devote a lot of space to developing a good understanding of the meaning and nature of money. This will be done gradually, moving from simpler to more complex treatments out of regard for the average citizen, who has been taught that this subject is beyond his or her capacity and must better be left to the "experts." These experts are naturally the great financiers, and their coterie of economists who serve them well with their many theories. This leaves the average citizen confused and afraid to learn the truth about this important subject.

Even most of our leaders, legislators, and highest executives have not learned the basics about money. This neglect makes them incapable either of understanding the economic problems that should be their concern or of coming up with any effective solutions. The most they can talk about is temporary palliatives.

Looking back at history and recalling the significant statements made by the "banking fraternity," as its members call themselves, we recognize that they have revealed their deep and very practical understanding of the nature of money and its many functions. They are the real authorities. Money is the center of their lives. They are the people who understand its true nature and how to use it to their own advantage. They, rather than the theoretical writers and proponents of various ideologies, are the practical experts who will be our teachers.

But in studying what the members of the "banking fraternity" said and did about money at various stages of financial history, we also learn of their ambitions and efforts, often devious and deceitful, to acquire the power to create and control the money systems of nations.

The Facts about Honest Money

You give up your time and energy to some productive enterprise. If you are working for a daily or weekly wage, you give up so many hours of your time, and so much of your physical and mental energy, in the production of something useful or valuable to society. Society acknowledges your contribution by giving you a *receipt* or some other form of *credit* for your services. This receipt in turn gives you a *claim* that entitles you or any other holder in a developed exchange economy to receive somebody else's contribution. This receipt or claim is also a promise assuring you that you will receive a value reasonably close to the value you contributed to society. This is the function of honest money.

But it is only society, represented by its government, that has the sovereign power to *tax* its citizens and oblige them to create value that will assure the holders of these receipts that they will be honored with delivery of value. This sovereign function of government is especially important when we speak of credit for *future* production. Both the receipts or credits received for value already in existence and the credit issued to enable future production serve as honest money, so long as the credit is issued by the community's government.

This definition of money has been the perception of the meaning of money by honest people through the ages. This understanding of money has been officially defined and acknowledged in England in the "Mixt Money Case Decision."[1]

People have always expected to receive value in return for their services to society; the money they earn is a claim to that value. However, this does *not* explain money as it exists today in the economies of almost all the nations of the world. Over 90 percent of all money today is not honest money at its point of origin. The money we in the United States have today, for example, has been created by the Federal Reserve banking system and is based on debt, not on production or

18

other wealth. It is a claim that has never been a receipt, because no value has been produced by the system.

It's like the banking system coming to pot luck suppers again and again without ever bringing a dish. Naturally, there will be less food for the rest of the people coming for supper and bringing dishes to share. This is what our present debt-based money system is doing to the nation's economy. It is presenting more plates (claims) for food than there is food on the table (wealth in the economy). Everybody gets smaller portions, while some people take something for nothing. If this sounds like the counterfeiting described in the Frigo Brothers story, it is. Private creation of money has allowed some people to become land lords of the world. It is the major cause of inflation.

In early American history, the power of creating money was exercised by the individual sovereign colonies, although not without interference from England (as we shall see in the chapter on that subject). To become states in the new nation, the colonies surrendered that power to the new government for the sake of unity, a truly patriotic gesture. It was a consolidation of their individual rights to be used now by the Congress of the new sovereign nation.

To assure that this would be done, the founders of the country embodied that provision in the Constitution: "The Congress shall have power . . . to coin money, regulate the value thereof, and of foreign coin, and to fix the standard of weights and measures" (Article I, Section 8, Clause 5). Clause 6 adds: "To provide for the punishment of counterfeiting the securities and current coin of the United States." And Section 10 of the same article confirms the fact that the states had relinquished the exercise of sovereignty along with the power to create money by forbidding them to continue to use that power. Clause 1 says, "No State shall . . . coin money; emit bills of credit." For any state to coin or issue bills of credit would be counterfeiting, punishable by the provisions of Section 8, Clause 6.

If coining money and issuing bills of credits by the states are unconstitutional and forbidden, how can it be constitutional for a private banking corporation to do so? It was a foregone conclusion that private corporations were excluded by that clause. If states issuing bills of credit would be counterfeiting, private corporations creating them would clearly be. But Congress has been maneuvered into just such a clearly unconstitutional surrender of this sovereign power to private banking interests.

These private banking interests now create our credit money, but they do not have the taxing authority necessary to maintain its value.

Nor do they have anything of value to give for those promises to holders. That is not honest, but it is the only money we have now. The land lords of the world manipulate the money supply as they create it, thus rocking the whole economy of a nation back and forth between depression and inflation. Periodically they shake out for themselves the value created by the productive sectors during prosperous times by contracting the money supply, causing a depression. A depression enables them to pick up the wealth by foreclosures with subsequent purchases at bargain prices, for their own gain. This procedure gives them more and more power over the citizens and widens the gap between the rich and the poor.

Thus the private banking interests regulate the value of the dollar instead of Congress. The dollar now will buy less than twenty-nine cents worth of goods and services at 1972 prices. This is not just exploitation but plunder, as some of their own people admit in their more humane moments. Instead of condemning the land lords of the world, most of whom have a stake in perpetuating the system, we invite them to admit its dishonest and exploitive nature and the need for changing it into an honest one. They have inherited traditions and a mentality whose time should end. Our appeal is to the innate compassion of human beings for whom love of their fellows is still a basic value.

Certainly it is not our intention to point the finger at the small local community bankers. They are trying to serve their communities within a system of faulty and unjust fractional reserve structures. Of course they do reap the gains for themselves that go with the system.

Money Is Essential to an Exchange Economy

Anything that is convenient and can be divided and/or counted so that a definite value can be placed on the fruits of production or services rendered can be used as honest money, so long as certain conditions are met. It can be a piece of metal like copper, silver, or gold; individual pearls, diamonds, or clamshells; or a piece of paper, as first used by the Chinese. The thing used need not have any intrinsic value. If it does, it may have a commodity value in addition to its value as money. The commodity value and the money value are seldom the same. Ninety-nine percent of the money used in the American exchange economy has been pieces of paper, either personal and business checks or Federal Reserve notes, with different figures on them counting the values in terms of dollars and cents. Now we are learning that even paper is not necessary. Billions of dollars are transferred electronically across the oceans or by satellite every day. Only the figures represent the debits and credits involved in the transactions. This could all be honest money if certain indispensable conditions are met.[2]

The Power of Money

In the history of humankind, there have always been people with a lust for power over others, people who wanted to be land lords, with tenants working for them. The historical chapters about the origin of our debt-based money system and about money in the thirteen colonies give us some idea of how the power struggle has been going on for centuries. This struggle has grown in intensity and scope with the increased opportunities that present themselves with the growth and development of new nations and civilizations.

The quickest and most efficient way to gain power over others and become a land lord of the world is to gain control of their means of sustenance, the production of goods, of their very livelihood. This is done by creating money as claims on what the "tenants" earn. That money entitles its bearers to take from the economy. If the money is not at the same time a receipt for something of value added to the economy, it will always impoverish those who produce the value.

With money one gains control over economic goods—their production, distribution—and services, and consequently over the people dependent on those goods and services. Those who create debt-based money[3] gain and exercise that control by creating credit for buyouts and monopolies and other so-called investments. But there is more. There is also the power to control the media and public opinion.

The Land Lords of the World Control Public Opinion

Great as is their power over the economy of a nation, the power wielded by all the land lords of the world over public opinion exerts an influence on all other areas of a nation's life. Besides the financial elite, the major industrialists, politicians, leaders of nations, special interests and ideologists, the directors and anchor people of the major media also participate as molders of public opinion. By means of the media owned by them and at their service, the land lords control virtually everything that goes on in the world. Wars are declared, sanctions imposed, presidents and legislators elected or deposed, laws enacted or repealed, secularism imposed on our society and into the education of our youth, innocent people unjustly imprisoned, aberrant sexuality and violence promoted. All this is happening to suit the agenda of the land lords of the world.

Baron Meyer Amschel Rothschild, founder of the international banking house of Rothschild, in a letter dated June 25, 1863, to induce his banker friends to vote for the Bank Act of 1863, wrote, "Permit me to control the money of a nation, and I care not who makes its laws."[4] The awesome power over the economy and of public opinion in the hands of the land lords of the world presents the citizens of every nation with an almost invincible obstacle to a victory over unjust and immoral structures in society.

Abraham Lincoln learned the hard way that "public opinion is everything. With it nothing can fail; without it, nothing can succeed." Those are his words after he failed to get the support of Congress in his struggle for financial reform in 1863.

Molding Public Opinion

Newspapers, periodicals, and electronic media are primarily news-reporting businesses that today are highly technical and sophisticated operations. In general, they try to be accurate in their reporting of events and activities in all areas in which they believe their readers might be interested. Their primary objectives are to attract as many readers as possible; to serve the ideologies or agendas of their editors, publishers, and advertisers; and to be profitable businesses for their investors.

All the media are effective vehicles of information and are used for molding public opinion and directing it toward certain objectives, some praiseworthy, others not. There is almost always a variety of material designed to serve the interests of the readers as well as of the editors.

Some media have a reputation for being more objective than others. For example, in the opinion of the author, the reporting in the *Wall Street Journal* is generally dependable, its articles and news stories are done in depth, and its editorials are thought-provoking. This does not mean, of course, that it reports everything or that it does not serve the interests of Wall Street. It does. When it comes to financial news, such as the Orange County derivatives debacle, or bank profits, or the constantly changing movements of the Federal Reserve Board chairman, the news is factual and credible. The *slant* on the news is that the loss was due to the investors' bad judgment.

It is not the purpose of the author to castigate or condemn the media or any other of the many institutions mentioned in this book. But facts must be presented in order to bring a message. The purpose is to help the average reader who depends on the media for all of his or her information to be alert to some of the strategies used to mold public opinion and thus be able to distinguish propaganda from bona fide news reporting.

What is said in this chapter about the media is incidental to the chapter's major purpose, which is to show the power of money over the molding of public opinion. Problems with the media arise when the major news services and networks (the "establishment" press) must serve the policies and directives of their owners and investors—the land lords who create and control money.

Here are a few instances that show how the media are forced by their owners to manipulate public opinion for the purposes of the land lords rather than the common good:

1. History books used in schools have been revised to withhold truth and information from the public that it needs to understand how the financial interests have worked throughout American history to control the nation.

2. After 1913, critical references or information about the Federal Reserve money system and its operations that would endanger private money creation or the use of fractional reserve banking have simply not been permitted to any significant extent. Such "protective" action was requested by Paul Warburg, the chief architect of the Federal Reserve system.

3. When politicians particularly vocal in trying to change or even amend the existing system, or call for accountability or a report of any kind from the "independent" Federal Reserve Board, are up for election or reelection, millions of dollars will be thrown in for the election of the "politically correct" opponents. Some great legislators have lost office that way.

   The Bilderbergers[5] meeting in 1991 in Baden-Baden, Germany, picked Bill Clinton as the nominee for American president. In 1995, in a meeting at Burgenstock, Switzerland, David Rockefeller said, "Never, not once, has Bill disappointed us." Another person in the group said, "We have to do something to save him." And Henry Kissinger chimed in, "Whatever the price . . ." The man they are afraid of is Pat Buchanan; they will do everything to stop him from being nominated.

American journalists were at the meeting: Peter Jennings, ABC's anchor; Thomas Friedman of the *New York Times*; Peter Kann of the *Wall Street Journal*. Yet the citizens never heard anything about this meeting from the network media. Why? A Swiss journalist managed to penetrate the meeting for the Swiss paper *Basler Zeitung*, which carried the story in its June 9, 1995, edition (as did many other European papers). James P. Tucker, Jr., a reporter from the U.S. weekly *Spotlight*, worked in tandem with the Swiss journalist and *Spotlight* was the only paper to cover the story in the United States. It is probably not coincidence that the network media hate and are trying to discredit and destroy *Spotlight*.

4. Where banking or other monopoly interests are concerned, such as NAFTA (North American Free Trade Agreement) or GATT (General Agreement on Tariffs and Trade), the media will be alerted that it is in their interests to support the bill (or oppose it if that is what the banking interests want). Advertising and credit will be denied if they don't take the "correct" position. This is not something new. It was the procedure used extensively in the banking fraternity's drive for the Banking Act of 1863.[6]

5. Legislators who oppose the desired action are smeared by a campaign of name calling, labeling, and working on people's fears of what will happen if they are elected. If it becomes necessary to retract any statement, the retraction is hidden in small print on some inside page. The image and the emotions desired remain in the public mind and consciousness. The retraction won't matter; the person's reputation will have been destroyed, and he or she will either fail to be confirmed or will give up the effort.

6. The media will emphasize the advantages of the bill, but never say who will benefit or why, never quote the whole wording of the bill. Opposing views will not find their way to print or the air.

7. The media will slant the news with adjectives and cartoons to get their point of view across. Calling opponents "extremists," "anti-Semitic," "anti-abortion" (never pro-life) "leftist," "fascist," "liberal," "conservative" are some of their favored terms. They never define

the label or give reasons for the label. They know that people tend to accept the label because they "read it in the paper" or "heard it on the news." Such name calling should be an immediate alert that what is being presented is propaganda, not news.

8. All the foregoing strategies for molding and manipulating public opinion appear in Hitler's *Mein Kampf*. These methods worked for Hitler; they still work. To make the procedures more efficient and the outcome more predictable, the media use polls. They slant the questions and the way they report the results. They "turn on the heat" where it's needed, then take another poll to see if the temperature is going their way.

Monetarism

The winner of the Nobel Prize for economics in 1976, Milton Friedman, is credited with the origin and promotion of the theory of *monetarism*. With its advent on the national scene starting as early as the 1960s, money itself became the central factor in United States economic policy. Monetarism said that the management of money alone would provide the solution to our economic problems. Financiers, politicians, economists, and the central banks started arguing about aspects of the theory and experimenting with them.

From the perspective of society as a whole, however, monetarism is a disease. Once it gets into the nation's blood, it is almost impossible to cure or eradicate. It feeds on human greed and lust for power and influence. It uses money as a claim on goods and wealth without giving anything in return. That greed is promoted even by civil authorities and civic organizations, which should know better, until it consumes the total personality of more and more people.

The virus was around long before Milton Friedman. For those infected with it, that is, just about everybody in our modern secular society, money is everything. It is the center of peoples' lives, the good of all their striving. *How* they get it, for too many people, is secondary. In fact, they don't even give a passing thought to the morality involved. All they know is that money gives them power and a claim on what others have produced. Add this obsession with money, this disease afflicting so much of our society, to the creation of money by a private banking system afflicted with the same disease and the result is a perfect formula for widening the gap between the few, who amass ever greater wealth, and the constantly increasing number of the poor and powerless. Just so that this does not sound out of touch with reality, witness two areas where the disease of monetarism has gone wild most recently.

In our society at large, we see casinos and lotteries and TV games being promoted by government and advertising agencies all around us. They constantly inject more and more of the virus of monetarism into society. With the promise of instant millions in the lotteries, they cultivate the mentality that with luck a person can gain something—in almost unimagined amounts—for nothing.

In the financial fraternity, the monetarist epidemic has gone out of control with the manipulations of newly invented financial instruments called *currency derivatives*. By speculating in these derivatives and manipulating them, international financiers have shown that they are able to destroy the currency of any nation at will almost overnight. New York speculator George Soros, who first targeted the English pound, made over one billion dollars overnight, then boasted that he would go after the German mark. Even members of the new aristocracy in Europe are alarmed by what Soros and speculators like him are doing to the European monetary systems, destroying the stability of their currencies. In early August 1993, French, German, and Italian banks showed a great deal of concern about the threat that this was to their currencies.

According to a June 8, 1995, report in the *London Financial Times*, as of the end of the first quarter of 1995, speculation is more rampant than ever, with U.S. banks profiting by $11 billion from derivatives sold as investments to public institutions (and causing them huge losses). At their meeting in Halifax, the Big Seven industrial nations took only token action against speculation. The whole financial community is sitting on a powder keg—and knows it.

Bankers Trust New York Corp. has discovered trading in derivatives to be a very efficient and quick way to plunder industries as well as currencies. This is just the tip of the iceberg of what is going on today in a society infected with monetarism.

An editorial in the August 2, 1993, issue of the *London Guardian* had this to say about the looting of currencies: "Europe must take the lead in persuading the rest of the world to take on the international speculators. Far too much profit is being made these days out of playing with money rather than from making things. The *daily* turnover of the foreign currency exchanges approaches a trillion dollars, only a part of which is linked directly to trade deals."

Money obtained by manipulating a nation's currency without producing wealth in return is simply dishonest money. It is counterfeit and those who create it are thieves. On the vast scale that it's now being done, it plunders a nation's wealth and economy.

Only a part of the daily one trillion dollars in foreign currency exchanges was "directly linked to trade deals." How big of a part was it? Dr. Norbert Walter, chief economist of the German bank, Deutche Bank, told a Frankfurt newspaper on August 8, 1993, that only about 3 percent of that amount was tied to trade in real goods. Ninety-seven percent was in transactions that played with the moneys of the nations involved, siphoning off real wealth to holders of financial paper, like George Soros, paper that gave them the right to claim goods for themselves that others have produced.

By the end of 1994, it was reported that Orange County, California, lost over $2 billion by "investing" in derivatives promoted by the bankers' trading institutions. The prospect of bankruptcy forced layoffs and higher taxes on the residents. At the same time, there were repercussions throughout the financial markets of the nation.

Such losses also have been reported on a smaller scale, bankrupting the budgets of school boards and political entities across the whole country. With trading in derivatives placed at over thirty-seven trillion dollars, paper laying claims to that much value far exceeds the value of the assets of the whole nation. Banking interests have at last discovered the ultimate tool for the plunder of the economies of all the nations of the world.

It appears that the financial banking structures of the whole world are fearful of destroying themselves. A major national example is the case of Mexico, with its 1995 devaluation of the peso during the closing days of December 1994. The big U.S. banks loaded Mexico with debt that was beyond its ability to handle, and then siphoned off Mexico's resources for the bonds.[7] This resulted not only in the decline of true wages for its citizens and higher prices for goods consumers have to buy, but the loss of $40 billion of American taxpayers' money through the Federal Reserve system. The winners? Citibank of New York and other big banks, which profited in the billions. The losers? The Mexican economy, American taxpayers, and, most of all, Mexican workers, who must work harder to survive.

It does not take much reflection or imagination to see that monetarism creates poverty in those who produce wealth and riches for the few who own and control the financial paper. It is sophisticated stealing of the fruits of the labor of honest, hardworking people. Monetaristic greed is at the bottom of the breakdown of all moral sense and responsibility and at the root of all economic and social evils.

Notes

1. Refer to chapter 7, where financial historian Del Mar gives the full decision.
2. Those conditions are spelled out in detail in chapter 20 below; a complete plan for establishing an honest money and banking system is presented in chapter 21.
3. Debt-based money is explained in chapter 5.
4. We shall see both of these quotations again in chapter 12 in the context in which they were originally made, along with a longer letter as an example showing how the money powers in that situation were controlling the media of the day.
5. See chapter 9.
6. See chapter 11.
7. President Clinton openly stated that Mexico has lots of oil to use as collateral in "bailing them out."

Chapter 5

The Origins of Legalized Debt-Based Money and Banking

Banking has its origins in antiquity. There have always been banks, even in marginally civilized nations, as long as there has been some kind of an exchange economy. Banks can and do serve useful functions in the economic development of nations, if honesty and a service motive prevail. But they can also create poverty and economic enslavement if they become almost exclusively industries with profit the predominant motive.

There were banks in other nations when merchants started the Bank of England. Nonetheless, it was that bank that developed ways of using money to make unprecedented profits for its owners while throwing whole nations into the slavery, debt, and their citizens into never-ending poverty.

Local Bankers and the Debt-Based Money System

Local community bankers generally are trying to do the best they can within a dishonest money system over which they have little or no control. Many, no doubt, are not even aware that the debt-based money system within which banking became an industry is dishonest by its very nature.

The creation of money by the private issuance of credit and lending it to a nation and its citizens, when that money is not backed by honest value, cannot be honest, no matter how honestly individual bankers give their services. It's a global version of the Frigo Brothers and their counterfeiting competitors who issued receipts and claims on cheese they did not produce. (Frigo Brothers microeconomics magnified millions of times.) The dishonest nature of the system introduced by the greedy and dishonest London merchants and bankers will be evident when we study its origins.

The Bank of England

The credit, or blame, for planting the seed that sprouted as the Bank of England, which now has grown into the international banking structure that virtually controls the economies of 178 nations, belongs to William III, prince of Orange and sovereign ruler of England, Scotland, and Ireland, jointly with Mary II. Here is the story.

A company of the rich merchants had under its control large stocks of gold and silver. Some was their own, and some of these were deposited with them for safekeeping. Safekeeping and lending deposited funds are what banks were for, so quite logically the group called itself the Bank of England. It could use that name because the members, together with their European banker friends, had control of virtually all the gold and silver, which was promoted as money by the Rothschild family. To enhance their profits, the bankers had been issuing ten times as many receipts for gold as they had gold deposited with them. They then lent those receipts as claims on gold, and collected ten times the interest that they would have received lending only honest receipts.

Issuing ten receipts for each ounce of gold meant that if all the holders of receipts presented their claims at the same time, they would find that there was only one ounce of gold in "reserve" to honor the ten claims. Either the first one could get the whole ounce and the other nine would get nothing, or all ten could get just one tenth of an ounce. This is basically what today we call *fractional reserves*. Yet the bankers collected interest on each receipt loaned as if it were good for a whole ounce of gold. Thus if they charged 10 percent a year on the loan, they would collect 100 percent a year in interest, a whole new ounce of gold for each ounce they had on deposit in the bank, thus doubling their deposited stock of gold in just one year.

Besides that new full ounce in interest income on the original ounce on deposit, the ten borrowers would still owe them the principal, in gold—a whole new ounce for each of the ten receipts loaned but backed by a single ounce in reserves. Meanwhile the debtors would somehow have to earn the gold with which to repay both the loan and interest. When the ten loans were repaid, each with a full ounce of gold, the bankers would have 1000 percent profit on the original ounce. Granting that all loans were repaid at the end of one year, that would be 1100 percent profit in just one year. Can you think of a better way to gain power and mastery over others? It's far more certain than a modern lottery. But it cannot be called honest.

They had discovered that depositors seldom claimed their gold. It was much handier for people to use the paper receipts to carry on business. So they managed to hide their dishonest practice from unsuspecting depositors. Besides being dishonest, this banking practice was also *illegal*. The bankers certainly didn't want to get caught and be prosecuted as criminals. They weren't worried about the morality of their practice, just the legality. So in 1694 they developed a scheme to legalize what they were doing.

They knew that William III didn't want the Stuarts to return to the throne. To defend against that possibility, he needed to raise an army. And to raise an army, he needed money. The British crown as sovereign authority had the power to create the money of the nation. But in their earlier history the merchants, under the leadership of Amschel Rothschild and his family, had maneuvered so that gold (and silver to some small extent occasionally) had become the only acceptable money. William didn't have enough gold or silver to raise an army. All his government had was enough for the immediate needs of the government itself.

William III's need for funds for an army provided a perfect opportunity for the Bank of England to force him to legalize its dishonest practices. So, under the leadership of William Patterson, the Bank offered William III a loan of 1,200,000 pounds at 8 percent interest, *on the condition* that it be given the right to issue notes to the full extent of its capital.

This would mean that the bank would lend the government 1,200,000 pounds in gold and silver. In return, besides interest, it obtained the right to issue bank notes as claims on the *same* gold and silver loaned to the government for raising an army. It could also lend out those notes and collect interest on them.

How did this work? First, the definition of *capital* changed with each step in the money-creating business. Initially it meant the 1,200,000 pounds—true value. After the value was loaned, the bank no longer had it. *Capital* now meant money—the paper notes the bank issued—not value. That money, plus its bonds from the government, plus whatever other gold it had constituted its total new *capital*. On the basis of this new capital, the bank could issue still more notes, again increasing its so-called *capital* (but not its value).

Eventually, of course, the government would have to repay the loan in full, plus the 8 percent, in gold and silver. Where would the government get that gold and silver after it had used the loan to provide for the army? That was not the concern of the bank. The government would either have to borrow it from somewhere or tax its subjects.

This was the first government debt to bankers used as a basis for money. From this time on, banks, not the government, would create money and that money would be based on debt, not value. The Bank of England was now the creditor and the real sovereign power; the government was the debtor, subjected to the bank's orders.

To repeat, what was the backing for the bank's issue of new money? It was the debt that William III owed to the bank. That money was as good as the gold, the people were told. But the government no longer had the gold, because it had used it for the purpose for which it had borrowed it. Now the value all depended on the government's power and ability to tax the citizens, who would have to pay the taxes in gold. Here we have *the beginning of ever-increasing levels of taxation to ensure the payment of interest on ever-growing government debt.* These taxes are necessary to support the growth and profits of a private banking system issuing its bank notes as money, based on debt.

After lending the government of William III the 1,200,000 pounds, the bank still had 36,000 pounds in gold left. Using that as a reserve, it issued 550,000 pounds more in bank notes, resuming the practice of lending ten times of what it had on deposit, only this time the bank increased the ratio from ten to slightly over fifteen times. The practice had been legalized when the bank was given authority to issue its own notes as money based both on its gold *and* on the government debt. The bank, now in control of the creation of money, felt secure in doing this. This additional money in its own notes gave it more power over the nation's economy. By 1696 it had added 1,750,000 pounds of its own notes to the *volume* of money in the nation it now controlled by debt.

There You Have It!

A national debt for the government, taxes for the citizens, and unlimited money-creating power and ever-increasing capital for the Bank of England.

That is exactly what we have in most countries today, including the United States. The only differences are the *size* of the debts and taxes and the *names* of the banks. (These factors in our current debt-based money system will be discussed further in chapters 7, 13, 14, 15, and 16.)

More on What Happened in 1694

By seeking the right to create money from William III, the Bank of England acknowledged that this right belonged to him as a sovereign, in the name of all the people. Now the bankers were the sovereign power, with a rich source of income as lenders and the power to manipulate the volume of money. By stimulating monetary inflation and production of wealth and then contracting the volume of money to cause depressions, they could amass huge fortunes for themselves at bargain prices. This ever-increasing wealth gave them greater and greater power over the politics and economies of their nation and eventually of the world. It enabled them to literally become land lords of the world.

In the meantime, the ordinary citizens were unaware of what had happened. After all, the bank was called the Bank of England. They trusted Mother England, a fact the bankers relied upon. Citizens were just pawns in the game.

This whole chapter can be summed up in the words of Psalm 94, verse 20, written about three thousand years ago. It originally was meant for judges, but applies equally well to our debt-based money system: "They do injustice under cover of law."

The basic principles adopted from the Bank of England and the European central banks by the Federal Reserve banking include:

1. The creation of money by private banks, which laid the foundation for making banking an industry.
2. A money system based on government borrowing from a private banking system, that is, a money system based on government debt.
3. Use of the taxing power of the government to pay the interest on the debt.
4. Subordination of the nation's economy to manipulation by financial interests for their own profit by means of alternate inflations and depressions.
5. Use of fractional reserves for unlimited usury and profits for the few at the expense of the many.
6. Use of the European bankers' expedient of commercial paper in addition to government debt as backing for a more "elastic" currency. This was proposed by Paul Warburg of the Central Bank of Germany, who was recruited by Wall Street bankers to help them design the Federal Reserve central bank (see chapter 12 for further

discussion of the Federal Reserve system). Warburg's proposal went beyond what was in practice by the Bank of England.

Chapter 6
Fractional Reserve

What Is Fractional Reserve?

The concept is simple: it means reserving part of what should be reserved. As applied to banking and the creation of money, it means the issued promises to pay (the Federal Reserve notes or "bills" in your wallet) are backed by only a small fraction, 10 percent or 5 percent—or even 0 percent since the Banking Act of 1980—as a reserve with which to honor the promises. Just what will the bank give you if you come with a Federal Reserve note? Until March 1933 you could request either silver or gold. But then, Pres. Franklin D. Roosevelt, following the Federal Reserve bankers' instructions, forbade the redemption of the reserve notes in gold.[1] So now, all you can get for a Federal Reserve note at the bank is another Federal Reserve note.

Not being required to fully back Federal Reserve notes with gold enables any commercial bank to lend ten or more times as much as the reserves it has on deposit with a Federal Reserve bank. The exact requirement at any time is determined by the Federal Reserve Board. The commercial bank can then collect interest on the whole amount borrowed. In other words, this system enables commercial banks to collect interest on money they don't have! That has been made legal for the first time in 1694 as we saw in the previous chapter.

Three Hundred Years Plus Is Enough—1694–1997

For three hundred years, the political struggle for the creation and control of the nation's money has continued. It has been a tug of war between patriotic citizens and the financiers with headquarters principally on New York City's Wall Street and in London.

We need to reverse what took place in England in 1694, and we need to be able to explain why it must be reversed. In doing so, we must observe these three points:

1. There can be no compromise with the call for complete and permanent repeal and removal of all five procedures legalized in 1694. They are the major economic causes of the problems of poverty and economic injustices in the world. These five procedures are:

- The creation of money by private banks or by any other private interests or banking institutions.
- A money system based on government debt.
- An economy subordinated to private banking interests and at their mercy.
- Banking as an industry that creates no wealth.
- Fractional reserve system.
   The use of commercial paper as a backing for credit may be considered a sixth structure that must be removed, but it did not originate with the Bank of England. It comes from Paul Warburg as a European central bank's practice.

2. Allowing any one of the five structures to continue would leave an opening for the return of all of them, with a vengeance. This has happened before in our history with incomplete and half-hearted attempts at reform.

3. We may not let down our guard once our objectives are achieved. Each generation in turn must be properly educated so that it can protect itself. If it isn't, the new aristocracy will surely not miss any opportunity it sees to regain these "keys" to unlimited profits and power.

A Modern Example of the Effects of Usury

As we approach the twenty-first century, the same oppressive usury is with us as in 1694, but it is practiced more boldly and on a vastly greater scale by the use of the fractional reserve idea and oppressively high interest rates.

The example given in the September 18, 1994, issue of *Our Sunday Visitor* is *symbolic* of the widespread practice of usury in Italy today. It tells about a couple, Francesco and Clara, who committed suicide on August 25, 1994. They left a note saying they could no longer go on trying to pay off an exorbitant debt on their small farm and airfield. "The Gaddi's debt bind is shared by one-in-five businesses in Italy, the Chamber of Commerce says. Usurers prey, too, on the unemployed and the poor. Borrowers say they are threatened with violence if they do not pay and some have turned to prostitution in order to make payments. . . . Moneylenders . . . force borrowers to pay 120–250% interest a month."

The article mentions the efforts of two clergymen involved in "Italy's new fight against usurers." One is Bishop Decio Grandoni of Orvieto-Todi, who warns that usurers are "penetrating more dangerously in the social fabric." The second is the Jesuit Massimo Rastrelli of Naples, known as "the anti-usury priest," who raises money to help usury "victims to pay off their loans." The article closes with this statement: "The Church is also working with labor and business leaders to get new laws passed against usury and usurers."

Unfortunately, that is little more than a Band-Aid solution. A better approach would be to help create and condition public opinion to support a complete change of the money system so that it could provide credit to the nation's citizens as a service of the sovereign nation. This would facilitate employment and make it unnecessary for the citizens to turn to greedy private money lenders. The plight of the Italian borrowers is repeated in many other nations. It is one indication of the havoc caused by the lenders, the International Monetary Fund, the World Bank, and fellow travelers.

Note

1. Silver was also involved to a minor extent, but because of the several changes in laws concerning its use, we will not pursue its history here.

Chapter 7
Money in the American Colonies

Colonialism in America

The development of a debt-based system in America was a carryover from sixteenth- and seventeenth-century *mercantilism*. Merchants of that period were the forerunners of modern capitalism. One of the basic principles they held was that gold and silver were essential to a nation's wealth. If a nation did not have mines or access to these precious metals, they had to be obtained by trade. This was the main reason for the competition among the major nations for the possession of colonies. Spain, Italy, Portugal, Holland, and England had an insatiable greed and appetite for gold; this led to the discoveries and settlements in both North and South America. England, of course, was the main player in United States history. This period was one of the most sordid chapters in human history. All the great explorers—Columbus, Cortes, De Soto, and Pizzaro—were active in the oppression, torture, murder, and enslavement of many native populations.

Manufacturing was forbidden in the colonies. All commerce was the monopoly of the mother country. The colonies were to serve both as markets for the exports of the mother country and as suppliers of raw materials, especially these precious metals. The goal was profit and wealth for the mother nation. Naturally, the merchants saw themselves as in control of this process of colonization—its profits, and the politics involved. The profits had to be in gold and silver. United States history shows that this was exactly the program that England tried to implement in the thirteen American colonies.[1]

After the war with Spain over the colonies ended, the British Crown was free to continue colonizing America. It encouraged private citizens to undertake settlements by granting them very generous charters. The first charter was granted to Virginia in 1606, the first for Massachusetts in 1628, and so on. Each colony was a separate part of the British empire but otherwise independent and a sovereign state with the power to make its own laws so long as they did not conflict with those of England. One of the powers each colony had was the power to create its own money system.

Although we will speak of the colonies as if all we say applied to all of them, it is important to note that the thirteen colonies were not the same. There were three different classes of colonies—charter, proprietary, and crown—each class with its own kind of a relationship with the British Crown. Within each class, each colony had its own character and goals. Within the limits of their charters, these colonies acted as sovereign states. To go into the complex individual financial histories of all these types of colonies would take us too far afield. So, with one exception, we shall limit our story to what can be said of all of them in common, while we pursue the account of Massachusetts, the strongest charter colony.

Development Impossible without Money

As the population of the colonies approached one million, with many different trades and occupations, there was a crying need to go beyond the primitive Dutch barter system that had served the earliest colonies but permitted only limited development. The colonies needed money, if they were going to make any progress in developing their commerce. What little money they had was English money and what other colonists brought over from Spain, France, and Holland.

With England in complete control of the money supply in the colonies, this money eventually ended up in London through taxes or in payment for imports. If the colonists wanted some of this money back, they had to send their products, the fruit of their labors, to England at any price it pleased England to pay for them. Thus for close to two hundred years, almost all the friction and troubles the colonies had with England were over money and money systems. If the colonies issued their own money, the Bank of England (through the Crown, which it had controlled since 1694) either taxed it away or destroyed it by sending shiploads of counterfeit money or through other intrigues. This finally forced the colonies into a war they really did not want. This is what Benjamin Franklin tried to tell the authorities in London. As we know, they wouldn't listen. Before we examine the experiences of the charter colony of Massachusetts, let's look at an event that had great influence.

The Mixt Money Case

The creation and issue of money was defined as the prerogative and function of the sovereign state by the Privy Council of England in 1604, in what is known as the *Mixt Money Case Decision*. Alexander Del Mar, in *History of Money in America*, writes:

> Money was a public measure, a measure of value, and, like other measures, it was necessary in the public welfare that its dimensions and volume should be limited, defined, and regulated by the State. The whole body of learning left by the ancient and renascent world was invoked in this celebrated dictum: Aristotle, Paulus, Bodin, Budelius; the Roman law, the common law, and the statutes, all upheld it; the State alone had the right to issue money and to decide of what substances its symbols should be made, whether of gold, silver, brass, or paper. Whatever the State declared to be money, was money.

London Merchants Seek to Defeat the Mixt Money Case Decision

Del Mar comments, "The decision greatly alarmed the merchants of London, and for more than half a century after it was enunciated they were occupied with efforts to defeat its operation."

The merchants were alarmed because they had contrived to acquire—by trade, discovery, plunder, piracy, murder, or enslavement of Latin American and African natives who were forced to do the mining for them the gold to be used as money. Greece and Rome and other nations disappeared as nations when the concentration of wealth reached the point at which only 2 percent of the population owned virtually everything. But even their merchants did not ply their greed on as large a scale as those in the New World, beginning with the Spanish, Dutch, Italian, English, and Portuguese. It was impossible for ordinary citizens to acquire money except by selling the fruits of their labor for whatever price the merchants gave them. Slaves, of course, acquired nothing at all. Naturally this shortage of money in the hands of the citizens caused distress and poverty throughout the nations that depended on gold as money.

Now the 1604 decision in the Mixt Money case had very clearly defined that money, its creation and regulation, was a prerogative of the State. This threatened the merchants' whole gold operation and the money system based on it. Gold was the foundation of their power; no wonder they were alarmed. But to ordinary citizens, the Mixt Money Case Decision brought some measure of hope.

It is very interesting to note that the 1604 Mixt Money Case Decision goes unmentioned in the latest encyclopedias and textbooks. Could it be that the successors of these merchants are protecting themselves by not permitting any of this information into our educational system? We'll look at such precautionary behavior that is practiced constantly by the land lords of the world of our day, which we'll see in more detail in chapter 13.

Massachusetts and the Mixt Money Case Decision

Massachusetts enjoyed the greatest freedom as a charter colony and took the most significant initiatives to provide its own money. Luckily, the colony had leaders and influential people who understood the implications of the Mixt Money Case Decision and of the power that they had over money as a sovereign state. So whether the merchants overseas were "alarmed" or not, the provincial government decided to use the right, granted by its charter in 1620, shortly after the Mixt Money Case Decision, to create its own legal tender.

This right was never taken away from the colony, although its implementation was interfered with when it came to opening a mint on October 19, 1652. But the Pine Tree shilling, which it minted, was channeled to London by the merchants where it was usually melted down, depriving the colonists of their newly created money. Still, this money served the colony to some extent for thirty-four years, until 1686 when the mint was suppressed by King William. The Crown managed to have this coin exported out of the country, leaving the colony again without money and in a state of depression. This rendered impossible any economic progress beyond that of again using some form of barter in order to provide for minimal human needs. No credit was available. All the fruits of this rudimentary economy ended in London through its control of coinage. There were other attempts made to issue promissory notes into circulation, including an effort to establish a land bank for such issue, but these were not accepted by the public and quickly disappeared.

The colony struggled with limited trade for forty years. Then, on July 3, 1692, it made its paper bills of credit, first issued on December 10, 1690, full legal tender. This meant the bills now could be used to pay all debts, both public and private; to finance the construction of the infrastructure needed for transportation; and to pay all expenses. The quality that made the paper legal tender and fully honest money

41

was the fact that the government accepted it in payment of taxes and recognized it as a lawful medium for settling all debts between the government and private individuals. The following wording on the notes issued by Massachusetts shows that they fulfilled that requirement: "The indented bill for ten shillings, due from the Massachusetts Colony to the Possessor, shall be equal in value to money, and shall be accordingly accepted by the Treasurer, and Receivers subordinate to him, in all public payments, and for any stock at any time in the Treasury. Boston in New England, December 10th, 1690. By order of the General Court."

The colony at last had its own honest money, without debt or interest to anyone. In fact, by granting long-term loans to its citizens for the purpose of starting businesses, it collected a low rate of interest, which was a source of revenue for it and reduced the need for taxes. The bills, of course, were accepted in payment of taxes, a critical requirement for any valid national currency. Taxation provides a government with the power to maintain an equilibrium in the money supply and therefore assure its stable value.

Eventually the other colonies followed the example of Massachusetts and accepted each others' bills, thus further increasing trade. Through their productive enterprises and commerce, using their paper money, the colonists developed a prosperous economy. They discovered that individuals did not need gold or silver or any other commodity; the receipts and the credit of the sovereign state were satisfactory.

This valid paper money was paid into use by way of public expenditures until there was enough to serve the orderly exchange of goods and services, with just enough taxation to keep the supply in balance with the production of wealth. *As this money entered the colonial economy, the next thirty years were a period of unparalleled prosperity and development*, more than doubling both population and wealth.

Benjamin Franklin described the conditions this way: "Abundance reigned in the Colonies and there was peace in all their borders. A more happy and prosperous population could not perhaps be found on the globe. In every home there was comfort. The people were generally highly moral and knowledge was extensively diffused."

When Franklin went to England as a representative of the colonies, he found poverty and hunger and streets filled with beggars. The officials assumed conditions were the same in the colonies. So they asked him how the colonies handled caring for the poor, how they managed to collect the taxes they needed to build poor houses. Franklin answered: "We have no poor houses in the Colonies, and if we had we would have nobody to put in them, as in the Colonies there is not a single unemployed man, no poor and no vagabonds."

When asked how he accounted for that prosperity in the colonies, Franklin said, "It is because in the Colonies we issue our own paper money. We call it Colonial Scrip and we issue enough to move all goods freely from the producers to the consumers; and, as we create our own money, *we control the purchasing power of money and have no interest to pay.*"

Evidently Benjamin Franklin was telling this to the wrong crowd. Gold and silver had been picked by the Rothschild banking family as the specie of choice to be used as money because the family held vast amounts of those metals and could therefore control the money supply and its value. Working with kings and other rulers who already were dependent on the bankers to some extent, the Rothschilds persuaded them to adopt their system. For the British at this time, that was the only worthwhile money for taxing or trading with the colonies.

The colonies, on the other hand, did not have gold or silver, or very little. This did not stand in the way of their prosperity once they followed the Mixt Money Case Decision and chose to use bills of credit for money, which had no value for the British. No specie is necessary to give money its value. All that is needed is for the issuing public authority to accept it in payment of taxes, make it legal tender in payment of all debts, and to *control its supply*, so that it is always in balance with values it produces. (Note that the *Constitution* gives Congress the power "to regulate the value of our money"—Article 1, section 8.5). It cannot regulate the value of money unless it has complete control over its creation.

However, when King William III surrendered the nation's sovereignty in 1694 to the private merchants' Bank of England for their gold and a debt, government decisions were now made only nominally by Parliament but actually by the English Board of Trade and the Bank of England. So now, when the merchants of the Bank of England heard of this prosperity in the New World, they promptly set out to exploit the colonies and plunder their wealth, just as they had in the mother country. They took the colonies' money away, contrary to the colonial charters, which the bankers did not consider themselves obligated to honor. So the colonies' prosperity did not last very long.

In 1720, the colonial royal governors were ordered to destroy the monetary issue of the colonies without regard to consequences. They carried out the orders by trick or threat—and ultimately by counterfeiting and sending shiploads of bills, thus destroying the value of those in circulation (cf. Frigo Brothers story)—causing a major depression in the colonies. Then, in 1741, the British Parliament (controlled by the Bank of England) suppressed the Land Bank of Massachusetts and forbade the colony to issue any more legal tender or bills of credit.

On June 28, 1749, the Resumption Act was approved by the king, as the Bank of England wanted. This act resumed gold and silver coin, which the colonists did not have, as the money demanded in payment of taxes and other debts. In 1764 these prohibitions were extended to the rest of the colonies. This was in direct violation of their colonial charters. What was the result? This is how financial historian Alexander Del Mar describes it: "Ruin stalked in every home; the people could not pay their taxes, and were obliged to see their property seized by the sheriff and sold for one tenth of its previous value. . . . Every sort of injustice was committed under cover of law."

The colonies did their best to arrive at a compromise, even sending Benjamin Franklin to London in their behalf. But to no avail. The Bank of England was determined to own and control the money the colonists used and to enslave them with debt. This is the same debt-based money system, inaugurated in 1694, that is in operation in the world today through the Federal Reserve, the World Bank, and the International Monetary Fund.

Concerning his efforts at compromise, Franklin wrote:

> The Colonies would gladly have borne the little tax on tea and other matters, had it not been that England took away from the Colonies their money, which created unemployment and dissatisfaction.

Here was the primary provocation for the War of Independence, although it is not the usual way history textbooks report the causes of the war. Even current financial interests do not want citizens to consider this the main reason for the colonists' decision to resort to war.

So the only honest, debt-free money system enjoyed in United States history was during the thirty-year period between 1692 and 1720 (plus perhaps a few years before the royal governors' restrictions took full effect). The Bank of England's debt-based money system had arrived on American shores. The next chapter will discuss how that system took root and developed, and the struggles, successes, and failures the new nation's citizens and leaders had with it in the period up to the Civil War.

More Reflections on the Early Colonists' Experiences

In every age and situation, some benefits came to the people even from a dishonest money system. Any system provides some money for an exchange economy that could not exist without money. Money always provided a measure of prosperity, temporary though it always is with debt-based money. The financial powers are clever enough to know that unless a cycle of prosperity is permitted, there will be no wealth produced, nothing that can later be plundered by means of a depression caused by a deliberately created shortage of money.

Note

1. The Louisiana territories under Spain and France had their own financial history, but their problems were similar to those in British colonies.

Chapter 8

Debt-Based Money Comes to America

Brief Historical Context for this Chapter

1774	September 1	British seize cannon and powder at Charlestown and Cambridge. Colonies prepare for war.
	September 5	The First Continental Congress convenes. The colonies try to form a confederation.
1775	May 10	Second Continental Congress meets in Philadelphia.
	June 15	Washington is named chief of the continental forces.
1776	June 11	The Committee of Five appointed to prepare the Declaration of Independence chooses Thomas Jefferson to do the writing.
	June 28	Thomas Jefferson presents a completed draft of the Declaration of Independence, saying he "turned to neither book nor pamphlet," but drew upon his own and the people's prevalent philosophy and feelings.
	July 2	Continental Congress takes final vote for independence.
	August 2	After much debate by the delegates of the attending twelve colonies, most of the fifty-five final signatures are affixed to the amended Declaration of Independence.
1777	November 15	The Continental Congress agrees upon the Articles of Confederation as a working arrangement for the independent and sovereign colonies, which now need to work

together for self-defense and perhaps to coalesce into a nation.

From 1775 to 1781, the War of Independence was fought amid great
sacrifices, loss of life, and hardships. Virtually the only money the
colonists had during all this time was their paper continental currency
and individual colonies' bills of credit, which had little value because
the Continental Congress did not have taxing authority, nor could it
make them legal tender. While the Americans were still in the throes
of war, and Britain saw the possibility of losing that war on the military level, the Bank of England interests were maneuvering to win the
war by means of a debt-based money system like their own.

The Confederation

On March 2, 1781, the First Congress of the Confederation met
to adopt officially the Articles of Confederation as the basis of the
government. The Articles continued in force until the Constitution was
ratified in 1789.

Seven months later, on October 19, 1781, the British army under
Cornwallis, composed of almost eight thousand men, surrendered. Alexander Hamilton, who would play an important role in the history of
the debt-based money system coming to America, distinguished himself as a colonel and a skillful commander in that final battle.

The American War for Independence was perhaps the greatest
event in the history of the nation. When it ended, the colonists had
gained for themselves sovereignty as a new nation and liberty. The
costs, in lives and possessions, were immense.

Alexander Hamilton's Bank of America

During the war a brilliant and ambitious young man, only twenty
years of age, received an assignment as secretary to George Washington. His name was Alexander Hamilton. From the age of thirteen he
had been attracted to business and finance and making money. He
studied at what is now Columbia University. There he met and made
many influential friends, especially among the bankers on Wall Street.
He admired their power and privileges and set out to learn their ideas
of private central banking, the same ideas upon which the Bank of
England had been founded in 1694.

While in the service of George Washington, Hamilton studied all aspects of finance—money, gold, silver, foreign exchange, and so on. During this time he also wrote letters to influential men in Europe about his ideas. He formed definite plans for a privately owned central bank like the Bank of England. In addition he intended to follow the teachings of Adam Smith's *Wealth of Nations* as his guide on economics.

In February of 1781, Hamilton left Washington's service. Now, only twenty-four, he felt ready to venture into the field of finance. He had studied, made contacts with bankers, and learned how a private central bank could use its power to destroy government-created money, which he knew he had to do before his central bank could gain exclusive control of the nation's money. He admired such power and wanted to be in a position to be able to use it. He would rely on the ignorance of the ordinary people about money matters.

The Confederation, with no gold or silver of its own and only limited amounts borrowed from France, Spain, and Holland, had to depend on its own weak continental currency and on the paper money of the colonies, each with its own issue. With this financial confusion and the burden of debt from the war, the colonies were under great financial stress. This gave Hamilton his opportunity. He wrote to a powerful member of the Continental Congress suggesting that favorable treatment of wealthy men would incline them to help the government out of its difficulties.

Immediately after leaving George Washington, Hamilton wrote to his friend Robert Morris, who was then superintendent of finance for the Continental Congress, outlining a very ambitious plan for an international central bank under the control of European capital. Morris, who was himself wealthy and had good European connections, obtained $500,000 from the king of France and subscribed all that remained in the continental treasury to the stock of the bank, a total of $254,000.

Thus, only three months after the war, Hamilton and Morris managed to get a charter from the State of Massachusetts and set up the Bank of America. However, the oppressed colonies were not about to surrender their hard-won independence to an international central bank, so this bank was rejected and failed.

The reason for bringing this failed Bank of America into our story at all is that it helps us to understand better the motives of Hamilton and Morris in their subsequent endeavors. For example, here is what Robert Morris wrote to John Jay, ambassador to Spain, asking for funds for the Bank of America: "I am determined that the Bank shall be well supported until it can support itself, and then it will support us."

John Adams, who became the second president of the new United States, expressed this estimate of Morris: "He has vast designs in the mercantile way, and no doubt pursues mercantile ends, *which are always gain*."[1]

United States Constitution Ratified

On July 2, 1788, Cyrus Griffin, president of the Continental Congress, announced that the Constitution had been ratified by the necessary nine states. The Federalists, under the leadership of George Washington and Alexander Hamilton, had worked hard to have it ratified and were happy with this announcement.

The Federalists comprised mainly the monied interests—merchants, professionals, and people with property. They wanted a strong central government patterned on the British government, to which many were sympathetic because it favored the interests of people like themselves. Therefore the colonies had been withholding ratification until they were assured that the Bill of Rights became part of it to protect themselves against a powerful central government's authority denying them the personal rights and freedoms they had fought for.

1788	September 13	The Continental Congress meets to prepare for the new government. It transacts its last official business on October 10, 1788.
	December 23	Maryland cedes ten square miles as the future site of government, the District of Columbia.
1789	April 6	George Washington is elected first president, John Adams vice president. Both are Federalists.
	September 11	Alexander Hamilton is appointed secretary of the Treasury.
	September 26	Thomas Jefferson is appointed first secretary of state.

Hamilton's First National Bank of the USA

Top priority during Washington's first term had to be bringing order to the finances of the new nation. The many debts and the confusion existing with the continental currency and other currencies in the colonies were serious obstacles to the development of trade and industry in the nation. Therefore the Federalists worked hard both to ratify the Constitution and to assume the many debts into one national debt that would also include the debt for the War of Independence.

Federalists, remember, were the monied and propertied people, the elites or aristocrats of the new world. This fact, and the fear of a huge national debt, caused a great deal of controversy between them and the more numerous ordinary citizens—the farmers and laborers. They were strongly opposed to the Constitution and didn't trust a central government so strong that the ordinary citizen wouldn't have much of a voice in it. That wasn't the citizens' idea of democracy. Thomas Jefferson, the author of the Declaration of Independence, was their leader and represented what became the Democratic-Republican Party. Its members were opposed to the principles and actions of the Federalist Party led by Alexander Hamilton, the new secretary of the Treasury and strong proponent of central banking.

Jefferson, who found fault with the Constitution because it concentrated excessively on the federal level, hoped nevertheless that the nine states would ratify it to ensure the good that it contained. But he wanted the other four states to hold off until the Bill of Rights amending it was accepted by the other nine. To Count de Moustier, in a letter dated May 17, 1788, Jefferson wrote:

> I see in this instrument a great deal of good. . . . There are, indeed some faults, which revolted me a good deal in the first moment; but we must be contented to travel on to perfection, step by step. We must be contented with the ground which this Constitution will gain for us, and hope that a favorable moment will come for correcting what is amiss in it.

A year earlier Jefferson had written to a Joseph Jones:

> With all the defects in our Constitution whether general or particular, the comparison of our governments with those of Europe, is like a comparison of heaven and hell. England, like earth, may be allowed to take an intermediate station.

Alexander Hamilton, on the other hand, whose failure with the Bank of America ten years earlier led him to find fault with the Articles of Confederation, worked hard for the United States Constitution and its ratification. He knew it would unite the colonies under one strong government and present him with better prospects to again undertake the formation of a central bank. It soon became evident that Hamilton was preparing to do just that. He and his friend Robert Morris would be cooperating again to accomplish that objective.

Under the leadership of Alexander Hamilton, the financiers promoted a First National Bank, which was patterned on the Bank of England with its power to create money based on the nation's debt and fractional reserves. Meyer Amschel Rothschild, founder of the International Banking House of Rothschild, had helped finance Great Britain in its war with the colonies and also, through intermediaries including Hamilton's friend Morris, had loaned money to the colonies. He now guided Hamilton in getting this new central bank established.

It did not matter to the House of Rothschild which side won the war. In either case it would profit. Financiers finance wars for one purpose only, to enhance their own profits through interest on government debt and by supplying munitions and hardware for the military. Patriotism is irrelevant; their goal is making money.

Hamilton remembered Amschel Rothschild's oft-quoted line, "Permit me to issue and control the money of a nation, and I care not who makes its laws." The founders and owners of the new central bank would have the power to control the economies, politics, and destiny of the new nation. In soliciting support for the scheme from the financial circles in London, New York, and in Congress, Hamilton held out the bright vision of great profits that would accrue to them from such an adventure. The congressmen were also promised opportunities for personal profit from the new central bank operation. Their support for the bill granting the bank a charter was needed and was obtained by appealing to their greed.

By founding a private central bank, which they called the First National Bank of the United States, Britain and its financiers with their American colleagues effectively won the war through finance, even though Lord Cornwallis surrendered on the battlefield. Britain's debt-based, fractional-reserve money system had finally come to America. Alexander Del Mar, eminent historian of that period and author of numerous books, including *The History of Money in America*,[2] exclaimed:

> Never was a great historical event followed by a more feeble sequel. A Nation arises to claim for itself liberty and sovereignty. It gains both of these ends by immense sacrifice and treasure. Then, when victory is gained and secured, it hands the national credit—that it is to say, a national treasure—over to private individuals, to do as they please with it!

John Adams, the second president, himself a Federalist like George Washington and Alexander Hamilton, had this to say after seeing the First National Bank in action for several years:

All the perplexities, confusion, and distress in America, arise, not from the defects in the Constitution or confederation, not from want of honor or virtue, so much as from downright ignorance of coin, credit and circulation.

The betrayal of its citizens so soon after the war, Del Mar says, "can only be attributed to the absence of such a body of knowledge on financial subjects as would have the statesmen of that day . . . profit by the experience of the past."

What a price citizens must pay because of a lack of knowledge! To avoid such tragic mistakes in modern times, we need to learn from these experiences of the early American colonists.

Two hundred years ago, it could have been true that there was "an absence of a body of knowledge on financial subjects." But today that is no longer true. This knowledge may be kept out of our public educational system, but it is readily available in our libraries and in the thousands of books written on these subjects. Del Mar had a bibliography of some four-hundred titles when he published *The History of Money in America* in 1899! So while there may have been an excuse for the early American colonists and their statesmen, including the first president, George Washington, for not having sufficient knowledge about financial matters to recognize the dangers in what was being proposed, there is no excuse for us. There is no excuse for remaining ignorant about money.

George Washington admitted that he didn't understand finance. He entrusted these matters to Alexander Hamilton. Upon the recommendation of Robert Morris, a wealthy man with international contacts, Washington had appointed Hamilton secretary of the Treasury. As we have seen, Alexander Hamilton's primary interests and sympathies lay with the financial interests and with using his understanding of money to advance their causes.

Washington's ignorance of the nature of money caused his country to lose to the monied interests the victory it had won on the battlefield. The nation was now in the hands of the banking fraternity.

The Opposing Views of Hamilton and Jefferson

The financial problems of the new nation and Hamilton's proposal for solving them by means of a private central bank chartered by the

United States provided the occasion for a fierce and celebrated battle between Hamilton and Jefferson.

This controversy was carried on by the two leaders with the help of two newspapers founded by the two opposing camps. *The National Gazette*, edited by Philip Freneau, promoted Democratic-Republican principles. Thomas Jefferson, along with James Madison, James Monroe, and Benjamin Franklin were the leaders of that party. The *Federalist Gazette of the United States*, edited by John Fenno, backed Alexander Hamilton and the Federalist cause. The famous *Federalist Papers*, written mostly by Hamilton, provided some of the ammunition for the battle.

The Main Principles of the Democratic-Republican Party

The Democratic-Republican Party's principles stemmed from the philosophy and convictions of Thomas Jefferson, expressed in the *Declaration of Independence*. They included the following:

1. A democratic order based on the individual freeholders, people who would be able to own land and property, not subject to laws that would keep title to lands and property within a privileged group or class. Though Jefferson and his associates considered themselves aristocrats and were independent proprietors, their sympathies were with the middle-class citizens who were the producers of real wealth. They identified with these people and with their desires to keep and enjoy the fruits of their labor in a system of government in which they would have an effective voice.

2. Confidence that ordinary citizens, acting through their representatives, could be trusted to govern themselves. On July 12, 1816, Jefferson wrote to Samuel Kercheval: "I am not among those who fear the people. They, and not the rich, are our dependence for continued freedom. And to preserve their independence, we must not let our rulers load us with perpetual debt."

3. A belief that people could learn and improve their skills. Jefferson believed in creating a true aristocracy of talented and gifted people who would be qualified for leadership and public office. This was not to be an aristocracy based on heredity or wealth but on virtue

and talents. In a letter dated August 30, 1795, Jefferson wrote: "I do most anxiously wish to see the highest degree of education given to the higher degrees of genius, and to all degrees of it as much as may enable them to read and understand what is going on in the world, and to keep their part of it going right; for *nothing can keep it right but their own vigilant and distrustful superintendence.*[3]"

4. An economic order based on people's initiative and industry, relatively free from industrialism and big finance. In his first annual message to Congress as president of the United States, Jefferson said: "Agriculture, manufacture, commerce, and navigation, the four pillars of our prosperity, are the most thriving when left free to individual enterprise."

5. Distrust of the power of big, centralized government. Writing to John Taylor in 1798, Jefferson commented: "It is a singular phenomenon, that while our state governments are the very best in the world, without exception or comparison, our General Government has, in the rapid course of nine or ten years, become more arbitrary, and has swallowed more of the public liberty than even that of England."

6. Wide diffusion of goods and wealth among the people who create them and sympathy for debtor interests rather than the interests of big creditors.

Federalist Principles

Alexander Hamilton was the leader of the Federalist Party. They were the new aristocrats (the elite), comprising the monied interests, people of wealth and substance, the Wall Street financiers and their banker friends, as well those associated with the Bank of England and other European bankers and merchants. Their aims were profit and power. With the power of money, they knew they could control both the producers of wealth and the government, just as the Bank of England did. Hamilton was fascinated by that kind of power. Federalist principles included the following:

1. A belief that the best government was one by the elite.

2. Distrust of the ability of the citizens at large to govern themselves; therefore the elite alone should be in control of all the executive

functions of government. The Federalists fought against the adoption of the Bill of Rights insisted on by Thomas Jefferson and the Democratic-Republicans. They believed those first ten amendments to the *Constitution* would interfere with the control they wanted to have over the new nation.

These were the two major ways the Federalists differed from the Democrat-Republicans as described above. Both parties were patriotic in their motives and believed their approach would best serve their country. The Federalists were for centralization of power and government and that that approach could very well be best for the country if the citizens remained ignorant. George Washington, a Federalist, was afraid that a democracy would fail for that reason. When he accepted it as an experiment, he warned the country about the absolute necessity of sound education for it to succeed.

The Nation's Financial Problems

The nation's obligations on January 14, 1790, were these:

Foreign debt to the French and Dutch	$ 11,710,378
Domestic claims	44,424,085
States' own debts (if assumed)	25,000,000
Assuming states' debts for the common war effort	21,500,000
Total	$102,624,463

There was a great deal of opposition, debate, and compromise concerning assuming some of those debts, but finally a political compromise was reached. Jefferson lent his support to Hamilton's assumption plan, while Hamilton gave Jefferson the support of his influence for fixing the site of the nation's capital in the District of Columbia. In July 1790 both proposals were approved.

On to the Central Bank!

In December 1790 Hamilton submitted to the House his plan for a central bank. He requested the Congress to grant him and his associates a charter for a private bank; it would be called the First National Bank of the United States.

Hamilton knew exactly what he wanted. His bank was modeled on the Bank of England. All the debts that Washington was worried about would be assumed and consolidated, and then the bank would buy those debts in the form of interest-bearing bonds from the government. The government would accept the obligation to pay the bond holders (the bank) interest on those bonds by taxing the citizens, a power that the bank itself would not have.

With the bonds in its vaults as reserves, the bank would issue bank notes to pay the government for the bonds. This would create for the government all the money it needed to pay off its debts at full value. Of course, the government's national debt would now be owed to the bank and the financiers. The bigger the debt, the more interest would be garnered from the government on the bonds.[4]

Could the national debt problem have been handled any other way? Thomas Jefferson proposed that an honest and constitutional measure would be to have the problem handled by the United States Treasury. Congress could make Treasury notes the nation's money instead of using the bank notes. Then it would not need to pay interest to a private banking system. The people's taxes would thus be lower. By its taxing power, it could control the supply and value of its currency as provided in the Constitution[5] to ensure freedom from both inflation and depressions. Why didn't Jefferson's view prevail?

Alexander Hamilton had learned well from his tutors on Wall Street and in England, and he carefully prepared the way in Congress before he presented his request for a charter on December 13, 1790. He held out to both congressmen and members of the financial community the prospect of great private profits that they could gain from the venture.

First, he gave the congressmen advance information that all debts would be paid at full parity, or 100 percent on the dollar. These men knew that money was in such short supply that creditors would be willing to give up their bills for a mere fifteen cents on the dollar. This advance knowledge enabled the congressmen to buy up all the paper cheaply before the farmers and creditors in outlying areas found out they could get full value. Thus the congressmen would make an immediate profit of eighty-five cents on every dollar when Hamilton's proposal for the bank was passed by Congress. Apparently Hamilton's reading of human nature's greediness was correct. Forty-five percent of the congressmen availed themselves of this opportunity to benefit at the expense of the citizenry.

But there were also ways to garner longer-term profits. Hamilton explained that the main source of permanent gains and income would be the interest on the bonds at 8 percent. But if the bonds could be gotten from the government at a discount of 50 percent, which in some situations could be arranged, the effective interest rate would double. The initial profits (over 560 percent!) could be used to buy more bonds for these permanent gains. Combined with some other procedures the bank planned to follow, they were told they could reasonably expect profits of 30 to 35 percent on their invested capital. Thus it is easy for us to understand that in spite of great opposition from the Democratic-Republicans and great leaders like Jefferson, Adams, and Benjamin Franklin, who had just died, the bill granting Alexander Hamilton and his associates a charter for the private bank passed on February 25, 1791.

George Washington doubted that Congress had the authority under the *Constitution* to pass such a bill and had the vice president, John Adams, prepare a veto. After hearing arguments from both Jefferson and Hamilton, who argued that the bill fell within the "implied powers" of the *Constitution*—an argument used, and misused, down to the present day. Washington was still not persuaded by either man's arguments. Believing that in cases of doubt the president's support should go to the cabinet officer whose department was directly involved, he supported Hamilton and signed the bill. Now the nation's debt problems were solved. *Or were they?* It was a good idea to consolidate the debts of the new nation and arrange to have them paid. It was also good to provide a supply of money, which the nation needed badly for the development of industry, commerce, and infrastructure. This, in fact, was one of the arguments that Hamilton had used to gain the support of merchants and industrialists. But at what price were these benefits purchased? The nation's hard-won sovereignty and independence were subverted to the same Federalists who opposed a true democracy in the first place. They got what they wanted by stretching the *Constitution* with Hamilton's "implied powers" argument, which set a precedent for manipulating the *Constitution* in the future.

Alexander Hamilton was a brilliant and very capable aristocrat in the English tradition. While he was instrumental in spelling out for his associates and the congressmen how to achieve great profits, he himself did not profit as he expected. His Federalist "friends" cast him aside after using him to get a central bank they could control.

The First National Bank

The First National Bank was a private bank for private profit. Initially the government furnished some of its capital and was allowed a minority interest, but in time this was completely eliminated. The word *national* was used to make the public accept the idea of a central bank more easily.[6]

Congress surrendered its sovereignty to this private banking system by giving it a charter to create the nation's money. And then the government went into debt to this private banking institution by borrowing its money. Hamilton's bank used the "fractional reserve" ploy to create and lend about three times its reserves, thus collecting more interest. Today the Federal Reserve uses virtually no reserves; the Banking Act of 1980 allows banks to use foreign bonds and their own debt instruments as so-called reserves. This is one in a series of more recent "improvements" on the system used by the first central bank.

The First National Bank also obtained an exclusive monopoly on all banking. In its historical situation, it was not able to enforce that provision completely, because some of the state-chartered banks issued their own notes to circulate as money. It was only in 1913 the Federal Reserve system, a successor of that first bank, finally achieved total monopoly and control of all banking.

The power to control the money supply of the nation made it possible for Hamilton's bank to contract or expand the supply at will. Thus it could create cycles of inflation and depressions from which it could increase its own wealth from foreclosures and bankruptcies.

It is important to note that the stock in trade of a bank is money and interest. This means banking is called an industry but produces no wealth for the nation's economy. Casinos and lotteries are the same kind of "industries." Banks were intended to be service institutions. Alexander Hamilton himself came to regret having established the bank. Only seven years of experience with the bank led him to write the following in a letter to Oliver Wolcott, the new secretary of the Treasury in the Adams-Jefferson administration:

New York, August 22, 1798

My dear Sir:

No one knows better than yourself how difficult and oppressive is the collection even of taxes very moderate in amount, if there is a defective circulation. According to all the phenomena which fell under my notice, this is our case, in the interior parts of the country. . . .

For these and other reasons I have thought well of, I have come to a conclusion that our Treasury ought to raise up circulation of its own. I mean by issuing of Treasury notes. . . . This appears to me an expedient

58

equally necessary to keep the circulation full. . . . It will be easy to enlarge without hazard to credit.

(Signed) Alexander Hamilton

Once established, however, the system Hamilton started continued to develop and become more and more entrenched, fighting off all challenges with the power that comes with money, its creation, and its control. Today this debt-based fractional reserve banking controls not only the economic destiny of the United States but the destinies of 178 nations through the three entities known as the Federal Reserve, the World Bank, and the International Monetary Fund, and their associated central banks and other subsidiary organizations.

Notes

1. Dewey's *Financial History of the United States*.
2. Alexander Del Mar, *History of Money in America* (New York: Gordon Press, 1973; originally published in 1899).
3. All emphases in text or quotations made in italics are the author's, not by the original author.
4. By February 1996 the national debt of the United States reached $5 trillion—a great problem for the nation and for the whole banking system as well.
5. Constitution Article 1, Section 8, Clause 5.
6. The same thing was done in 1913 when the word *federal* was chosen to help get the Federal Reserve Banking Act enacted.

Chapter 9
The New Aristocracy

Introducing the Land Lords of the World

Almost all American citizens believe that the United States is a democracy. The facts are that we are going through the motions of democracy while being ruled by a new aristocracy. This is true of virtually all more or less stable nations of the world.

The media are very aware of the presence of such an aristocracy in the world. If we read our newspapers carefully, we notice terms such as "the elite," "the media elite," "the social elite," "the financial elite," "the establishment," "oligarchies," and so on, in their reporting and commentaries. I use the term "land lords of the world" because they exert effective control over the financial, political, and social structures, and economic development of the world.

What Kind of Aristocracy?

In itself the concept of an aristocracy is not bad. It means rule by the best (*aristos* is the Greek word meaning "best"). The idea of an aristocracy had its origin in the writing of Plato and Aristotle. To have the best, the most intelligent and capable people in charge of government sounds like an ideal worth striving for. It was also Jefferson's ideal.

George Washington belonged to the propertied upper class and considered himself an aristocrat; he had serious misgivings about ordinary citizens being able to govern themselves under a democratic form of government. Nevertheless, he cooperated with his fellow citizens to adopt the "experiment" of representative democracy. Alexander Hamilton held the same views and was also an aristocrat. I call these men members of the new aristocracy to differentiate them from an aristocracy based on hereditary nobility. It is new in that sense, not in relationship to time.

There have always been certain people in society set apart as in some way better than others and more capable of being its rulers. The nobles and titled aristocracy before the new aristocracy also collected tribute, just as the new aristocracy today collects ever-increasing taxes and plunders the wealth of the nations of the world. However, it was the merchants from mercantilist days who perfected the mechanisms for building and perpetuating a more powerful aristocracy than ever existed in the history of nations.

Those mechanisms were money, gold, and debt, not just money as a medium of exchange but as something with which they could exert control outside of the conventional and legal channels of government. This new aristocracy is today the world power that rules virtually every nation, regardless of its external form of government. It is made up principally of the financiers of the world and includes the big banks, the central banks, the Federal Reserve, the International Monetary Fund, and the World Bank; the great captains of industry, international finance, and the media; and the investors and capitalist structures financed by unearned money.

One might not exactly call this a conspiracy. There is some competition among the central banks as they jockey for power and control, and among the media and other institutions. It is difficult to judge in every instance, however, whether the differences are genuine or contrived to mislead the citizens, as has often been the case. These "elite" of our society, though not necessarily all of them, make up a number of secret groups. The three major ones are the Council on Foreign Relations (CFR), the Trilateral Commission (TC), and the Bilderbergers. The bonds that hold them together are (1) maintaining and defending their own privileged position; (2) forming a world government under the United Nations with themselves as the secret rulers of the world's peoples; and (3) always striving for more profit, power, and advantage for their members. The following descriptions of the three groups will outline some of their respective activities.

The Council on Foreign Relations

An organization called the British Royal Institute on International Affairs was founded by the English financier Cecil Rhoades (also founder of the Rhoades Scholarship program) to promote reuniting the United States to the British Empire. The Council on Foreign Relations (CFR) was founded in 1921 by J. P. Morgan and other international bankers as the American branch of the British institute and was intended to be comprised of American citizens only.

The CFR, however, went beyond the British institute. Its specific task was to condition Americans to accept world government as a desirable solution to the problems of the world. It did not do much until 1939, when David Rockefeller took over as chairman, and it was funded heavily by the Rockefeller, Ford, and Carnegie foundations. Though now eighty years of age, Rockefeller is still very much its master.

The CFR publishes the quarterly journal *Foreign Affairs* and other literature and could be called the public relations and propaganda arm for the Trilaterals and the Bilderbergers. Almost all the key personnel in the United States government, especially in finance and foreign affairs, have been picked from the CFR ranks by all the presidents since Franklin Roosevelt (regardless of which political party was in power). In effect, these are the elite, the establishment that runs the country, largely according to the wishes of the Trilaterals and Bilderbergers. The rest of the citizens of the United States may well wonder just how much of a voice they have in the supposedly representative democracy.

Some of the New Aristocrats of the United States

Below is a sampling of CFR membership. The latest list comprises over three thousand people taken from banking and finance, big business, industry, the media, politics, and academia. Membership is by invitation only and can be terminated at any time.[1]

General meetings are open to all members, but, because many members may be only passive members—as in any organization—not much is done in these meetings. The seminars, workshops, decisions, and other significant activities are restricted to certain members and are highly secretive.

In Government

Pres. Bill Clinton belongs to all three groups. He was chosen to be front-runner for the presidency and to be supported by the media before the primary elections. Naturally, the other candidates would run out of money and be forced to drop out. President Bush had also been a member, but in the judgment of the "elite," Bill Clinton would serve their objectives better. So they dropped Bush, just as two hundred years earlier the new aristocrats used and discarded Alexander Hamilton, who was also one of their own.

Other members of the Council on Foreign Relations in government today are Albert Gore, Jr., Vice President; George Stephanopoulos, Director of Communications and four other top officials of the White House Staff; Warren Christopher, Secretary of State and thirty-seven other officials in the Department of State; Les Aspin, Secretary of Defense, with ten others in that department; Colin L. Powell, Chair of the Joint Chiefs of Staff; Anthony Lake, National Security Advisor; James Woolsey, Director of Central Intelligence; Laura Tyson, Chair of the Council of Economic Advisors; Lloyd Bentsen, Treasury Secretary, with six other top treasury officials; Alice Rivlin, Office of Management and Budget; Bruce Babbitt, Interior Secretary; Henry Cisneros, Housing and Urban Development; Donna Shalala, Health and Human Services; and thirty-four members of the United States Congress. Several Congressmen are also Trilaterals.

In the Media

Some well-known names include the following:
CBS—Dan Rather, Henry Schacht, five others.
NBC—Tom Brokaw, John Chancellor, Marvin Kalb, Irving Levine, and nine others.
ABC—Barbara Walters, Diane Sawyer, three others.
PBS—Robert McNeil, Jim Lehrer, three others.
AP—Katherine Graham, two others.
Reuters—Michael Posner.
CNN—Daniel Schorr, W. Thomas Johnson.
U.S. News—David Bergen (a Trilateralist).
NY Times—eighteen members of the CFR, two on the Trilateral Commission.
Time, Inc.—seven members.
Newsweek / Washington Post—fourteen members.
Wall Street Journal—three members.
Reader's Digest—two members.

In Industry

Listed here are just some of the more widely known company names with members of the Council on Foreign Relations on their board of directors: General Motors, Ford, Chrysler, Exxon, Texaco, Shell, Mobil, Tenneco, Deere & Co., AT&T, American Express. Many business and industry leaders are also Trilateral members.

The Federal Reserve System and Big Banks

All are loaded with CFR and some TC members on their boards. Among the banks are Chase Manhattan, Chemical Bank, Citicorp, Morgan Guaranty, Bankers Trust, First National of Chicago, Manufacturers Hanover, Bank America, and the Securities and Exchange Commission.

The Trilateral Commission

The Trilateral Commission was organized by David Rockefeller, the chairman of the Chase Manhattan Bank, July 22–23, 1972, at Tarrytown, New York. It was to be an international version of the CFR, but much more selective, with membership from Western Europe, North America, and Japan. All members must be believers in the "new world order."

The goal of achieving a world government as a federation of nations was being opposed, so this commission was planned to smooth the way for such a government by first forming regional associations of nations, an effort undertaken in cooperation with the Bilderbergers. Almost all the United States Trilaterals are multinational corporate executives or international bankers and members of the other two groups. The Rockefeller oil interests also have played an important part in this organization.

Trilaterals, who include about 320 members, met in Hyatt Park in the nation's capital on March 27–29, 1993, for their 1993 meeting. In 1994 they met in Tokyo in the Okura Hotel on April 9–11. They called their propaganda section to meet at a Council of Foreign Relations forum in Washington two weeks before the Tokyo meeting. The purpose of that emergency meeting was to save the most-favored-nation trade status for Red China. This status was being opposed by some congressmen on account of China's serious human rights violations. But for the new aristocrats, the prospect of the immense profits to be gained from the vast markets and the great natural resources in China, especially the newly discovered oil reserves to be exploited by international financiers, was more important than human rights.

Just as they pushed for NAFTA at their 1993 meeting, around which they would build the American Union as a bloc of the one-world government, so now they are promoting the Asian-Pacific Union as their third bloc. Both of these would be added to the European Union and patterned on it in order to meet their overall objective of a single world government. The Red China markets, with over a billion people, are just as important for that Pacific Union as Canada and Mexico were for NAFTA and the American Union. Three former secretaries of state spoke in behalf of allowing Red China the most-favored-nation status, which it received May 22, 1994. The members of this new aristocracy are doing a great job in getting the United States Congress to help implement the objectives of the Bilderberger policy decisions and to promote the one world agenda.

The three trading blocs could then be molded into one world, which the new aristocracy, the land lords of the world, would find easier to control. This, of course, would mean that the individual nations would lose their sovereignty. The drive for a United Nations army to enforce their will is well under way. The expedition into Somalia was the first experiment in using such an army. It didn't work out quite as planned because nations still treasure their own ethnic traditions and their sovereignty. Trying to force the nations to give them up only results in more wars and basic human right violations.

The Bilderbergers

The first conference of a very select group of leading bankers, statesmen, industrialists, and politicians was held in 1954 at the Bilderberg Hotel near Oosterbeck, Holland. Hence the name "Bilderbergers."

Unlike the CFR, the Bilderbergers are an international association of several hundred members from the United States and Western Europe, almost exclusively the NATO countries (more recently the former Soviet Union countries and the Eastern bloc countries were invited). Here the Rothschild family is the dominant force, although the American Rockefeller influence is also very much in evidence. This is the senior policy-setting organization for the whole world, but especially for the European sector, leaving many of the American concerns to the Trilateral Commission. The Bilderbergers have vice presidents for the individual major industrial nations.

It was the Bilderberger group that developed the plan to divide the world into three major regions: the European Union, the American

Union, and the Pacific Union. This was done at their secret meeting in Vouliagmeni, Greece, in the spring of 1993. In 1994 they met secretly at the Kalastajatorrpa Hotel in Helsinki, Finland. One of the main concerns at that conference was the future of Russia.

Examples of Bilderberg Decisions

During the weekend of May 11–14, 1989, on the island of La Toja off the Atlantic coast of Spain near Pontevedra, it was decided that British prime minister Margaret Thatcher had to be removed, and orders were given to the contingent from Britain to work for her defeat. The reason was that she refused to yield British sovereignty to the European superstate that was to emerge in 1992. Thatcher was later replaced by John Major.

Extraordinary steps were taken to preserve the secrecy for the June 8–11, 1995, Bilderberg conference at Niewalden on Mount Burgenstock, Switzerland. Local police asked the Swiss army to guard the hotel and protect the participants. Only the participants had access to the hotel, and a special helicopter brought them there. Preliminary reports say that the participants were not happy; things were not going their way, and David Rockefeller, who was confident that a world government would be in place by the year 2000, revised his estimate to 2002. The attendees were disappointed with the many populist movements around the world and the resistance of nations to giving up their sovereignty. However, Bill Clinton is the "best" president they have had in a long time, and they committed themselves to do everything possible to get him reelected. They also concluded that Pat Buchanan must be stopped at all costs.

Bill Clinton, a long-time Trilateral, was summoned to his first Bilderberg meeting in Baden-Baden Germany in 1991. At their meeting in Spain in the spring of 1992, he was picked as the favored candidate for the presidency. There is an understanding among the secret groups that once their candidates are in office, they do not attend the meetings personally so as to maintain the secrecy, but they send trusted assistants to represent them. Dan Quayle was able to attend the 1990 meeting on Long Island personally because it was just overnight from Saturday to Sunday morning and could be kept secret. He came back with the instructions that American taxes must be increased. President Bush obeyed, in spite of his "read my lips" pledge. This no doubt contributed to Bush losing the election.

The Real Rulers of the World

Many members belong to more than one group. All three groups are cross-related by their directors taking part in each other's decisions and cooperating in carrying them out. For example, although it was the Bilderbergers who decided to "retire" Margaret Thatcher, it was the Trilaterals who more recently did the same to Japan's prime minister Morihiro Hosokawa. They were "uncomfortable" with him and unsure that he was "reliable." His "retirement" took place on April 8, 1995.

These new aristocrats are the real political and financial government of the nations of the world. Some call them the shadow government, but actually it is the democracies that are the "shadows," a status volunteered by President Wilson for the democracy of the United States.[2] They are so vastly powerful that the very thought of their dominant position in the world tends to intimidate ordinary citizens. Through their conglomerate of debt-based money systems, they control and dictate the finances and politics of the 178 nations of the world that belong to the International Monetary Fund and the World Bank with their parental ties to the Federal Reserve system and the central banks of the world.

The new aristocrats look upon ordinary citizens pretty much as the aristocrats of Washington's day did—as a mob of largely ignorant people who don't know what is good for them and are not capable of governing. They believe it is up to them, the "elite," to determine the agenda and govern us.

Yet, as the last conference of the Bilderbergers at Burgenstock, Switzerland, and the Copenhagen, Denmark, meeting of the Trilateral Commission show, they are not invincible. They are depressed by the current nationalist mood of America and the resistance throughout the world of nations trying to defend themselves against the threats to their sovereignty, which they perceive as coming from the one-world government notion. In other words, the land lords of the world are vulnerable when large enough numbers of ordinary people get involved in protecting the freedom and ethnic identity that come with national sovereignty. From the time of Paul Warburg's drive to pass the Federal Reserve Act in the United States, the new aristocrats have lived in fear of the people, whom they have thus far managed to manipulate and deceive, just as Warburg said they would.

The Land Lords' Agenda

The following are major points in the agenda of the new aristocracy:

1. Dividing the world into three major economic regions, the European, American, and Pacific Unions. The European Union has already been established. The next priority was to get the American Union going by adopting NAFTA. David Rockefeller, in his capacity as a policy leader in the Bilderberg group, announced that he fully expected that NAFTA would be extended to all the Western hemisphere by the year 2002.

The third step is to start moving toward the Asia-Pacific Union. That was the top priority of the 1994 meeting. Former presidents—the Trilaterals Carter, Reagan, and Bush, and Bilderberger Ford—did well following the orders of these land lords of the world. But none of them were as bold and open in carrying out their agenda as President Clinton. Going to Seattle on November 19, 1993, to start promoting the Pacific Union, Clinton told those present that he would disregard any restrictions made by Congress on placing American soldiers under foreign commanders, despite the fact that such restrictions had already been added to the defense appropriation bill he had signed into law. Clinton said: "I construe it as not restricting my Constitutional responsibility and authority as commander in chief, including my ability to place U.S. combat forces under the temporary tactical control of a foreign commander."

2. Installing a global UN army to give the UN enforcement power.

3. Forcing so-called democracy on other nations.

4. "Helping" the new democracies by imposing debt-based money system "reforms" through the World Bank and the International Monetary Fund. Those nations' economies must be able to pay the interest on the debts that are created for them. In addition, they must provide a market for our industry and pay for their purchases with their raw materials and agricultural products at whatever price our big monopoly corporations choose to give them—a new colonialism!

Finally, they must not be allowed to develop industries or infrastructure or increase their populations. This would make them too strong and a threat to our national security at some distant future time.

This is not just idle speculation, as the *NATIONAL SECURITY STUDY MEMO 200* of 1974 makes clear.

The Memo

All the above policies have been adopted by the new aristocracy and are being promoted constantly. In 1974 a detailed secret plan to limit world population growth was drawn up by the U.S. State Department, then headed by Secretary of State Henry Kissinger, a prominent Trilateral and member of the Council on Foreign Relations. The document was dated December 10, 1974, and consisted of 198 pages of typewritten text. It was called the *NSSM 200 (National Security Study Memo 200)* and was immediately classified as a secret National Security Council document. It was declassified on July 3, 1989, and made available to the public at the National Archives in Washington.

In its 198 pages, the document goes into very specific procedures for keeping certain nations and their populations weakened economically, militarily, and by limiting their growth, so that they will not present a "threat to the national security." Thirteen developing nations having strong growth patterns are targeted in this document as the ones in which these policies are to be implemented. They include Iraq, Brazil, and other Latin American and Asiatic nations. Keeping this in mind will help us understand the four billion dollars spent last year to promote contraception and abortion in those nations, especially the sterilization of half of Brazilian women, and the Desert Storm operation in Iraq, with its subsequent starving of a quarter of a million people, many children. It also illuminates why through economic sanctions and the delaying tactics in responding to Bosnia and the rest of the Balkans' call for assistance in defending themselves and their sovereignty.

Jacqueline R. Kasun, professor of economics at Humboldt State University at Arcata, California, says of the policies detailed in this document, "There was no backward movement on the commitment to these policies. It's always been forward. Because the groups that are behind these policies are extremely powerful and very well financed and they have, above all, very important connections in Congress."[3]

NOTE: The names used throughout this chapter are illustrative only to show how the three branches of the land lords of the world are involved in the affairs of our nation. The offices held by them may be held by someone else when this book is published. That is irrelevant to the theme of the chapter. The source of updated information is given in a footnote of the text at the appropriate place.

Notes

1. For a copy of the CFR annual report, which includes a list of current members, write to the Council on Foreign Relations, 58 East 68th Street, New York, NY 10021. Members who do not wish to have their names listed, however, may have them omitted. How many of these unlisted members exist is unknown.
2. See "The Great Deception" in chapter 12.
3. Jacqueline R. Kasun, *The War against Population: The Economics and Ideology of Population Control.* (Harrison, NY: Ignatius Press, 1988).

Chapter 10
Was There Ever Debt-Free Money?

Debt-based money, the kind we have in virtually every nation in the world today, is the worst kind of money because it is an instrument for looting the economic resources of every nation where it is found. There has been money used by nations, however, including our own, that with reservations could be classed as honest money. That was the money based on gold or some other specie or commodity. Used honestly, this type of money served the needs of commerce quite well for centuries. But in all nations where it was used, it proved to be a very efficient tool with which to concentrate the true wealth of the nation into the hands of the few who had the possession or control of the specie.

Adopting gold as the standard for money under the influence of the merchants and their bankers in the fifteenth and sixteenth centuries brought on some of the most shameful and disgraceful chapters in the annals of human history.

Some Ancient History

The use of specie brought down nations in ancient times as well as in modern times. All kinds of things or animals were used in different nations as specie, which represented human beings' productive effort. In ancient Greece, for instance, in 1194 B.C.E., oxen were used for money. The golden armor of Glaucus was valued by Homer at one hundred oxen. To buy such armor, one first had to raise or earn the hundred oxen. It wasn't gold that bought the oxen, but the other way around. Coins of cheap metal, more easily available to the ordinary citizens than oxen, were used later on, and whenever that happened the people prospered.

The money lenders always fought against using cheap and plentiful things as money because they could not control the supply; it was easily available. They wanted something rare to be used, which they could get their hands on but ordinary citizens would find difficult to acquire. The people would then have to borrow that money from the lenders at interest, and work twice as hard to repay both the loans and the interest.

So our modern specie-based or debt-based money systems are nothing new. It is the same story that has been repeated over and over. Citizens have at times been given good and wise direction and beneficial laws have been proposed from time to time in the course of history. But for the most part, the people either have not taken the time to understand what is going on, or understanding it, have only gone halfway to cooperate with their patriotic leaders. Citizens today behave much the same.

By 595 B.C.E. in Attica, the money lenders had succeeded in destroying the people's cheap money, as they usually do when the people get careless and uninvolved. In the end the money lenders owned almost everything, with the people in debt to them and a mortgage stone at the corner of nearly every piece of land. It sounds very much like what has happened and is happening to thousands of farmers in the United States today. On the verge of violence, both parties in Attica agreed to have the philosopher Solon arbitrate the matter.

Solon drew up a code of laws, which he said would save Attica from bloodshed and ruin provided all accepted and obeyed them. First, he abolished all interest. The money lenders naturally refused to accept that. The people, foolishly hoping they might get to charge interest and get rich too, turned this proposal down. Although Solon managed to save Attica from violence and ruin with other changes, the way was left open for the money lenders to regain their privileged position and impoverish the citizens again. The reform—as with our own attempts in the United States to reform the money system—stopped short of doing the job right.

Croesus, king of Lydia, asked Solon if the laws he had made for the Athenians were the best that could be given them. Solon said, "Yes, the best that they were able to receive." This prompts us to ask ourselves, Is the debt-based money system the best *we* are capable of receiving? Or do we have the political will and the knowledge that will make us capable of changing it to a debt-free system?

This very short historical sketch of the money situation in ancient Greece provides evidence of the inadequacy of specie as money and of its use by the privileged class to divest the ordinary citizens of the wealth they produce by their labors. In ancient Rome the story would be similar. As far as we know the Chinese history of money, it too used gold as far back as three thousand years, no doubt with resulting usury practiced by the lenders. The Chinese also seem to be the first to have used paper money.

Successful Debt-Free Money Systems in the Middle Ages

Debt-free money is real, practical, and honest; it has been used for a long time and has always brought prosperity to the community using it, without either inflations or depressions.

The first instance in reliable recorded history in which bills of credit were successfully used as debt-free money was in the city-state of Venice. Here the government established the Bank of Venice in 1171. In order to conduct the war that it was engaged in at the time, this government was forced to issue bills of credit through its own government-owned bank in the form of tallies. The tallies could be transferred from person to person and used as a medium of exchange.

There was no specie backing this money, no promise to redeem it for anything else. But the government accepted these credit tallies in payment for all taxes due to it. This was debt-free, valid money in its simplest form. It met all the requirements for debt-free, interest-free, honest money. This brought a new dimension to the whole concept of money that enabled commerce to take a more positive turn as a factor in the civilization of nations.

Characteristics of the Venetian Banking System:

1. Money was issued by the government's own treasury bank, giving the government full control of the volume of money and its value.
2. Because they retained their value, the bills were a good vehicle for storage of wealth. They were preferred to coin by a premium of 20 percent.
3. The bills were not subject to be redeemed in any specie over which speculators could gain monopoly control and thereby channel the fruits of production into their own hands.
4. This money did not create a debt for the government to owe to any private banking institution.
5. Bills were accepted by the government in payment for taxes and all other payments due to the government. (This is essential both to

make the money legal tender and to enable the government to control the volume and value of money in circulation.)

6. As far as deposits by the people were concerned, the bank paid some interest on these for the first three hundred years. Interest was abolished completely in 1423. With the value of the money being stable, the people were satisfied to have the bank keeping it safe for them.

How Long Did the Bank of Venice Last?

It survived 641 years! What were the results? The inhabitants were happy; there were no depressions, no inflation, and not a single panic![1]

The Bank of Genoa, another city-state bank, operated by the same principles as the Bank of Venice but was established a little later. It was the first bank of record to issue bank notes, as the private Federal Reserve banks do today. The difference was that they were bank notes issued by a government-owned bank, not by a privately owned bank as are the Federal Reserve notes we have today.

These two city-states, along with Florence, were the financial centers of the world for many years. Operating as they did, they provided the people with a dependable and honest medium of exchange and kept the money lenders at bay. It was *not* a system that would give a few people much of a chance to become rich and a privileged class at the expense of the general public.

The Merchants Take Control

But beginning in the fifteenth and sixteenth centuries, the merchants of Europe began to gain influence with the ruling classes. By mutual favors they promoted the use of gold as specie to be used as money in their commerce. The Rothschild family bankers were the leading promoters of this.

By 1609, the search for gold was in full swing throughout the world. In that year the first private commercial bank was established in Amsterdam, the center for the commerce of the day. Gold was king, so it was adopted as the specie backing for the bank notes. On that basis the bank served commerce quite well and profited handily from the interest charged on its loans for almost two hundred years. But eventually greed took over. The bank loaned more than the specie it had to redeem its notes and deposits, an example of how the fractional reserve idea gets into the blood when greed takes over. The bank failed in 1790, the first banking institution issuing notes on a specie basis to fail.

The Bank of Hamburg, founded in 1619, operated the same as the Amsterdam Bank but was a bit more conservative and did better. With these two banks under good government control, Holland grew rich and prosperous and avoided panics. However, these banks did not give the money lenders quite the freedom that they wanted, so they moved on to London, where the monied merchants and bankers were in full control and on their way to acquiring much greater riches through their now well-established money system based on government debt. That was the new and totally dishonest dimension in banking legalized by King William III in 1694 (described in chapter 5).

Prior to that sad date, England also had an ingenious debt-free money system similar to the ones in Venice and Genoa. It had been adopted by Henry I in 1100. This early English money consisted of tallies made out of wood with no intrinsic value and no specie backing. But they were accepted by the government in payment of taxes and all other dues, the essential requirement to make them legal tender. England also prospered using these tallies as money and avoided panics for almost six hundred years, until that fateful day in 1694. With the advent of the government-debt based system, the nation was soon plunged into depression and unemployment.[2]

Debt-free Money in America

There was debt-free money in America from 1690 to 1720 in the colony of Massachusetts.[3] Beyond that there were just a few short interludes with debt-free money in America; the rest is a story of panics, depressions, and inflation with debt-based money controlled and manipulated by the financiers.

In 1861, Pres. Abraham Lincoln persuaded Congress to issue debt-free and interest-free money in the form of "greenbacks" in order to finance the Civil War when the bankers wanted 24 percent to 36 percent interest for their money. That story is in the next chapter.

More Recent Examples of Debt-free Money in Use

While some of the older examples of the use of debt-free money lasted for hundreds of years, the more recent ones have been of short duration. There are a number of reasons for this. One is that the land lords of the world are more numerous and more alert to new opportunities for profit and extending their dominion. They are quick to see the potential in an emerging nation or a nation enjoying prosperity. They want to cash in on this wealth and not let the nation become an example of greater freedom from debt and prosperity than the nations already under their control. They perceive such freedom as a threat to their privileged position.

Witness the example of the early colonists' efforts to issue their own money and to enjoy some measure of prosperity versus the imperialism of the Bank of England cashing in on that prosperity (as described in chapter 7), and today the example of the Eastern European nations after the breakdown of communism struggling against the imperialism of the International Monetary Fund and the World Bank. The same motives and procedures operated in both cases.

Latin America and Russia

Are the internationalist banking representatives really concerned about helping Russia and the Latin American countries with their proposed reforms? There is too much nervousness and excitement in their statements and too much arrogance in the way they make their demands for us to accept such a possibility. Further, we know the nature of the "reforms" will lead those nations into more debt that in turn will allow more opportunities for looting of their already shaky economies.

The State of Guernsey

Guernsey, one of the Channel Islands off the coast of France, is an area of fewer than twenty-five square miles. It depended on income from military occupation during the war of 1812–14 between Britain and France. The island was self-governing and had a parliament called the State of Guernsey. Its total population at the end of the war was between six thousand and seven thousand. The money in use at that time was the bank notes of the Bank of England, since the island belonged to Britain. But with the end of the war, Britain had no more use for Guernsey and the supply of Bank of England notes dried up.

With no money as a medium of exchange, practically all economic activity and employment came to a halt and the people faced starvation. The island had abundant natural resources—building stone and other materials and good farm lands—but its infrastructure—the harbor, roads, and buildings—were in disrepair and unusable. The only passage across the island was a rutted road about seven feet wide, barely passable by an ox cart.

Neither people nor their previous governors had faced such an extreme situation before. Now they became aware of political and economic issues and began thinking about how to solve their problems. A committee approached the governor to ask his advice on how to get money to hire people to build a market house, which they needed badly. He knew that it is the state's sovereign prerogative to provide the money for its citizens, so he suggested that Parliament issue sufficient money based on an honest estimate of the cost of the market house as a credit to be paid out into circulation for the construction of the structure. The new market house was completed and opened on October 12, 1822.

The paper money issued would be accepted by the government in full payment of taxes with the guarantee that the money could be retired and cancelled after two years, if necessary. This made it full legal tender, and it was accepted by everybody. As the new currency was paid out into circulation, it expedited the exchange of goods and services of the citizens so successfully that other issues of money were brought out for other public works. Roads, schools, and other markets and businesses were built.

A small liquor tax, rentals of stalls in the market and other buildings, and increased maritime trade produced enough revenue to support the government with no or very little taxation. The population doubled with the advent of this prosperity. There was no bank on the island to challenge the legitimate creation of the citizens' money by their sovereign government. The great prosperity and high standard of living was taken advantage of by international bankers who then entered the picture, but the government still exercises much control over its money.

The Singapore Miracle

The total land area of Singapore is almost ten times that of the state of Guernsey. It comprises an island and fifty-seven islets off the coast of the southern Malay peninsula and is linked to it by a causeway. It became an independent nation on August 9, 1965. A Singapore government spokesman described conditions there prior to its independence: "It had no natural resources. Crime was rampant, secret criminal societies had considerable power, prostitution and drug addiction were widespread. The country was poor, its slums notorious."[4]

Sixteen years later, in 1981, scholar Dr. Martin A. Larson visited Singapore to learn firsthand the facts about what was already being called Singapore's economic miracle. What he found was "A modern civilization, with all cultural amenities. . . . Almost everyone had modern housing; and those who retire enjoy generous pensions without any cost to the younger and producing generations. Furthermore, there is almost no public welfare; out of 2.5 million, only 12,000 receive such largess."[5]

Bringing the information up to date, the Cox News Service in April 1994 noted: "Not quite 30 years after gaining its independence, Singapore has risen from the malarial and crumbling remains of a weary colonial outpost to become the unchallenged pearl of Southeast Asia. Its residents' average income is second in Asia only to Japan. Fully 84% of Singaporeans own their own homes and more than half own stocks. But Singapore has refused to accept rising crime." What the People's Action Party, which is still in power today, has accomplished corroborates the report by the Cox News Service. "The result has been astonishing," Holburt says. "Singapore is one of the safest cities on earth and its people among the most prosperous."[6]

Leslie Lengel, who accompanied her husband to Singapore, reports that it was as though they "were living out a fantasy from another world. 'I love it,' she said, ticking off the attributes that invariably seduce first time visitors to this city-state: its squeaky clean streets, orderly traffic, friendly cosmopolitan inhabitants, and most of all the near-to-total absence of crime. 'It's a wonderful experience. . . . We feel very safe.' "[7]

Stories in the media do not recount this success story. Instead, they report something "negative" about Singapore, such as the strict controls on crime, drugs, news media, money, and so on. The land lords of the world look on such a healthy economy as a threat to their own debt-based money and banking system.

Dr. Larson tells us what he learned on his visit:

1. There is no such thing as fractional reserve banking in Singapore.
2. All currency is issued by the government and is redeemable either in specie or in bonds. Even though specie is used, it is strictly controlled to prevent abuse.
3. The government, not a central bank, is responsible for fiscal policies.
4. There is no government debt, debt-based money system, or government interest payment to a banking institution.

5. Generous interest is paid to private bond holders.
6. Deficit spending is forbidden.
7. Retirement funds are put to work to build and upgrade infrastructures.
8. The money system is a genuine debt-free system.

The results of the honest debt-free monetary system instituted in Singapore can be realized anywhere. There is, of course, much more to the Singapore story that is not given here. For example, the financial services help with the building of infrastructures and industry in their neighboring countries, as reported by *The Wall Street Journal*, are nothing short of fantastic.

Criticism from the land lords of the world, who try to discredit this story, says, "Yes, maybe it worked in a small country, but it won't work in a great industrial nation." *The contrary is true. What works in a microeconomy will be both intensified and multiplied in the macroeconomy.* The same causes will produce the same effects on a bigger scale. We have considered that aspect in chapter 3, and we have seen the truth of that observation verified by comparing the results of the state of Guernsey's experience with those of Singapore, which is almost ten times bigger. What couldn't a debt-free money system do for the United States!

Modern Germany

In Germany after World War II, industry and agriculture were devastated and in ruins. It was stripped of all its movable assets, gold, fuel, and so on. A quarter of its homes were destroyed. Famine and hyperinflation added to the people's misery. Konrad Adenauer and his finance minister, Ludwig Erhard, went far beyond what Lincoln did (next chapter). They took away the central bank's power to create fractional reserve money and gave the people debt-free money created by the sovereign power of the government based on the only value they had, land. Within six months inflation was cured and the stage was set for its "economic miracle" of the 1950s. Debt-free money worked better in a big country! The results lasted even after the financial land lords regained a restrained power over money creation when the political leaders let down their guard.

Notes

1. Stephen Colwell, *Ways and Means of Payment*, 1965 reprint of 1859 ed.

2. David Devant and Nevil Maskelyne, *Our Magic*, 1982 reprint of 1946 edition, and Jonathan Elliot, *Funding System of the United States and Great Britain*, Notable American Authors Series, 2 vols., 1992 reprint of 1845 edition, 1,299 pp.

3. The details in chapter 7 and the very significant Mixt Money Case Decision of 1604 are worth reviewing at this point.

4. Quoted by Jonathan Holbert, *The Wall Street Journal*, March 28, 1994.

5. Martin A. Larson, *Spotlight*, September 21, 1981.

6. Holbert.

7. Quoted by the Cox News Service.

Chapter 11

Land Lords of the World Take Over the Nation and the World (1862–1997)

Establishing the First National Bank of the United States in 1791 was a major breakthrough for the international banking community. But it did not turn out to be a complete victory; some of the states continued to charter state banks with the power to issue their own bank notes, which were used as currency.

The states had just surrendered their power to issue money to the Congress of the United States in Article I, Section 8, Clause 5 of the Constitution. But now after Alexander Hamilton's use of the "implied powers" expedient to justify Congress delegating powers to a private bank that were reserved to it by the Constitution, the states may have figured that they could disregard the fact that they had given up their power over money to the new national government. So they continued to issue their bank notes along with those of the new so-called national bank. And henceforth the provisions of the Constitution would mean whatever those exercising the real sovereignty wanted them to mean.

Because the First National Bank was not yet in total financial control of the whole nation, and the *bank's very existence was challenged and opposed by great masses of the population*, there ensued a battle royal for the next seventy-two years, until 1863. That year the National Bank Act of 1863 put the bankers in a much stronger position; fifty years later, in 1913, they finally achieved total control of all banking through the Federal Reserve Act (*see* chapter 12).

The struggle was like a great football game, going on for over 120 years. The two opposing teams were the Federalists, starting the game with Alexander Hamilton as their captain, and the Democratic Republicans, with Thomas Jefferson as their leader. The Federalists represented the international banking interests and local merchants. Later they disavowed that name, when they were losing the game. The Democratic Republicans eventually dropped the word *Democratic* from

81

their name and were simply called Republicans. They stood for the nation's property owners and the general population.

Thomas Jefferson

It appeared at times that the people were going to win. They had the advantage when Thomas Jefferson was elected president for two terms. Following the same principles and convictions that he expressed in the Declaration of Independence, even with Hamilton's bank already there with a twenty-year charter, Jefferson established an honest, wise, and economical government that would be a model for future presidents to follow. He believed that government should meet fully and promptly all its obligations within its own generation and *not impose heavy debts on future generations*.

Instead of burdening the people with new taxes, through prudent and frugal management, he abolished all internal taxes; he dismissed all the officers who had administered and collected them; his secretary of the Treasury Albert Gallatin, reorganized the national finances; and so, with only one-half of the former income, he and Madison in ten years reduced the public debt from $83 to $45 million. This was an accomplishment without parallel in the history of modern governments.[1]

Lincoln's "Greatest Blessing," Debt-free Money

During the Civil War, armies and a navy had to be maintained. Wars have always been great occasions for the international bankers, because under the debt-based money system, both sides of the conflict can be forced to borrow money from them to finance the wars. This always adds to the nation's debts and the bankers' stock of bonds bearing interest. Wars bring untold devastation of human life and resources for the citizens at large but great profits for the big banks and munitions makers. The additional bonds also mean that the children and grandchildren will have taxes to pay for many generations to come. This is all inevitable unless the people choose to change the debt-based money system.

When Pres. Abraham Lincoln and his secretary of the Treasury, Salmon P. Chase, applied to the bankers and lenders of New York City for loans to pay his army and carry on the war, the bankers wanted

24 percent to 36 percent interest, payable in gold. Lincoln and Chase refused to borrow on those terms; they were then told that "if the government didn't want the money at that figure, why, they [the bankers] could loan it the Southern Confederacy."[2]

Very much disturbed and worried, Lincoln sent for Col. Dick Taylor, a close friend in whom he had great confidence. Lincoln asked Taylor for advice on how to solve the problem of financing the war. The recommendation Lincoln received is clear from a letter that Lincoln wrote to Taylor acknowledging his services:

My Dear Colonel Dick:

I have long determined to make public the origin of the greenback and tell the world that it is Dick Taylor's creation. You had always been friendly to me, and when troublous times fell on us, and myself surrounded by such circumstances and such people that I knew not whom to trust, then I said in my extremity: "I will send for Colonel Taylor; he will know what to do." I think it was January, 1862, on or about the 16th, that I said so; you came, and I said to you: "What can we do?" Said you, "Why, issue Treasury notes bearing no interest, printed on the best banking paper. Issue enough to pay off the Army expenses and declare it legal tender."

Chase thought it a hazardous thing, but we finally accomplished it and gave the people of this Republic THE GREATEST BLESSING THEY EVER HAD—their own paper money to pay their own debts.

It is due you, the father of the present greenback that the people should know it, and I take pleasure in making it known. How many times have I laughed at you telling me plainly that I was too lazy to be anything but a lawyer.

Yours truly. A. Lincoln[3]

With the help of Thaddeus Stevens, chairman of the House Ways and Means Committee, Lincoln was able to persuade Congress to pass the Legal Tender Bill of 1862, authorizing the issue of the debt-free money. The U.S. Treasury then issued United States notes printed with green ink. Because of this, they were called greenbacks. They were not redeemable by anything except other greenbacks; no gold or silver was promised because the Treasury didn't have any. What made them sound debt-free money and full legal tender was the Act of Congress and the inscription on each bill: "Legal Tender in Payment of All Debts, Private and Public, Including Taxes." The first issue was $150 million, which was sufficient to pay all soldiers and to provide for all current needs of the army and navy. No taxes were needed and no interest was due to the bankers. The people accepted the new money that was paid into circulation gladly and at full dollar value.

International Bankers Alarmed

Shortly after the United States issued the debt-free greenbacks to help finance the Civil War, the bankers of England became greatly alarmed at the threat this raised to all international bankers. When they saw that this money was working very well, their controlled newspapers sounded the alarm throughout Europe. *The London Times*, for instance, wrote: "If that mischievous financial policy, which had its origin in the North American Republic during the late war in that country, should be indurated down to a fixture, then that Government will furnish its own money without cost. It will pay off its debts and be without debt. It will have all the money necessary to carry on its commerce. It will become prosperous beyond precedent in the history of the civilized governments of the world. The brains of all countries will go to North America. That Government must be destroyed or it will destroy every monarchy on the globe."

Please note these points in the above editorial:

1. The source was the international bankers, whose whole life was money and debt. They knew what they were talking about.
2. For a government to create its own money was "mischief" for international banking; it threatened its very existence.
3. If such a government-created money system were to become established, the country would prosper.
4. Problems with deficits and the national debt would be solved.
5. All other countries would lose their talented people to such a country, or, more likely, would want to institute a similar system. The editorial appealed to the European rulers, indebted to the international bankers, to destroy the government that dared to use such a system. The bankers knew that if the rulers followed the example of the United States, they too would get out of debt. This would destroy, *not* their own nations, but the existence of international bankers.

It is significant that the editorial never mentioned the word *fiat* or inflation, the criticism current media would hurl at Lincoln's system. The London bankers knew better. Their own notes were fiat money too.[4] That editorial, coming from international bankers who understand the nature and functions of money and debt perfectly, is a superb witness to the validity of all the positions about debt and money, and their implications taken in this book.

Responding to the Emergency

Alarmed that Lincoln intended to make this debt-free money permanent, the bankers hurriedly convened at Washington, D.C. just four days after the passage of the Legal Tender Act. Bankers from New York, Philadelphia, and Boston were present. Their purpose was to plot emergency legislation to stop Congress and Lincoln from getting too far with issuing money the bankers could not control.

They invited the Senate Finance Committee and the House Ways and Means Committee to meet with them in the office of the secretary of the Treasury on January 11, 1862. They then stayed on in Washington conferring with Secretary Chase and mobilizing their forces, lobbying, bribing senators and congressmen, and harassing and ridiculing Lincoln—all the usual tricks they had used before and continue with their ever-increasing power to use to this day.

When Lincoln's Legal Tender Bill came up with the request for another issue of $150 million in greenbacks, it was passed and signed on February 25, 1862. Lincoln got this and one more similar request from Congress, but *with a big surprise.*

An *Exception Clause* was added on the reverse side of all greenbacks from then on. The whole printed endorsement now read: *"This note is legal tender for all debts, public and private,* **except duties on imports and interest on the public debt,** *and is receivable for all loans made to the United States."* The Act of March 3, 1863, authorized a third issue with the same restrictions.

This was the bankers' emergency solution. With that exception clause, the newly-issued greenbacks were no longer full legal tender. The people didn't notice the difference, but the bankers did. With that change, the government would not accept the new notes from the people in payment of taxes or duties on imports that were then in effect, and the banks would not accept them from the government in payment of interest on its bonds. In other words, now the bankers could tell the people the greenbacks were no good. Naturally, they would not tell them that it was their manipulation of Congress that put that exception clause on the back of the greenbacks.

So the bankers told the people the new money was no good, but, since the people had it on their hands, the banks would accept it from them in exchange for their bank notes—at a discount. The banks would give the people thirty-five cents on the dollar. But why would the banks want that money at all, if it was no good? Would they be accepting a loss of sixty-five cents on the dollar?

No, they had also made plans to cover that situation. They were going to make an immediate profit of sixty-five cents on the dollar. Remember, the exception clause also said, *"and is receivable for all loans made to the United States."* So, while the government could not use greenbacks to pay its interest bill to the bankers, the banks could use greenbacks *at face value* to buy more government bonds on which they could draw more interest. Thus the bankers turned the situation to their advantage at the expense of the citizens. This was a very successful emergency solution to the bankers' problem with the debt-free greenbacks.

The Confidential Circular from Number 3 Wall Street

While things were now going their way, with the threat of the greenbacks averted, the big bankers wanted to improve and consolidate their position and make it more permanent.

Concurrently with their plotting of emergency action, they prepared legislation for Congress for a new, permanent, privately owned banking system of national banks. A "Hazard Circular" was prepared and issued by Ikleheimer, Morton, and Vandergould of New York City to their "friends and clients." The bankers requested that the circular be regarded as "strictly confidential."

The circular spelled out in detail the great potential for profits that the new Banking Act bill would present for them. The message is introduced in these words:

> The great debt the capitalists will see to it is made out of the War [the American Civil War] must be used to control the value of money. To accomplish this, the government bonds must be used as a banking basis. It will not do to allow greenbacks, as they are called, to circulate as money any length of time, as we cannot control that, but we can control the bonds and through them the bank issues.[5]

Bankers were called upon to contact their senators and congressmen immediately and to withhold support or lending to newspapers that opposed the bill. Notice that while the national banks were private institutions, they still called themselves "National" in order to make the people believe they were government entities. The National Bank Act of 1863 was sponsored in the Senate by Sen. John Sherman and by Congressman Samuel Hooper in the House; it was enacted on February 25, 1863.

From this experience with the bankers, Abraham Lincoln learned that *"public opinion is everything. With it nothing can fail; without it, nothing can succeed."* Those are his words after he failed to get the support of Congress in his struggle for financial reform in 1863.

The Response to the "Hazard Circular" in the 1860s

After the passage of the Banking Act of 1863 and the skillful dissemination of the circular outlining the great possibilities for huge profits from the provisions of that act, numerous national banks were chartered between 1863 and 1929.[6] All wanted to partake in the great profits that were promised.

Depressions and Inflations

The banks were now free to use their power to create depressions and inflations, as suggested in point 15 of the "Hazard Circular." Only three years after the Banking Act of 1863 was passed, the Contraction Act of 1866 was passed by Congress. It would bring on a depression, famine, and hunger.

On December 4, 1868, E. G. Paulding, a banker and congressman from Buffalo, New York, wrote to Secretary of Treasury McCullough, asking him to carry out the provisions of the Contraction Act: *"You no doubt know, to a certain extent, you have control of the currency of the country, and I think that you will of necessity contract moderately."* The banker congressman said that there would be *"plenty of money for at least one year to come,"* but then the contraction should start. It did.

In 1866, the country had almost $2 billion in currency. By the end of 1867, there were 2,386 business failures, as opposed to 520 the year before. This continued progressively until in 1874 there were 5,832 failures, a million men out of work, wages down, and many strikes. The following year failures increased to 7,740 more; in 1876 the number was over 10,000. That year there were three million unemployed, foreclosures, riots, and starvation. The Contraction Act had accomplished its purpose. The depression was a success for the money changers. They could pick up the failed businesses and foreclosed properties cheaply with funds from their debt-based money and then start a boom and on to inflation.

The next major depression, or "panic" as it was called, came in 1907. That provided the financiers with the occasion for the creation of a central banking system by the Federal Reserve Act in 1913, which is in force today with many amendments, all giving ever fewer people greater control over all banking and reaching out to virtually all other nations. The amount of manipulation of public opinion, deceit, and corruption that went on during the last half of the nineteenth century and the first quarter of the twentieth staggers the imagination. The history of the rest of twentieth century up to the present day shows how the nation's economy has been rocked to and fro between depressions and inflations.

Historical Witnesses

The following quotations reflect the judgment of some honest and knowledgeable people in positions of responsibility:

1. Salmon P. Chase, secretary of the Treasury during Lincoln's presidency, regretted his part in getting the National Bank Act passed. Chase called it: "My greatest financial mistake of my life. It has built a monopoly that affects every interest in the country. *It should be repealed*, but before this can be accomplished, the people shall be arrayed on one side and the banks on another in a contest such as we have never seen in this country."

2. The Money Commission created on August 15, 1876, consisting of three senators, three members of the House, and three cabinet secretaries, has this to say in a report given March 2, 1877: That the disaster of the Dark Ages was caused by decreasing money and falling prices, and that the recovery therefrom and prosperity... were due to increasing supply... will not be surprising... when the noble functions of money are considered.... Falling prices and misery and destitution are inseparable companions. It is universally conceded that falling prices result from contraction of the money volume.... The highest moral, intellectual, and material development of nations is promoted by the use of money, unchanging in value (Vol. 1, 50–51).

3. Secretary of the American Bankers Association James Buel sent a letter in 1877 to all its members:

   Dear Sir: It is advisable to do all in your power to sustain such prominent and weekly newspapers, especially the Agricultural and Religious Press, as will oppose the greenback issue and that you will withhold patronage from all applicants who are not willing to oppose the government issue of money. . . . To repeal the Act creating Bank Notes, or to restore to circulation the government issue of money will provide the people with money, and will therefore *seriously affect our individual profits as bankers and lenders. . . . See your* Congressman at once and engage him to support our interests that we may control legislation."[7]

Situation Today

Let's take as an example a relatively small bank, not listed among the twenty-five top banks of the nation. The January 15, 1994, issue of the *Milwaukee Journal* carried this news story by business reporter Jack Norman:

Nine senior executives at Valley Bancorporation will pocket $16.3 million in cash when the sale of the big Appleton bank to Marshall & Ilsley Corp. is completed next month, according to a document released this week. . . . The biggest payment will go to Peter Platten, III, Valley's president and chief executive officer and a central negotiator in the merger. . . . Mr. Platten will get $3.3 million in cash because his job at Valley will be terminated. As an added bonus, he'll also be given enough extra money "to offset fully . . . the amount of any golden parachute excise tax owed" on the $3.3 million.

At many firms, including Valley, the golden parachutes are payable even if the executive is hired by the acquiring firm. . . . Indeed Platten will become vice-chairman of M&I at a salary of $375,000 a year plus an annual bonus of at least $225,000. . . . In addition Platten will get options to buy 100,000 shares of M&I stock. Platten owns 150 shares of Valley stock, which will be exchanged tax-free for M&I stock worth about $5.8 million."

Valley chairman Gus Zuelke, 72, who will not take a position at M&I, will receive $100,000 a year for the rest of his life, along with a car, an office, and other benefits. . . . Executives at M&I and Valley have not said whether lower level employees may lose their jobs as a result of the combination of the two big banking systems.

This is just one small example of how the structured banking system works today. When one considers the big New York banks, both the corporate profits and the salaries reach scandalous figures. Recent stories in the *Wall Street Journal* publicized a certain bank giving its sixty or so top executives bonuses of $5 million each for the year in addition to salaries in the millions. One CEO was given a salary of

$25 million. He was supposed to be the highest paid executive. It is not the purpose here to single out any of these banks or people, but merely to provide a glimpse of how the goals promised by that "Hazard Circular" are being met by debt-based money created by banks through the use of fractional reserves, all at the expense of the ordinary citizens. It is difficult to see how there can be any just relationship between the services these CEOs give to the community, for which they receive such compensation, and the services of ordinary citizens who have to produce the wealth these salaries and bonuses claim.

Notes

1. Martin A. Larson, *The Federal Reserve and Our Manipulated Dollar* (Old Greenwich, Conn.: The Devin-Adair Co., 1984).
2. Charles Bonsall, *Money, Its Nature and Function* (Appleton Encyclopedia, 1861), p. 296.
3. Quoted in *The New York Tribune* (December 6, 1891).
4. Fiat money is described fully in chapter 20.
5. The circular is quoted in its entirety in Appendix B. It gives a good insight into the motives and operations of the international and big national bankers. It sums up all the provisions of the Bank Act of 1863.
6. Robert Friedberg, *Paper Money in the United States*, 12th ed. (Coin & Currency Institute, 1989).
7. K. C. Howe, *Who Rules America* (J. Cononoughy, Gordon Press, 1980 library edition).

Chapter 12

The Federal Reserve Banking System

The Need for Banking Reform

There is no question but that at the beginning of the twentieth century the United States stood in need of some kind of banking reform. This was recognized by legislators who were planning genuine reform using an asset-based money system. There was also a powerful faction in Congress that stood for government issue of money, as Thomas Jefferson, Andrew Jackson, Benjamin Franklin, John Adams, James Garfield, Abraham Lincoln, and even Alexander Hamilton (after his frustrating experiences with the Bank of North America and the First Bank of the United States, which he had worked so hard to establish for the Wall Street bankers).

Both approaches were anathema to Paul Warburg and the financiers. They bitterly opposed them because either one would take away their privileged position to issue money based on government debt, along with the European option to issue commercial paper, which Warburg favored.

Paul Warburg was a banker from the great Warburg banking family in Germany. When he emigrated to the United States, he was helped by Rothschild funds to purchase a partnership in the Kuhn & Loeb banking firm on Wall Street and was eventually hired by the Wall Street bankers to help them establish a central bank.

At the time there were about twenty thousand national and state banks, stock saving banks, and trust and loan companies, with about sixty-five hundred of them issuing their own bills of credit to circulate as money. This often caused much confusion and great losses when many of them failed. So the idea of a central bank bringing order into the chaotic banking situation was in itself a good idea. But the issue was who would create the money and own and run that central bank, the government or a private banking corporation? Warburg understood the choices clearly and said that if the Treasury created the money, it would be the central bank, which was true. Warburg's job was to help the bankers establish a private central bank, with them having the power to create money and lend it to the government.

The Federal Reserve System

There has been a lot of controversy about the Federal Reserve banking system and much written pro and con. While the original thirty sections of the Federal Reserve Act could be printed in a twenty-four page book back in 1913, when the act was signed by President Wilson, now the whole act with all its amendments and changes requires more than eight hundred pages. Even the current members of the Federal Reserve Board themselves don't know all the provisions, many of them are either contradicted by others or obsolete. What the board does know is how the system works to make money for its member banks. *The Federal Reserve is the commercial bankers' bank, a private corporation owned by them and founded for their benefit. It creates the money for the nation, lends it to the government and the citizens, and uses its banking services in the pursuit of the highest attainable profits for its member banks, especially the top twenty big banks.*

Who owns the big banks is not public knowledge. It is certain that many of the owners are internationalists, but who these people are we don't know. The Federal Reserve is a highly secretive establishment and has always resisted efforts of people, including the government, to pry into its affairs or obtain information about its activities. So, complete information or accounting is never available. At one of the recent hearings Mr. Henry Gonzales, chairman of the House Finance Committee, asked Federal Reserve Board chairman Alan Greenspan for tapes of some board meetings. Mr. Greenspan told him, "It's none of your business what is in those tapes." The previous chairman of the Federal Reserve Board, Paul Volcker, when asked by President Reagan for a report, replied, "The Board Chairman reports to no president."

The intent of those refusals, they tell us, is to defend the independence of the Federal Reserve banks. Yet the perception that most people, even many community bankers, have is that the Federal Reserve banking system is a government agency. That perception is totally false. It was never intended to be a government agency. Its founders intended just the opposite—to avoid the least involvement or interference by the government while allowing some meaningless appearances of government involvement in order to deceive the public. In this they have succeeded.

The public, naturally, is confused and has abandoned trying to get to the truth. This is the way the planners wanted it to be. They knew that the people who understand the system would be too busy making money to interfere, while those who do not understand it will give up the effort. The result: nobody will bother the Federal Reserve.

Dr. Martin A. Larson, in *The Federal Reserve and Our Manipulated Dollar*, presents a scholarly explanation that is relatively short yet thorough and objective.[1] The book devotes 130 pages to the Federal Reserve, which is quite sufficient to give one a good understanding of the basic functions and strategies of the Federal Reserve system. Many other books provide the history and a description of the system that are more detailed but no more enlightening.

But for anyone who wishes to gain a real insight into the forces that propelled the drive for banking reform, there is hardly a more authentic way than to read the words of the man who was most responsible for the directions into which the reforms were aimed and ultimately led to the passage of the Federal Reserve Act of 1913. That man was Paul Moritz Warburg. In his monumental two-volume book of 1,750 pages on the Federal Reserve system,[2] Warburg tells his own story and the story of the evolution of the Federal Reserve system devised principally by him and under his leadership.

But Warburg does not tell the whole story. It is understandable in a book about himself and his own efforts for banking reform in our country that he would omit things that would cast him in an unfavorable light.

Paul Warburg, a central banker and immigrant to this country from Germany, was raised in the traditions of European central banking procedures, goals, and strategies. He lived and breathed in an atmosphere filled with the ambitious schemes of a banking community that would eventually make central banking based on debt and fractional reserves the powerful tools of today's bankers. Warburg's lucid style makes his book on complex financial issues easier to read than most books on these subjects, in spite of its length. He writes from great personal convictions, with persistence and dedication. *There is very much that one can learn from his book*, not only about the goals and structure of the Federal Reserve banking system but also about the strategies and procedures that must be used to regain for the common citizen what he obtained for the elite.

Above all, from beginning to end, *Warburg places great emphasis on the fact that the major effort must be the constant education and formation of public opinion.* Financiers and bankers found in Warburg a man of great talent, patient and shrewd, and truly brilliant in the many areas of finance and banking. But for an account of his intrigues and other devious activities, which he does not relate, we must look to other sources, especially to a book published by Prof. Henry Parker Willis from the University of Chicago.[3]

Willis points out that there are many very important and significant omissions in Warburg's book. Warburg does not describe all the secret, conniving intrigues and deceptions that went on between himself and the most powerful bankers in the United States in order to get a central bank established, one with the money-creating powers that *both Congress and the people were so bitterly opposed to.*

Warburg does not even mention the secret two-week "duck hunting" expedition in November of 1909, when a group of bankers and their experts under the leadership of Senator Nelson Aldrich and Warburg boarded a bonded private railroad car in Hoboken, New Jersey, and headed for Jekyll Island, off the coast of Georgia, officially on a duck hunting trip. During that time they put together the legislation that would give them the central banking system they wanted. The bill was introduced in Congress as the Aldrich Bill on January 16, 1911, but was so clearly a Wall Street bill that it did not even make it out of committee. It was too evident that the "ducks" were to be the American citizens.

For the next three years, it was up to the brilliant and cunning Warburg to help the big bankers figure out how to bypass opposition from Congress and the people and accomplish what they wanted. It would have to be done through more manipulation of public opinion and politics.

Warburg was given a leave of absence from the international banking firm of Kuhn & Loeb & Co., where he had purchased a partnership with $500,000 from his European friends, the Rothschilds. He was given an annual salary of $500,000, an astronomical figure by the standards of his day. The bankers wanted him to devote his time exclusively to the task of creating the strategies and manipulating public opinion for the proposed central banking system.

Warburg set out at once to "educate" congressmen and other influential people and build consensus for a privately owned and controlled debt-based central banking system to be established by Congress. He knew it would have to look like something other than a central banking system, however, because neither the people nor

Congress were ready to accept that. They had seen what such banking practices had done in England and Europe. Warburg spent as much as seven or eight hours with each banker and legislator on an individual basis in order to garner support.

Although Warburg often claimed patriotic motives, the central banker in him never forgot to remind prospective beneficiaries from the passage of the Federal Reserve Act of the great profits, power, and control the Federal Reserve banks would give banks both in this country and in the whole world. Great profits were, of course, exactly what the big bankers were after.

We saw in the last chapter that the same greed for profits led to acceptance of the Banking Act of 1863. The "Hazard Circular" spelled out how those profits were to be made under the provisions of that banking act. But the Banking Act of 1863 failed to give the financiers a complete monopoly. The Federal Reserve Act was designed to accomplish that and also to expand greatly what was promised in the "Hazard Circular."[4]

The magic conduit through which wealth and its production are channeled into the bankers' hands is fractional reserves, as we saw in chapter 6. But nowhere does Warburg speak of fractional reserves. He does, however, express his desire to see usury laws abolished wherever they exist. This shows he was well aware of the usurious nature of the kind of banking he advocated. A big part of the book discusses the central bank as a "reservoir" for reserves, which are to be available to banks within the system, especially the smaller ones with inadequate reserves, without adverting to their fractional use.

Planning to Deceive

Because both Congress and people had been steadfastly opposed to a central bank, Warburg and his colleagues suggested that it appear as something different—a federal agency. The private Federal Reserve bank notes would be the nation's money; the government would be "merely the issuing agent." It would print the money for the Federal Reserve banks. They would pay the Treasury for the paper, about 1.75 cents per bill, regardless of denomination. This will leave the people with the impression that the government is issuing the money, because it is printing it. This plan was described by one of the principal proponents of the bill in a letter to Warburg dated August 17 , 1913: "The present method of providing for issuing Federal Reserve Notes is also a compromise. Mr. Glass recognizes, as do others who are interested in the Bill, that the Federal Reserve Notes are really Bank Notes, and that the government is 'merely the issuing agent.' They are to be redeemed primarily by the money furnished by the Federal Reserve banks. The statement that they 'purport' to be an 'obligation of the government is to satisfy the radicals' " (Warburg 1930, 1:680). The people and congressmen opposed to a central bank were the "radicals" mentioned.

The Federal Reserve banking system promised the country a depression-free and inflation-free economy and a stable dollar, something that everybody wanted. However, a debt-based money and banking system is capable only of creating inflation and depression alternately for the banking elites' profit objectives, not preventing them. Still, the promises sounded good and would help get the act passed. They were never intended to be kept, and never could be kept. To continue with the deceptions, the Federal Reserve Bank would be divided into twelve Regional Federal Banks to avoid the suspicion of forming a central bank. In practice, however, the Federal Reserve Bank of New York, would be the bellwether that the other eleven banks would follow. Finally, calling the system *Federal* would help hide the private character of the system.

The Great Deception

The big breakthrough for Warburg and the bankers came when Woodrow Wilson was elected president of the United States. This was basically the result of manipulation of the politics of the day. Wilson not only actively assisted their deceptions but voluntarily went far beyond the help they expected. He told Carter Glass that he would make the Federal Reserve notes to be issued by the Federal Reserve Banks *"obligations of the United States."* Carter Glass was stunned, and said:

> I was for an instant speechless. . . . There is *not* any government obligation here, Mr. President. . . . It would be a *pretense* on its face. . . . Was there ever a government note based on the property of a banking institution? . . . The suggested government obligation is so remote it could never be discovered.

President Wilson responded by saying, **"Everything you say is true; the government liability is a mere thought. And so, if we** can hold the *substance* of the thing and give the other fellow the *shadow*, why not do it and save our bill?"

What a betrayal of the American people and government by an American president! Three years later, after seeing the Federal Reserve system in operation, Wilson admitted he had been deceived. He then regretted what he had done:

A great industrial nation is controlled by its system of credit. Our system of credit is concentrated. The growth of the nation therefore, and all our activities are in the hands of a few men. . . . We have come to be one of the worst, one of the most completely controlled and dominated governments in the civilized world—no longer a government by free opinion, no longer a government by conviction and the vote of the majority, but a government by the opinion and duress of small groups of dominant men.

Running for a second term, Wilson said from his campaign train:

The masters of the government of the United States are the combined capitalists and manufacturers of the United States. It is written over every intimate page of the record of Congress, it is written all through the history of conferences at the White House, that the suggestions of the economic policy in this country come from one source, not from many sources. The benevolent guardians, the kind-hearted trustees who have taken the troubles of government off our hands have become so conspicuous that almost nobody can write out a list of them . . . the big bankers, the big corporations. . . . *The government of the United States at present is a foster child of the special interests.*

Under the latest amendments to the Federal Reserve Act, the board can do almost anything it wishes in regard to the reserve requirements. It can accept commercial paper or foreign bonds as reserves or it can relax the lending powers of its local member banks to the point where they are unlimited, requiring zero reserves. Or it can choke off just about all borrowing by calling for 22 percent reserves, which the local banks may not have on deposit. This would force the local banks to call in or to refuse to renew some of their loans. There are also a number of other ways it has to restrict credit and the money supply, the principal one being the open market operations in the bond market. This always causes at least a recession if not a depression.

As an example of what happens regularly, let's take the situation of a farmer who has made payments on the principal and interest of his loan for two years. The third year the Federal Reserve has restricted the lending powers of the member banks (by increasing the reserve requirements and in other ways), causing a depression. It was a bad crop year for the farmer, and the prices for the farm commodities he did have to sell hit bottom, so he couldn't pay anything on either principal or interest. The local bank foreclosed on his mortgage and sold his property for what it could get in the depressed market. The farmer lost his whole life's investment and the family home besides. He had explained his situation to his local banker, who was sympathetic and would have extended his loan to help him save his farm, but there was nothing he could do because he was forced by Federal Reserve regulations to call the loan. If he did not, the Federal Reserve would close the bank and take it over. This is exactly what happened and continues to happen to thousands of farmers thanks to the Federal Reserve system and its powers over virtually all banking. When it comes to the big banks, which it wants to keep alive because they are a big part of the system, the Federal Reserve makes their losses "obligations of the United States" and candidates for bailouts.

Who Benefits from Federal Reserve Banking?

The operation of the Federal Reserve system of banking has proved beyond all doubt that those who create the money of a nation derive all the benefits. Some good accrues to the citizens at large. Even debt-based money brings a measure of prosperity. But the time always comes when the Federal Reserve Board chooses to contract credit and the money supply. That is done for a purpose, the same purpose for which the bankers acquired the power over the money system in the first place: private profits. To justify their actions to the public, they always claim an acceptable reason, such as "keeping inflation in check," which the public neither understands nor questions. Deception has been the modus operandi for so long that they will never give the public the real reasons for their actions.

Fear of Politics

The Federal Reserve system did not deliver on its promises during and after World War I, and was blamed for the 1929 depression. Warburg, who often expressed his fears for the bank, came to its defense, again *emphasizing its independence from government control. Yet he said it must have the support of the president* and of an organization that would fight off all attempts to endanger the system:

"The Federal Reserve system can only expect to succeed in keeping itself clean (from government control), if, on the one hand, it can count on the wholehearted protection of whoever, from time to time, fills the presidential chair at the White House, and on the other hand, upon the unwavering active support of the people" (Warburg 1930, 2:768).

"In addition . . . a constant campaign of education should be carried on which would tell the people what the Federal Reserve system does for them, and how desperately important it is to keep it clean and inviolate [from politicians]. If politicians sense . . . attacking the integrity of the System they must fear to be wiped out at the next election, they will take jolly good care to keep their hands off" (Warburg 1930, 2:769).

In other words, the politicians, who are supposed to represent the people, must "keep their hands off" the Federal Reserve system. Indeed, the financial power of the system will ensure that they are "wiped out at the next election" if they dare to oppose the system. The operators of the Federal Reserve system put on a bold front; they are fully aware of their power. Yet *they are constantly fearful that political action, which gave them their privileged position, could also take it away*. *And it could*.

It is with good reason that these people live in fear. They are engaged in an operation that is grossly dishonest, usurious, and oppressive. There are now over eight hundred organizations in our country that recognize this and are involved in different ways in moves to repeal the Federal Reserve Act. Dozens of states' legislatures are on record with memoranda calling for the repeal. The Von Mises Institute at Auburn University is a powerhouse teaching thousands of economists both in its courses and workshops the evils of Federal Reserve banking. At least ten million of our citizens are of one mind on the question. For the past ten years, the movement against the Federal Reserve system has grown progressively stronger.

What Happened to Our Gold?

We cannot close this chapter without taking note of a most devastating period of plunder of the nation's gold by the Federal Reserve. This took place during President Franklin Delano Roosevelt's administration. The depression of 1929–1933 provided the opportune moment for the Federal Reserve System to loot the people of the gold they had earned. How did they earn it? By working for the Federal Reserve notes with which they were paid; promises were redeemable with the delivery of gold. The people earned the gold, but the Federal Reserve decided to keep it and not redeem its notes, as promised.

By executive order, legislative acts, and many deceptive maneuvers by international bankers, gold was taken out of circulation. In fact, it became illegal for people to own any. President Roosevelt was the very accommodating tool the Federal Reserve Board needed to achieve its goals. To make it appear (in dealing with the public, it is appearances that count) that the Federal Reserve didn't want any gold either, it decided to "get rid of it." How? It *sold* it to the U.S. Treasury!

The Treasury naturally was expected to pay the Federal Reserve for the gold, even though the gold rightfully belonged to it in the first place. What would the Treasury pay for it with? The Federal Reserve wanted gold certificates. So the Treasury issued gold certificates, which gave the Federal Reserve the right to claim the gold again any time it wanted to. In the meantime, the gold would be shipped to the Bank for International Settlements (BIS) for safekeeping in its vaults in France, where the U.S. Treasury couldn't touch it.

This gold maneuver was triple plunder: first, from the citizens; second, from the U.S. Treasury, which paid for what rightfully belonged to it; and third, from both through the gold certificates, which the Federal Reserve can use to get the gold back any time it suits its purposes.

An Alert

The gold, to which the Federal Reserve still has a claim in the form of gold certificates, could be a trump card if the movement for monetary reform forces financiers into a corner. They will play that card to regain their monopoloy over the creation and regulation of money if they lose it through the political action of citizens. U.S. citizens must be *alert* to that possibility in our efforts for monetary reform.[5]

The above "alert" was written in 1992. As of September 1995, the Federal Reserve is in no danger from political action. But together with the International Monetary Fund and the World Bank, the whole financial system throughout the world is in imminent danger of collapse because of its own weight. The house of cards built up hastily through worldwide speculation in debt instruments called *derivatives*, which claim over $40 trillion of wealth, is about ready to topple, because the wealth promised does not exist.

The financial elite are "whistling in the dark," while publicly claiming there is no danger and promoting derivatives as good investments, while at the same time unloading them on public entities (counties, pension funds, schools) that have already suffered losses of more than $3.073 billion, with total debt involving infrastructures amounting to $1.2 trillion.[6] They themselves are running for cover, buying gold, gold futures, gold stocks, and also aluminum, copper, and tin.

Their food monopolies are buying up the world supplies of foods, especially grains, through futures markets. They are playing their trump cards in a different way in order to control the true wealth, while letting the public hold paper promises. It is a preemptive strike at the use of the gold certificates. They want to be in total control of gold and its production before the time comes when they monetize it again.

Notes

1. Martin A. Larson, *The Federal Reserve and Our Manipulated Dollar* (Old Greenwich, Conn.: Devin-Adair Co., 1975).
2. Paul M. Warburg, *The Federal Reserve System, Its Origin and Growth* (New York: Macmillan, 1930).
3. Henry Parker Willis, *The Federal Reserve System*. Reprint of orig. 1923 ed. Wall Street & Security Market Service, 1975 145.95 0–405–07246–5. Ayer.
4. The correspondence among the Rothschild Brothers of London; Ikleheimer and Vandergould, bankers in New York City; and John Sherman, member of Congress from Ohio, is quoted in many good financial history books and is omitted here. However, the text of the "Hazard Circular" is given in Appendix 2.
5. Details for that reform are in chapters 20, 21, and 22, which include the precautions to be taken so that gold will never again be used as money.
6. Figures are from the annual meeting of the National Conference of State Legislators held July 15–20, 1995, in Milwaukee, Wisconsin, reported in *Executive Intelligence Review* (August 18, 1995).

Chapter 13
Debt, Deficits, and Depressions

Debts Begin with Borrowing

When tax receipts are insufficient to cover budgeted expenses, the U.S. Treasury is authorized by an act of Congress to borrow the money from the Federal Reserve banks. Instead of creating it by it sovereign right, Congress lets the banks create the money. The banks do that gladly on one condition: that the government issue bonds that oblige the government to repay the principal *plus* interest. The government is then in debt to the private Federal Reserve banks. Its bonds are mortgages on the true wealth of the nation.

This is the procedure: the government issues the bonds. The Federal Reserve banks "buy" them, paying for them by entering a deposit to the account of the United States Treasury for the amount borrowed. By that single entry, the Federal Reserve "creates" the money for the government. The Treasury can then issue checks against that deposit to pay its bills and various entitlements, such as Social Security. (Of course, some of the government's expenditures are paid from the proceeds of income, Social Security, and various other taxes.) The government checks are then deposited by the recipients to their own accounts in the commercial banks with which they do business. That increases the money supply in the nation's economy. The debt-based commercial banking system continues creating money for the economy in the same way, by credit entries of money borrowed, subject to regulations of the Federal Reserve Board. Taxes, of course, do just the opposite. They decrease the supply of money in the nation.

The National Deficits and Debt

For many years now, the government has not been able to collect enough in taxes to avoid a deficit each year. This deficit is roughly the size of the interest payment due on the national debt. This indicates that taxpayers no longer are able to carry the burden of the interest payments. Without them, the budget would be in balance. In 1995 there would even have been a slight surplus. So the treasury department states.

However, other sources report that the Treasury hides the true deficit by taking credit for about $300 billion of Social Security Trust Fund surplus. Without that credit the true deficit would be that much higher.

The Treasury keeps on borrowing and adding to the debt. As of February 22, 1996, the government has borrowed from the private banking system a total $5 trillion. That national debt is growing at the rate of more than $1.2 billion *a day*, which for the whole year is more than the reported amount of the annual deficit. Evidently the government is borrowing more than we are told about. The national debt quadrupled in the last ten years from $1 trillion plus to $5 trillion. Prospects are that it will at least double during the next ten years. But, strangely, we must not talk about that debt. The crusade is against the deficits. There has to be enough money in the Treasury for the government to be able to pay the interest due. The Clinton administration was instructed by the International Monetary Fund even before Mr. Clinton's inauguration. "To increase taxes and cut the expenses." The statement was repeated a little later to the Economic Council. Naturally, the administration and its millionaire experts, who have all committed themselves to *respect the independence of the Federal Reserve,*" with all its satellites, the International Monetary fund included, got the message.

How does the International Monetary Fund manage to tell the U.S. government what it *must* do? That's a long story. It shows that we have surrendered our sovereignty to the power of the debt-based financiers. Chapter 19 will throw more light on this. Here we advert to the fact that the IMF wants to make sure there will be enough money in the U.S. Treasury to assure that the bonds of all 178 nations in the IMF will be "performing investments" paying interest. Not only do U.S. taxpayers have to pay interest on our national debt, but we must be ready to bail out the nations that can't. To do so means raising taxes and cutting expenses to the bone. Then in four years we *might* get the deficit down to about a half. That is the message. If we don't do that, the banks could foreclose on all the property in the nation, as was done in Greece over two thousand years ago. This would ruin the whole system, of course. The game would be over for the bankers as well as for the rest of the country.

Whatever Congress and the administration do about the deficit will be no more than using a "Band-Aid" solution. Major surgery is needed to remove the root cause of the bleeding (see chapters 20–24). With or without a balanced budget amendment, it is and will remain impossible for Congress to balance the budget or repay any debt without wrecking the country unless it first replaces our debt-based money system with a debt-free system.

Get Rid of the Debt?

The one fact that stands in the way of the best efforts of honest people to come to terms with the national deficits and prevents us from solving the problems debt creates is that *the national debt is our money.* Our money is debt-based money. It is created by the Federal Reserve banks when the government goes into debt to them by issuing its bonds. That is our whole problem.

If by some magic we were to get rid of the whole national debt, it would destroy over 90 percent of our money and create a nationwide panic. Or, raising taxes enough to get rid of the deficit and even to touch the debt would remove enough money from the economy to cause a major depression. This is elementary economics. All taxes, for whatever purpose, have the effect of removing money from the economy. If that is not replaced by new money added to the money supply for productive purposes, it has to result in depressing the economy. What problems would that solve? None at all. It would be a self-defeating operation.

To propose a trust fund for debt reduction, as some have done, is not an answer either. No trust fund has been honored, including the biggest one of all, the Social Security Trust Fund. So what guarantee would taxpayers have that a new one would fare any better?

Everyone knows that government is bloated and that there is a lot of room for cuts. Here Ross Perot and the UNWS organization have some excellent ideas; so did the Grace Commission, which Congress authorized but neglected to follow its recommendations. All those efforts follow the thinking and example of one of our most successful presidents, Thomas Jefferson. But in the end, with all the social programs that people have come to expect from their government, there is a limit beyond which the budget cannot be cut. Even with the *possible* cuts, the end result inevitably would be a deficit financed by more government borrowing, and more debt. That is the logical sequence under our current debt-based money system. There is no way we can get out of our predicament without jettisoning the debt-based money system and replacing it with a debt-free system (as explained in chapter 10 and with more detail in chapters 20–24).

About Foreign Debt

Pretty much the same game is played in all 178 nations that are members of the International Monetary Fund and the World Bank with the Federal Reserve banks as sponsors. The following quotation is from a Geneva-based press service digest quoting the general secretary of the Council of Churches in the Philippines, Feliciano Carino: "Foreign debt is the symbol and specific instrument whereby world resources and economic growth are controlled. They are controlled for personal profit and to perpetuate their dominance over the rest of society and the world by a few powerful sectors of national and international society. This foreign debt is the instrument by which that segment of society makes nations serve its own interests instead of these nations. Thus these privileged few become the real governors imposing their will through the control of capital and loans using their superior arms and political power where they feel it's necessary."

The nations accepting loans become perpetually dependent and no longer masters of their own destinies. Their foreign debt undergirds the power their creditors have over them, a power to manipulate the credits and economies so that the nations no longer have any real sovereignty and control over the community relationships of their own citizens (*National Catholic Register*, December 6, 1992).

Depressions

The creation of depressions follows these steps:

1. There is a deficit in the government budget.

2. Having exhausted its ability to get more revenue from taxes, the government borrows, because it has no other way to acquire needed money, given our present debt-based money system.

3. Having received interest-bearing bonds from the government, the privately owned Federal Reserve banks create money that then enters the money supply of the nation and increases it. The money

supply also increases every time a person borrows from a commercial bank. The one exception when borrowing does not add money to the nation's money is when a person borrows earned money from private individuals or credit unions. In those cases new money is not created by using fractional reserves; the money borrowed is already in existence.

4. When the Federal Reserve, which is the commercial banks' bank, instructs the banks to encourage borrowing, more and more people borrow. Thus more and more money is created and added to the money supply, the economy "heats up," prices go up, and inflation results. The Federal Reserve has several ways of doing that: lowering the reserve requirements, juggling interest rates, Open Market Committee operations, and others. Its actions are always highly secretive. News stories and figures released serve more to keep people confused than to clarify the Federal Reserve's purposes.

5. This created inflation usually runs about a ten-year cycle. For the last two decades, it has been a continuing phenomenon with nervous off-and-on manipulation of interest rates. By inflating the money supply, industry and commerce are stimulated into producing more wealth. Entrepreneurs and farmers are encouraged to borrow and get themselves deeper in debt and mortgaged to the bankers. They all hire more people at higher and higher wages. Unemployment figures go down. Production of wealth and services expands. After all, the cow called Economy has to go to pasture for a while before she can be milked again.

6. Eventually, however, milking time comes. Through the instrumentality of the Federal Reserve system—with its various options such as raising reserve requirements—credit and the money supply are contracted, loans are called, mortgages are foreclosed, and thousands of farms and businesses are taken over by the banks. Industries have to let the employees go. With accelerating unemployment, people can't buy what has been produced, forcing plant closings. Distress and lack of confidence grips the nation. Food lines and shelters for the homeless show up around the country. The nation is in a planned depression. In the meantime, the big banks are doing just fine.

7. The process continues. The government is blamed and called upon for programs to end the depression. This gives the new aristocracy

an opportunity to milk the government also, which now has to borrow from the banks for programs to "stimulate the economy." This adds to the national deficit and debt and increases the amount of interest the banking system can collect. Increasing taxes on citizens and industries that are already overtaxed won't help; to do so would only deepen the depression by removing more money from an already short money supply.

8. After the infusion of money, the wobbly economy gets on her feet and is again "sent out to pasture." The newly borrowed money created by the Federal Reserve system and banks, of course, will increase our national debt. So, the process starts all over again with new inflationary pressures to fatten up the cow and her milk supply.

The reasons for inflation and depression given by the new aristocracy experts and economists and their media will be different. They always have been. They are given in arcane and technical terms to make sure that the people in general don't catch on.

No Recession for the Banking "Industry"

While the economy is depressed and 16 percent of people unemployed (more than twice the "official" figures), millions homeless, and millions of others struggling to make ends meet, the banking industry has been doing just fine. All during 1992–93 and into 1997, the *Wall Street Journal* carried stories about how well the banks were doing. The March 19, 1993, issue of the *Milwaukee Journal* headed the following news item from Washington, D.C.: *"Bank Profits Soar"*:

> The nation's commercial banks earned a record $32.2 billion last year, the government reported Tuesday. The figure, nearly twice 1991's earnings of $17.9 billion, prompted FDIC officials to all but declare the banking industry's crisis over.

How did the big bankers do so well with the rest of the economy in a depression? That was a master stoke of genius! Here's how it was done.

United States leaders needed help from the Federal Reserve with high interest rates. They needed them lowered to get out of the depression. So amid wide acclaim by the media, the Federal Reserve did its "patriotic duty" and lowered the interest rates again and again. Everyone cheered. But something else happened that the public did not hear about, or heard very little. Lowering the interest rates gave the big banks a good excuse to lower the interest rates even more for the banks' depositors. As a result, the net interest and margin of profit for one hundred top banks *rose* from 3.81 percent to 4.65 percent in 1990 and again to 5.77 percent in 1991, the highest ever. The much publicized lowering of interest rates was supposed to help industry, and it did help some industries like the housing industry a little, but most of all it helped the banking industry to achieve record profits. This for an "industry" that produces nothing and isn't even supposed to be an industry but rather a service!

While the lower interest rates were supposed to make it easier for business and industry to borrow money to spur the economy, the biggest banks preferred *not* to lend it to them. They chose rather to buy more government bonds and other Treasury debt instruments. The banks found this more profitable and safer, without the risks associated with business ventures. With the interest on bonds guaranteed by the nation's tax payers, the banks couldn't lose. The comptroller of currency found that as of July 1, 1992, the total bank assets of those banks were made up of $627.5 billion in Treasury obligations and $598.4 billion in outstanding business loans. This was the first time that banks had more government bonds on their books than business loans, according to New York business writer John Crudele.

Dr. Aldo Milinkovich, a former Treasury examiner, not a private financial consultant, commenting March 29, 1993, on these maneuvers by the Federal Reserve, said: "I wouldn't call this shameful scheme a policy. I'd call it plunder."

A Voice from the Past about Debt

An editorial by Philip Freneau was published over two hundred years ago in the January 23, 1792, issue of the *National Gazette*. Freneau's editorial is a **classic example of satire**. But first, a bit of background.

Many people know something about the *Federalist Papers* of Alexander Hamilton, a scholarly piece of work. There was also a newspaper called the *Gazette of the United States* at the service of Hamilton, edited by John Fenno. *Opponents* of the central bank promoted by Alexander Hamilton and associates were led by Jefferson and Madison. They established a rival newspaper called the *National Gazette*, which Phillip Freneau edited. Some of Freneau's objections to the Hamiltonian program included:

1. Hamilton's economic measures favored the few moneyed interests rather than the many ordinary citizens;
2. A party machine was organized and the army strengthened in such a way as to suggest an intent to control rather than represent the many;
3. Both Hamilton and Washington considered themselves aristocrats. They favored the educated, the clergy, and the press, and they were fearful of "mob rule" in a democratic form of government. They preferred to see what Hamilton called "gentlemen of principle and property" in command.

Rules for Changing a Republic into a Monarchy

Freneau also tried to counteract Hamilton's plans because he was bitterly opposed to debt as a basis for money. *He foresaw the consequences of debt.* (Note how accurately his fears have been realized in our banking and money systems today, over two hundred years later!) The satire in Freneau's editorial begins with the heading: *"Rules for Changing a Republic into a Monarchy."* The "monarchy" in this case is the central bank. There are fifteen "rules" in the editorial, which is quite lengthy. The following are excerpts from it.

Rule 4. In drawing all bills, resolutions, and reports, keep constantly in view that the limitations in the *Constitution* are ultimately to be explained away. Precedents and phrases may be shuffled in, without being adverted to by candid or weak people. . . .

Rule 5. As the novelty and bustle of inaugurating the government will for some time keep the public mind in a heedless and unsettled state, let the press during this period be busy in propagating the doctrines of monarchy and aristocracy. For this purpose it will be particularly useful to confound a mobbish democracy with a representative republic. . . . Review all the civil contests, convulsions, factions, broils, squabbles, bickerings, black eyes, bloody noses of ancient, middle, and modern ages; caricature them into the most frightful forms and colors which can be imagined; and unfold one scene of the horrible tragedy after another till the people be made . . . to tremble at their own shadows, . . .

Then contrast with these pictures of terror the quiet of hereditary succession, the reverence claimed by birth and nobility, and the fascinating influence of ribands and garters, cautiously suppressing all the bloody tragedies and unceasing oppressions that form the history of this species of government. . . .

Rule 6. If by good fortune *a debt be ready at hand*, the most is to be made of it. . . . Get as much debt as can be raked and scraped together. . . . Advertise for more, and have the debt made as big as possible. . . . Make it as perpetual as possible. . . . Next to that get it into as few hands as possible. . . . Modify the debt, complicate it, divide it, subdivide it . . . postpone it. . . . To be brief, let the whole be such a mystery that only few can understand it . . . to clinch their advantages over the many.

Rule 7. It must not be forgotten that the members of the legislative body are to have a deep stake in the game. This is an essential point, and happily is attended to with no difficulty. A sufficient number, properly disposed, can alternately legislate and speculate, and speculate and legislate . . . until a due portion of the property of their constituents has passed into their hands. . . . All this be carried on under cover of the closest secrecy. Should a discovery take place, the whole plan may be blown up.

Rule 8. The ways in which a Great Debt . . . will contribute to the ultimate end in view are both numerous and obvious. (1) The favorite few, thus possessed of it, whether within or without the government, will feel the staunchest fealty to it, and will go through thick and thin to support it in all its oppressions and usurpations. (2) Their money will give them consequence and influence, even among those who have been tricked out of it. (3) They will be the readiest materials that can be found for a hereditary aristocratic order, whenever matters are ripe for one. (4) A great debt will require Great Taxes; great taxes, many tax-gatherers and other officers; all officers are auxiliaries of power. (5) Heavy taxes may produce discontents; these may threaten resistance . . . and will be the pretense for a standing army to repel it. (6) A standing army . . . will increase the moral force of the government by means of its appointments, and give it physical force by means of the sword . . . forwarding the main object.

Rule 9. The management of a great funded debt and extensive taxes will afford a plea, not to be neglected, for establishing a great incorporated bank. The use of such a machine is well understood. If the *Constitution*, according to its fair meaning, should not authorize it, so much the better. Push it through by a forced meaning and you will get in the bargain an admirable precedent for future misconstructions.

In fashioning the bank, remember that it is to be made *particularly* instrumental in enriching and aggrandizing the elect few, who are to be called in due season to the honors and felicities of the kingdom preparing for them. . . . The bank will admit the same men to be, at the same time members of the bank and members of the government. The two institutions will thus be soldered together and each made the stronger. Money will be put under the direction of the government and the government under the direction of money. To crown the whole, the bank will have a proper interest in swelling and perpetuating the public debt and public taxes, with all the blessings of both. . . .

Rule 11. As soon as sufficient progress in the intended change is made and the public mind prepared . . . in order to render success more certain, it will be of special moment, to give the most plausible and popular name that can be found to the power that is to be usurped. It may be called, for example, a power for the common safety or the public good, or, "general welfare." If the people should not be too enlightened, the name will have an imposing effect. . . .

Rule 12. The expediency of seizing every occasion of external danger for augmenting and perpetuating the standing military is too obvious to escape. . . . A military defeat will become a political victory, and the loss of a little vulgar blood will contribute to ennoble that which flows in the veins of our future dukes and marquesses.

Rule 13. The same prudence will improve the opportunity afforded by an increase of military expenditures for perpetuating the taxes required of them. . . .

Rule 15. Neither lungs nor pens must be spared in charging every man who whispers, or even thinks, that the revolution on foot is meditated, with himself being an enemy of the established government. . . . Let the charge be reiterated and reverberated till at last such confusion and uncertainty be produced that the people, being not able to find out where the truth lies, withdraw from the contest; . . . the above will be abundantly enough for the purpose. This will certainly be the case if the people can either be kept asleep so as not to discover, or be thrown into artificial divisions so as not to resist, what is silently going forward.

Should it be found impossible, however, to prevent the people from awaking and uniting; . . . should all who have common interest make a common cause and show an inflexible attachment to republicanism in opposition to a government of monarchy and of money, why then . . .

The editorial ends on that note, implying that we can draw our own conclusions. Remember that this editorial was written in January 1792. It was too late to stop the central bank that Hamilton promoted. Congress had already given Hamilton and his associates a twenty-year charter in 1791. But the *National Gazette*, with Freneau as editor, was effective nevertheless.

The people woke up and took action. They elected Thomas Jefferson vice president in 1796 and then to two terms as president in 1800 and 1804. Following Washington's precedent, Jefferson declined to run for a third term, so the people elected his vice president, James Madison, for two terms as president.

So the people did make a big difference for a period of more than thirty years. During this time the influence of the central bank was wisely controlled by these two presidents, and when the charter expired, it was not renewed. The Federalist Party itself likewise expired. The country had its problems with Great Britain but still made good progress economically.

With two hundred years of hindsight, we can see how accurately Freneau foresaw the effects of "the international imperialism of money," to use the phrase of Pope Pius XI from his encyclical *Quadragesimo Anno*. Unfortunately, the citizens let down their guard and that "monarchy" Freneau described is now in place on a vast scale. It embraces not only our nation through the Federal Reserve banking system, but virtually every nation in the world through the International Monetary Fund and the World Bank.

The United States is influential enough that the rest of the nations will follow if they see improvements in our economy and society in general. If we choose to correct our debt-based economy, they will also do so. This is not idle speculation. It is the judgment of people who understand the implications of every move in the field of finance and banking—the world's financiers themselves.

These people expressed their alarm at the prospect of what such action would do to their power as far back as 1862 (see their statement in chapter 11). Chapters 20 to 24, without minimizing the enormous challenges that we are facing, will address in a spirit of confidence and hope what we can to do to make the United States an example for the other nations of the world.

Another Deficit

In our preoccupation with the national budget deficit and debt, it is easy to forget that there is another deficit in our society. Often it touches our well-being and happiness more than the financial woes. Even if it is not the root cause of our economic problems, it contributes to them very significantly. This deficit is a moral one.

Dishonesty, deceit, and greed are rampant in our society. A true sense of community is lacking. Constant vigilance and support for morality, religion, and education, indispensable for good citizenship, are needed if the United States is to endure as a representative democracy. Love is a perennial debt we have to one another, one we may allow to remain and must continue to try to repay.

How Much Is One Trillion Dollars?

By the time this book will be published, our government debt will be more than $5 trillion. That is an incomprehensible figure to our citizens. In its February 20, 1978 issue, the *U.S. News & World Report*, when the government debt was approaching $1 trillion, presented five different measures to give us some idea of how much a trillion dollars is:

1. One trillion silver dollars stacked up would reach as high as 5,661,000 Empire State Buildings.
2. One trillion paper $1 bills would stretch 3.5 million miles beyond the sun, for a total of 96,907,000 miles.
3. One trillion dollars at average 1977 prices would buy 172,051,000 autos, or 18.8 years of U.S. output.
4. At 1977 prices, one trillion dollars would buy 18,416,000 new houses.
5. Shopping 24 hours a day 7 days a week, it would take someone 19 years spending $6,000,000 an hour to spend $1 trillion.

The last three measures need to be adjusted for the depreciated dollar we now have. But today the debt is over $5 trillion, not $1 trillion. What a burden this places on our children and grandchildren in our current debt-based money system! It obliges them to produce the value claimed by this debt or endure a standard of living lowered by that amount.

Chapter 14

Taxes, Taxes, and More Taxes

Who is there who does not know what taxes are? They are an all-pervading phenomenon in our society. The distinctive characteristic of taxes is that they are an obligation imposed on an individual by the government, and the government *will* collect "come hell or high water."

Over and over, we read of farmers evicted from their homes and losing everything they worked for over a lifetime, businesses closed, records confiscated and hauled away by tax agents armed as for war. At times this tax "weapon" is also used for political reasons, with some tax obligation contrived.

One difference between taxes taking a share of what you work for and the plunder that goes on constantly by means of our debt-based money and banking systems is that taxes are not quite as hidden as the looting that occurs through the operation of the money system. The following story and ones like it are repeated daily throughout the country.

North Chicago School Board voted 5–2 to dissolve the school district, which has 4,350 students. The district is heavily burdened with high local taxes and finds itself unable to finance its services (*Milwaukee Journal*, March 27, 1993).

Excessive Taxes' Effect on Consumers

Today even low-income wage earners, earning just $10,000, pay $765 FICA tax. Another $765 from their employers makes a total of $1,530 taken out of one low-income person's labor just for Social Security taxes. Add all the other taxes and interest on borrowed money and anyone can see why consumers have little left to spend on what industry produces and has to continue producing to maintain employment. They also are afraid that future taxes may take even more away from what they have and hesitate to spend more than they have to.

If the top 5.67 percent of income recipients, those with adjusted gross incomes over $88,000, paid a tax of 43 percent on their incomes, as some experts propose, it would not be necessary to tax the other 94.33 percent at all! Doing this would give the bottom 94 percent group a little more money to spend. But such an exorbitant tax added to all the other taxes would leave the 5.67 percent group, largely professionals, with virtually no incentive to work at all. Besides being unjust, it would be counterproductive in the long run.

Taxes already consume more than half of what people earn. Taxes plunder the economy almost as much as the debt-based money system does. These two forces keep citizens busy working harder than ever for the *land lords of the world* while trying to make a decent living for themselves and their families. In 1992 the U.S. tax burden from all levels of government was $6,119 for each person (*United States News and World Report*, February 8, 1993).[1] This, of course, refers only to direct taxes. It does not include "hidden taxes" (see below).

Officials bemoan the price tag on various plans for social services, claiming such plans could depress the economy and job growth over the next few years. But it's not the plans as such that depress job growth and the economy. That is done by the taxes required under our present debt-based money system to pay for them.

Some congressional leaders tinker with different options to cut some taxes but usually conclude that none of the options would give the economy the quick boost a tax credit would. Elementary economics! A tax credit, or better yet a tax cut, would leave more money with which consumers could buy the products of industry and encourage employment. Although we are working with much higher figures today than in 1964, the Revenue Act of 1964, which cut both income and corporate taxes, proved this rather simple point in a very dramatic way.

Revenue Act of 1964

Economic advisor Walter W. Heller of President Kennedy's Council of Economic Advisors explained to President Kennedy that a tax cut would get the economy moving again, result in greater employment, move people into higher income brackets, and thereby increase government tax revenue. Kennedy understood Heller's reasoning and wanted to enact a tax cut but was bitterly opposed in Congress. The most effective opponent was Sen. Everett Dirksen, who stalled the bill in committee for sixteen months. President Kennedy was assassinated during that time, but President Johnson finally got the proposed tax cuts into law on April 22, 1964. The results, just as predicted by Mr. Heller, were almost immediate.

What did the Revenue Act of 1964 accomplish? First, it reduced by $11.5 billion the income and corporation taxes of the country. Thus consumers' paychecks gained an almost immediate increase in disposable income, and $1 billion more from industry's higher after-tax profits was distributed in dividends. This consumer spending produced income for other people, which again was spent and turned into income, so that by the year's end $44 billion was added to the gross national product.

What would those tax cuts do to the national deficit? Would they increase it, as so many in Congress feared? Contrary to those fears, it helped cut the deficit nearly in half, from $8.2 billion to $4.4 billion. The higher revenues were the result of the big gains in profits and personal income. This was the "supply side economics," which held that increasing taxes loses money for the Treasury, while decreasing taxes raises the tax revenue. President Reagan followed the same "school of thought" and the advice of his Council of Economic Advisors and lowered the taxes. That is why the Federal Reserve Board chairman Paul Volcker had no use for him. Jack Kemp shares in Reagan's thinking also.

Supply-side economists give different reasons for the validity of this thinking. But whatever force other arguments have, the thinking is certainly valid on the basis of the fact that taxes remove money from the money supply and depress the economy, if the supply is not promptly replaced by newly created money. Whatever depresses the economy naturally will lower the income base upon which the Treasury can collect taxes. Lower taxes will leave more money in the economy and increase the income base and collections.

Further evidence that tax cuts have these results is that when President Johnson's cuts were repeated almost twenty years later under President Reagan, the result was six years of continuous prosperity. The media called the process "Reaganomics," while President Bush called it "voodoo economics." Bush, with his tax increase in 1990, helped to bring about our current economic problems, thus helping to prove that the opposite of tax cuts will also have opposite results. President Bush followed instructions from the Federal Reserve.

An Honest Money System

The above experiences with tax cuts took place within the context of our present debt-based money system. All the tinkering that is going on now in Congress is also done with the debt and deficit-based money system as a premise. If the tax reduction principle has been found valid in achieving such sizable gains in employment and in the whole economy within a basically faulty and dishonest money system, what great results could the nation not achieve within an honest and production-based money system! Such a system would vastly reduce taxes.

The January 24, 1994, issue of the *Milwaukee Journal* reports an Associated Press release about Treasury secretary Lloyd Bentsen's visit with Prime Minister Morihiro Hosokawa in Tokyo the day before. Bentsen had "no . . . reticence when it came to Japan's economy, calling on Hosokawa's government to cut taxes quickly as a way to stimulate its economy out of a recession and boost demand for imported goods." That was sound economics. If that would be good for Japan's economy, why not for the U.S. economy?

There is no claim that steps to increase productivity and reduce the national debt are going to be easy ones. (See chapters 20 to 24 for more about such steps.) But there is no alternative to making the profound and radical change from our debt-based money system into one that is debt-free and honest, if we are to avoid condemning our children and grandchildren to ever greater and greater economic slavery.

If we do *not* change the system, it will demand ever higher taxes and lead the United States into total bankruptcy and repudiation of its debts, with unforeseeable but undoubtedly violent consequences. Those are the fears in Germany right now, and the United States is not far from that position. It will be reached when the tax burden for the payment of interest on the national debt becomes greater than the citizens can bear. We are not far from that point.

How Are Taxes Extracted from the Citizens?

Taxes are collected in four basic ways. First there are the visible direct taxes: property tax, sales tax, state income tax, federal income tax, FICA (Social Security), fuel taxes, license fees, unemployment compensation, and in some places city or county income tax. Add them all up.

The second, third, and fourth ways are all "hidden" taxes. The first hidden tax that businesses and industry must pay in addition to their state and federal income taxes is the costs of employee retirement and health benefit plans and, at times, various penalties or assessments decreed by some regulatory bureaucracy. Any tax, direct or hidden, necessarily ends up as a tax on consumers, hidden in the higher prices they must pay for products and services.

A second hidden tax is inflation, the most brutal, deceitful, and regressive of all taxes. When a government deficit is covered by borrowing, money is added to the money supply. This dilutes the value of everyone's earnings, savings, pensions, and welfare checks. Every dollar is worth less.

Everybody seems to take it for granted that inflation is some kind of a virus from outer space that attacks cyclically. We accept it as something we can't do anything about. We try to provide for it by forever demanding higher prices and wages and getting more dollars, which constantly lose their value. The extra value goes to line the pockets of the *land lords of the world*, who have produced little or no true wealth to add to the economy from which the new dollars will make their claims.

A third hidden tax is loss of productive activity. It has been estimated that besides the direct financial costs to maintain the huge labor force needed, the value of the time lost to the production of wealth by these people who have to use it to collect the various taxes, keep all the records and prepare the tax returns for the government agencies exceeds $1 trillion. This represents a loss of that much potential wealth for the nation's economy

Yet the dollars spent for all that record keeping and tax collecting, which add nothing of real value to the economy, are figured as part of our Gross National Product. That distortion becomes yet another inflationary factor.

How Bad Is Unemployment?

Worldwide, unemployment is very bad indeed according to reports from almost every industrialized country; it is even worse in the less developed countries. Some figures point to as high as 40 percent of the labor force unemployed. In some poor countries that the United States "punishes" by economic sanctions for political reasons—countries like Haiti or Iraq—unemployment is as high as 70 percent and the people are being starved to death.

118

But here we will discuss the unemployment figures in the United States. Official figures from the Department of Labor at the end of December 1993 showed that only 6.4 percent of the civilian labor force was unemployed. But that is not the whole story.

The figures don't include those who have not made an effort to find a job during the preceding four weeks. They are assumed not to be in the labor force and looking for a job anymore. Of course, they could have given up because they could not see any hope. How many of these people were there? We don't know, but estimates are close to 5 percent.

Nor do those figures include those who were forced into part-time jobs, even one hour a week, either because they couldn't find a full-time job or for some reason were unable to hold one. These too were considered employed and therefore not included as unemployed. If we add both of these "no count" categories, we get 16 percent as a more realistic figure on full-time unemployment.

The above statistics deal only with the people in what is defined as the civilian labor force. Evidently, those on welfare or in the military are not in that work force. The military performs an essential service for the country, and the poor unable to provide for themselves, have to be taken care of in a self-respecting nation. But from the point of view of the nation's economy, they are consumers, not producers of wealth and value. Only indirectly do these groups trigger the activity of industry by being at least partially effective consumers, claiming a bit of production by the limited dollars they receive. How many people are in those two groups? We don't have the exact answer, but we know it is substantial—a minimum of twenty million. Add to the above the fact that nearly forty million people are in low-income employment receiving wages that don't raise them above the poverty line and we get a fairly accurate picture of the employment needs in our country.

How Do High Taxes Cause Unemployment?

All the taxes mentioned above decrease the taxpayers' purchasing power. Taxes that the unemployed and low-income people have to pay, especially inflation, which raises all prices, make it impossible for them to purchase even adequate food, clothing, and lodging. Without purchasing power, millions of people are left with unsatisfied needs and wants, while industry and other producers do not have a market for their products and must lay off employees. Taxes the middle class pays cut into this group's ability to buy other products of industry to maintain their higher standard of living. This likewise contributes to unemployment. Further, to keep up a higher standard of living forces some people to seek employment who otherwise would choose volunteer or other unpaid work. This decreases job openings for others.

High taxes on industries cut into their ability to show a fair profit on investment, to pay good wages, and to finance expansion or improvements internally. Further, high taxes force them to raise prices on their products, an increase passed on to consumers already limited in their purchasing power.

Finally, entrepreneurs, who provide most of the jobs in our country and take sizable risks to do so, are often bankrupt or discouraged by the burdens of high taxes and bureaucratic regulations. Thus even more jobs are lost.

What Is the Proper Function of Taxes?

On the federal level, the major use of the government's sovereign power of taxation should be to regulate the value of the dollar as provided for by the *Constitution*, Article I, Section 8, Clause 5. This would not be a big tax. Running Congress and other government services would *not* require taxes with a debt-free money system. (*See* chapters 21 and 22).

Without government borrowing money from a private Federal Reserve banking system, no taxes would be needed eventually for payment of interest. This would result in a saving of $302 billion a year from the budget, at least (1993 figures). The income tax was enacted by the Sixteenth Amendment for the specific purpose of enabling the government to pay interest on its borrowing from the Federal Reserve system once the Federal Reserve Act of 1913 was passed. It is possible that with a new debt-free money system the income tax would no longer be needed. Whatever taxes are needed could be collected through the new U.S. Treasury banking system. (*See* chapters 21 and 22). This would free 116,425 employees for productive work and save over $549 billion (the total cost of collecting $1 trillion income taxes for 1990. Figure from Internal Revenue Service and Tax Foundation, Washington, 1992). This in itself is more than the current deficits.

Thomas Jefferson was able to send the tax collectors home even within a debt-based money system. Besides providing government services and cutting the national debt by half, he was able to make the famous Louisiana Purchase.

Finally, Social Security should not be a problem for the Treasury. The present Social Security taxes are not fully a tax but more of a saving for retirement. It adds a social function for those in our society who are incapable of providing for their own minimum security in old age and health care. The taxes are fully adequate if the trust fund is honored and not used to finance other nations' wars. With a debt-free money system, adequate employment, and a stable dollar, no regular "cost of living increases" would be needed.

What about Taxes for Health Care?

Guaranteed health services for everybody do not appear to me to be the proper function of the government. *If* the government provides a debt-free money system and a stable dollar, which clearly is its sovereign responsibility for the nation, the people will be able to afford their own health insurance or services as they wish, with greater freedom and self-respect. The government can no more guarantee health for everybody than it can monitor their unhealthy and irresponsible choices and lifestyles, which lead to health problems.

The government health care programs as promoted are an unacceptable intrusion into the personal lives and free decisions and choices of ordinary citizens, professionals, and the private business community. Such programs would impose yet another intolerable bureaucracy in a nation already burdened with too many of them. The private sector is capable of making improvements to health care, which is not as bad as the government wants people to believe. In spite of the anecdotal cases of people who "fell through the cracks," the majority of those who need care receive better care than any top-heavy bureaucracy would deliver. There will always be some imperfection in any delivery system, and more so in a bureaucratic system run by government.

Where there are evident serious abuses, as in the legal profession and in insurance industries, the government has a clear responsibility. But there will always be failed situations, in the private sector as well as with government bureaucracy in control, that will be exploited by the media, when a lack of love in human hearts allows greed to prevail.

Naturally, before a debt-based money system is instituted, health care for the needy will be a major government responsibility and a big problem. Once that is accomplished and opportunities for adequate employment enable most people to assume full responsibility for their own health-care needs, government involvement should be minimal and limited to much lower numbers of those who are in some way disabled and truly underprivileged.

Note

1. Quotations of figures used throughout the book are recent enough to be valid in 1997 when the same financial environment still prevails and is nearing a climax of some sort.

Chapter 15

Inflation and Depreciation of Money

What Is Inflation?

The word *inflation* is bandied around in the press and by writers on economics, but they seldom define what they mean by it. It's just something they assume everybody is afraid of, like a virus or epidemic that every now and then comes from outer space to attack the economies of poor humanity. Supposedly the only cure can come from the Federal Reserve Board chairman.

Financial writers take for granted that the Federal Reserve Board chairman knows when inflation is coming, and the only way he can prevent or cure it is by an injection of higher interest rates into the economy. This seems to be his only remedy to lower the fever of what he calls an overheated economy.

The truth of the matter is that inflation is caused right here on earth by *the land lords of the world*. These people need to stimulate production of wealth by easy credit and money expansion so that there may be wealth around for them when they are ready to harvest it by a depression.

Honest but ignorant citizens hardly suspect who the architect of such procedures is: the Federal Reserve Board itself! After many tries, the chairman has the system "down pat" and has many ways of both feeding the flock and then leading it to be shorn, while keeping it from knowing where it is being led. Not defining what inflation is, many well-intentioned economists search for and argue about the causes of and solutions for inflation. Some tell us that raising taxes is a cure for inflation. Others say that raising taxes causes inflation. They argue the same way about interest rates and the money supply. What is the exact function of these actions in regard to inflation? Are they the cause or the cure, or maybe the result of inflation? None seem to know for sure.

This confusion exists because *inflation* is a generic word. The inflation that most people experience in their everyday lives and worry about is *price inflation*. When citizens see their taxes raised tenfold in fifteen years on the same piece of unimproved property or the price of their automobile or a piece of meat triple when newspapers and financial writers are talking about a 3 percent inflation rate, they know that somebody is not telling the truth.

Wages have also gone up or been "adjusted for inflation," a term used constantly, but somehow people have to work harder and harder to stay even, often with both spouses working to support families that only one breadwinner used to be able to support. Those at the bottom of the economic ladder, especially those in service jobs, have fallen behind. They have to pay the same inflated prices for necessities as everybody else without having the money with which to do it. The result is that the gap between those who have and those who don't, keeps widening, with the ranks of the poor getting bigger. It is evident that somebody is not figuring those inflation rates and adjustments correctly.

Those who blame the "cost of living increases" on inflation are begging the question. *Why* does the cost of living go up? *Why* do the prices keep rising? If the dollar had a stable value, the only cause for a price increase or a decrease would be the law of supply and demand. That would affect only the commodity or product in short supply and for a limited time, not the total price structure.

When a first-class postage stamp was two cents, one could buy fifty of them for a dollar. Today the same service costs thirty-two cents and one can buy only three instances of it for the dollar instead of fifty. That is a dramatic example of what happened to the value of the dollar, of how wise it was for the retired person to have saved two thousand dollars and to get only six cents of his or her dollar in value upon retirement.

What Causes Price Inflation?

What is often called the monetarist reason for price inflation is "too much money chasing too few goods." That is a valid observation as it stands, but where does that excess of money come from? Who created money that was not based on value and production? If price inflation is "too much money chasing too few goods," the obvious solution would be to increase the production of goods or decrease the money supply or both. But how to implement these options is what gives the economists and financial writers their headaches and brings about the confusion in their many proposals. The basic reason for their problem is that most of them are writing within an environment of a debt-based money system over which neither they nor the government have any effective control.

The control of the money supply depends on the will and design of the human beings who run the private Federal Reserve banking system. Their purpose is to serve the bankers' interests. When they tell the gullible and unquestioning public that they are raising the interest rates to control inflation, the higher rates give the banks a higher profit on loans and make credit costlier for industry. This restricts production, thus contributing to inflation (the "too few goods").

At the same time, the Federal Reserve may lower the reserve requirements, which encourages the banks to lend and increase the money supply (the "too much money"). Both actions contribute to inflation. What the Fed does, and the reason it gives for its actions to the public, are not the same. It is impossible to find a permanent solution to money inflation or price inflation when it all depends on the will of those who operate the money system for private gain and who are never open about what they are doing.

The Consequences of Price Inflation

We have already seen some of the consequences. Let's follow the process step by step.

1. Both money inflation and price inflation heat up the economy so that more goods are produced.

2. The relationship between goods and services produced and the money supply becomes distorted and gets out of control.

3. Well-to-do people feel good about their situation, have more money in their pockets, can buy more goods and service, and are able to invest more, enjoy life, and worry only about what investments will help them to cope with still more inflation.

4. Less fortunate and/or less resourceful people, and those depending on fixed incomes, have to pay the same higher prices for everything

and feel poorer. Even if they too have a little more money, they have to skimp more.

5. Labor sees the cost of living going up and demands higher wages.

6. The dollar is diluted and loses value. Investments made in poorer times with hard-earned money lose their value. It takes more money to stay in the same place economically.

7. Taxes go up. The well-do-do look for tax havens. Poorer people find these taxes harder to pay.

8. In the average income family, both spouses are forced to seek employment to keep the family afloat financially. Families headed by a single parent slide further down the economic scale.

9. Higher prices tend to become permanent. People begin to accept the new level fatalistically as a cycle caused by forces beyond their understanding or control.

10. Consequently, people come to expect regular cost of living increases in order to be ready for the next cycle. This helps make inflation an ongoing phenomenon.

This inflation-based mentality demonstrates that human beings are not disposed to accept less of anything. They are more concerned about getting more dollars than the dollar's value. The end result is that the gap between the rich and poor widens and the ranks of poor increase.

Life without Inflation: a Reflection
The reader is invited to reflect and construct his or her own vision of life without inflation by reversing the above consequences of inflation. Such a vision is likewise incorporated into the total vision presented in the concluding chapter.

Chapter 16
Some Basics for a Decent Life on Earth

Infrastructures

The quality and shape of our infrastructures determines to a large extent the quality of life we enjoy in our communities. All we need to do in order to see that the maintenance and improvement of many basic infrastructures in our country have not kept up with the needs of our citizens is to drive through the streets of almost any city and to read its local press.

Everywhere we find streets and roads in disrepair, as are many of the major interstate highways; bridges are in bad shape; public transportation facilities are inadequate in most of the country. It's all a poor reflection of the pride of a great nation and *prima facie* evidence that we have not been good builders and stewards of adequate infrastructures and of the environment.

Access to safe water and flood control are urgent problems in many areas of the First World. Shortages of water in other parts of the world, both for minimum health and irrigation, are critical. Many water, sewage, and garbage disposal systems in American communities are antiquated or inadequate; in other parts of the world, they are worse or nonexistent. The list is almost endless.

Current Prospects for Improving Infrastructures

We have heard a great deal of election campaign rhetoric about "investing in America." This would include the infrastructure, the politicians said, and education and health care were thrown in for good measure. To provide for all of this, President Clinton announced a program that would call for spending the "grand total of $20 billion" and, of course, new taxes to pay for it.

What President Clinton and the media didn't say is what happened to the surplus in the trust funds that were set up specifically for some of these infrastructures and for which various fees and taxes were collected. According to a study by the Congressional Budget Office reported in May 1992, the airport and airway trust fund had a surplus of $24.8 billion, and the highway trust fund had a surplus of $19.5 billion. Why weren't those funds used for the purposes for which they were built up by fees and taxes?

There are many other funds set up for specific purposes. Among them are Social Security, Medicare, and military and civilian employee retirement funds. The surplus, according the Congressional Budget Office report, came to a total of $970.1 billion at the end of 1991, forty-eight times the $20 billion President Clinton asked for in new taxes on energy. What happened to that $970.1 billion? The government had to "borrow" it, we are told, for things like foreign aid, more military equipment for other nations, and congressional pay raises, excursions into Panama and Iraq, contraceptive devices for Latin American countries, condoms for school children, and so on. What guarantee do we have that the new taxes we are asked to pay are not going to be "borrowed" the same way?

The Sovereignty Resolution

Efforts are now being made to introduce in Congress what is known as the Sovereignty Resolution. It has been proposed by an Illinois businessman, Ken Bohnsack, and calls upon Congress to create constitutional, interest-free money to "fund necessary and legitimate needs of our communities and nation, such as bridges, roads, water/sewer/waste disposal systems, (and others). . . . [The resolution] will permit tax-supported bodies . . . to borrow money directly from the U.S. Treasury interest free, as authorized by Article I, Section 8, Clause 5 of the Constitution."

This resolution holds out before us the prospect of increased production and employment, a better condition and quality of infrastructures, schools, and local utilities, lower taxes, lower interest payments by local governments, and lower interest rates for all.

This is a very important step in the right direction, but only a step. If this one step is not followed with all the rest of the steps necessary to make this change permanent, the whole nation will stumble badly and fall, as has happened with similar efforts in our past history. The shortcomings of this worthwhile initiative are these:

1. It represents the grafting of healthy tissue on a cancer-ridden body without removing the cancer and its causes. The Federal Reserve system of debt-based money is the cancer. Without repealing the Federal Reserve Act and turning over the twelve Regional Federal Reserve banks to the U.S. Treasury and Congress to be run by the U.S. Treasury in a professional manner, the Federal Reserve Board will still be able to use its awe-inspiring power to punish the Congress that has dared to pass such a resolution. The moneyed interests did exactly that in 1863 after Lincoln crossed them. Should such a resolution be adopted, the Federal Reserve Board has the means first to create inflation and then follow it with devastating depression. It is quite capable of such retaliation.

2. There is no chance that a resolution like this actually will be adopted or implemented because neither Congress nor the citizens have been adequately prepared for it by a sound and thorough educational effort. Further, the administration is 100 percent committed to following the instructions from the Federal Reserve Board and its associated institutions.

Nevertheless, we must applaud Mr. Bohnsack, for initiating this grassroots movement and the process of education. Although only a beginning, it is an excellent beginning indeed! But the plan must be developed further (as suggested in chapters 20–24 of this book) and much more education and formation of public opinion must take place.

We dare not do less. It will be difficult because we will be confronted and opposed by the virtually unlimited power of the *land lords of the world*, their money, and the media. They will deny us access for our educational efforts. But there is also power in our numbers and our knowledge, love, and commitment (described in another chapter).

On a Positive Note

Mr. Bohnsack's resolution has the support of the Michigan State Legislature, the Illinois State Senate, all the counties of Montana, all the townships of Ohio, all the cities of Illinois, and the United States Conference of Mayors representing fifteen hundred cities with populations of thirty thousand or more.

The resolution also has the support of the Community Bankers Association of Illinois, which shows that honest community bankers who strive to serve their communities recognize a movement that will serve the infrastructure needs of the nation. The Illinois state branch of Ross Perot's "United We Stand" has also gone on record as supporting. Hopefully the rest of this organization, with over four million paid members, will follow suit.

This is all a great accomplishment and shows that there is a solid base among the citizens of our country on which to build the foundation for a permanent reform of our money system.[1]

The Environment

The environment and ecology are here to serve both the short-term and long-term needs of people. We must be sure, however, that we follow true scientific principles, not just the propaganda of special interest groups. There needs to be a balance between needs of people and their environment, which has been entrusted by the Creator for humanity's responsible use, enjoyment, and stewardship.

Population

Propaganda for the United Nations Population Conference of September 1994 in Cairo, Egypt, promoted formation of plans to get rid of three and one-half billion people (out of the present five and one-half billion). Two billion people is the upper limit of what this earth can support, the propaganda says. So it was *not* a conference to help the populations of the world find access to an honest and equitable share of this earth's economic goods, but one aimed at depopulating the world.

Instead of treating people as a major resource contributing to the economies and well-being of nations, the conference looked upon them merely as consumers and polluters of the environment. That propaganda was based on the statements of two professors, Russian professor Viktor Danilov-Daniljan, and Cornell University professor of ecology David Pimental. Against that propaganda, the German association of agro-chemical industries, the Industrieverband Agrar, tells us that even with the present technologies "fifty billion people worldwide could be nourished at a high quality standard."

Our role is not to correct what the Creator has done, but to correct what we are doing by getting rid of our greed and the usurious debt-money systems that plunder and loot the hard-earned goods that both people and the environment produce. It is love of people as our greatest productive resource that will harness our minds and technologies to serve them, that will bring true economic freedom and respect for human rights, rather than hatred that seeks to limit or get rid of them. Jacqueline Kasun completely demolishes the scientific assumptions of both the environmentalist and anti-population propaganda in her book *The War Against Population*.

Pope John Paul II's Memorandum to the Nations

In a memorandum the pope calls the draft formulation by the Conference on Population an "act of treason against the principles of the UN Charter." It "violates fundamental aspects of human dignity and freedom, downgrades marriage, endorses abortion, and promotes selfish, obsessive forms of sexuality."

Instead, what the Conference on Population should be concerned with is "the well-being and development of peoples, the growth of world population, the rise of the median age in some industrialized nations, the fight against disease, and forced displacement of whole peoples." That is the true formula for peace in the world, as proposed before by Pope Paul VI in the encyclical *On the Development of Peoples*.

Moral Environment

When we speak about our stewardship of the environment, we need to begin with ourselves and our own lifestyles. If we fail to reverence our own bodies by the use of drugs and by other excesses or deficiencies in food and drink, no ecology or health program can make up for these failures.

Pope John Paul II summed up the primary issues of ecology very well when he said, "Simplicity, moderation and discipline, as well as a spirit of sacrifice, must become part of everyday life, lest all suffer the negative consequences of the careless habits of the few."

Greed and the constant drive for ever-greater profits are major causes of the abuse of our environment and of the contamination of a truly healthful food supply for our people. That should be self-evident to any thinking person in touch with the kind of denatured food that is offered and promoted by suppliers and their advertisers. Such food is not intended to provide a healthy environment for people but to return the greatest profits for investors.

More important than an unpolluted environment for our bodies is the environment in which both children and adults can develop healthy minds. It needs to be first of all an environment of respect and reverence for one another and for our dignity as human beings.

Widespread pornography and the gross disrespect for sexuality in both men and women, and lack of reverence for honesty and truth create a pollution of the worst kind. They endanger the wholesome educational environment needed for the education of our future citizens.

The Natural Custodian of the Land

Modern family farmers love the land and nature just as their ancestors did before them. But greed for profits has virtually destroyed the family farm. The nation's food supply is now largely in the hands of the big farming corporations, whose primary objective is profit. For them, care for the soil and for the food that they produce are subordinated to their endless quest for greater and greater profits. Their definition of efficient production does not include reverence for the environment and natural resources such as topsoil. For corporations, production is efficient only when it gives them "a competitive edge" in the marketplace and greater profit for their shareholders.

Love for the land and reverence for the environment make family farmers the best natural guardians of the environment. With a deep and personal respect for the earth, family farmers are the most reliable custodians of the land and producers of food for a healthy people. But to survive, farmers must be able to make a decent living for their families on the farm. They are unable to do that when they have to compete or contend with the big corporations and their manipulations of the markets, unfair tax structures, inadequate credit, and below parity prices for their products.

True modern farmers are a far cry from the so-called dirt farmers of the past. They understand the scientific basis for ecological farming that respects the soil and produces quality food. But they must be given a chance by a fair economic and political system that looks upon them as entrepreneurs, part of the infrastructure of the nation and essential for the sustenance of its people and their economy. To deprive farmers of that function by subjecting them to competition from the big food monopolies that are able to buy foreign food products produced by farmers of other nations at starvation wages will destroy the livelihood of both. It is a short-sighted policy that loots foreign land and destroys the future productive capacity of our own lands.

The first obligation of a nation is to be able to feed its own people, to make sure that its productive capacity for food is intact within its own borders. It cannot do that by throwing its family farmers to the wolves of the so-called free markets. The argument is often made that the big importers and exporters of our food supply make it possible for the consumers to obtain food at lower cost. However, in the process our farmers are destroyed, as well as the farmers of the exporting nations, who are forced to produce at starvation wages and are thus destroyed or kept in perpetual poverty. The solution is not in impoverishing the primary producers of our food supply, but in a stable economy that enables the *consumers* to be employed at wages that make it possible for them to pay the producers a fair price for the food they eat.

Note

1. As of September 1995, there is no further information available on the current status of this resolution. Given the lack of interest in politics by the citizens at large and their inertia when support of their legislators is called for, it is unlikely that this resolution will pass. To succeed, any such move will need far more educational effort and involvement from the citizens. It is opposed to the entrenched power of the *land lords of the world* and will never have the support of the media.

Chapter 17
Investment and Capital

True Wealth

Wealth, either derived from the possession of a natural resource or from productive efforts of people, is what a sound exchange economy is all about. It provides the citizens of a country with all the necessities of life and with a base for the services they need.

The production of wealth, the services based on it, and the education or training necessary to prepare for both, in their turn provide employment opportunities. That should enable people to obtain an honest and just share of the wealth produced and of the services necessary for the support of a life of human dignity for themselves and their families.

Honest Earned Investment

The word *investment* is used very loosely in all the current theoretical writing on economic issues and news stories. Without defining the term, the articles are not really intelligible to the person in the street, often not even to the one on Wall Street. Honest investment should mean investing of ourselves or of real value that we acquired honestly, or of the money we earned by contributing commensurate value to the community. It also includes credit issued by legitimate government authority for development of community infrastructures and facilities. That kind of honest investment produces more wealth for the economy and provides employment for the nation's citizens, who are then able to share and enjoy the fruits of their creativity.

Unearned Investments

Most of the time, the word *investment* as used in the media does *not* mean investing anything; instead it refers to debt-based money created as credit by a private banking system or acquired through manipulation of financial instruments like derivatives.[1] These claims on the wealth earned by honest investment and labor are nothing but plunder. Witnesses to the truth of that statement are found in countries where privatization and market and financial reforms have been instituted by the International Monetary Fund and the World Bank (more about that in the next chapter).

Demanding privatization of economies in Russia, Latin America, and other Third-World countries has the major purpose of providing "investors" with the opportunity to buy up the produced and natural wealth of these countries at bargain prices. A public sale with no other competitors having any money to bid always provides bargains. It gives the "investors" a quicker way to turn profits. Further, if the big banks who provide funds for these speculative loans lose, the U.S. taxpayers will bail them out. Recall the $500 billion savings-and-loans bailouts.

George Soros is a recent example of the kind of "investor" discussed here. Almost overnight he made $1 billion trading currency derivatives. In reporting the story, the media used the word "earned," another abused term. Soros did not contribute anything of value to any nation's economy in order to earn anything. Rather, he almost destroyed the British pound and set out brazenly to go after the German mark next, according to the story in the media. The Federal Reserve banks and other central banks defended the practice.

Honest Capital Produces Wealth

Capital is essential for an economy based on the production and exchange of goods and wealth.

But the capital that comes from credits created by a private debt-based banking system is not true capital, just speculative debt-based money. Defenders of that kind of capitalism point to the prosperity of the industrialized nations, where such capitalism had been practiced. Yes, any kind of money stimulates production, but after those periods of prosperity, there always have been depressions or recessions that plundered the wealth created by that capitalism.

For countless families, such "prosperity" forced the employment of both husband and wife just to keep above board financially and to provide some of the necessary consumer goods for their families. The workers are praised for such productivity, which enables American industry to be competitive. But not a word is said about the worker's job insecurity in a system in which "investors" periodically skim off the fruits of the workers' industry.

The rich "investors" also have other options that the less affluent, who depend only on honest earnings for their money, do not. Faced with higher taxes, they "invest" in tax-free municipal bonds; or, if the "investors" are the big banks, government bonds. Roughly one half of the $5 trillion government debt is in the form of government bonds, which are lying in the vaults of the Federal Reserve Banking system and doing nothing for the economy except drawing interest from the taxpayers. The bonds are a safe and sure "investment" for the banks. With them in their vaults, and the government doing the job of collecting the interest from the taxpayers, they need not take any risks in the marketplace by lending to productive industry or business.

Capitalism and the Entrepreneur

"Capitalism, like the family, is not an institution that can become obsolete . . . as long as human societies persist. Human needs and numbers annually increase; science and technology provide their continuing surprises. . . . No nation can grow and adapt to change except . . . that its productive wealth is diversely controlled and can be freely risked to new causes, flexibly applied to new purposes, steadily transformed into new shapes and systems. . . . The capitalist system succeeds and thrives because it gives room for the heroic creativity of entrepreneurs . . . even though the greatest of capitalists, the founders of the system—were in some sense 'robber barons.' " So speaks George Gilder, program director of the International Center for Economic Policy Studies and chairman of the Economic Roundtable at the Lehrman Institute.

It is true that the free entrepreneur holds an important key to a productive economy and to the solution of the problem of unemployment. However, we still have the so-called robber barons with us, in greater force than ever; they inhibit the development of an economy dependent on entrepreneurs by denying them access to adequate and dependable credit at reasonable interest rates. Nor do we have "productive wealth . . . diversely controlled." The major part of it is under monopoly control.

The robber barons have been identified as owners and operators of the private debt-based money system with their associated big industries and monopolies. They constitute an "international imperialism of money" and do their robbing throughout 178 countries of the world in far more sophisticated ways than the robber barons of the past. They are using the Federal Reserve system, the International Monetary Fund, the World Bank, and fellow travellers, not to promote genuine and free entrepreneurs and industry (the purpose for which they were supposedly organized), but for siphoning off the wealth and fruits of human labor of these countries. Anyone following what is being done by these institutions in Africa, Asia, Ibero-America, Russia, and most recently in Mexico will recognize the most colossal robbery the world has ever seen, outdistancing by far the robber barons of mercantilism or of old-style colonialism.

This chapter was intended simply to expose the "tip of the iceberg" of fictitious and dishonest so-called investments. These are made by the use of a highly usurious and exploitative system of banking with dishonest debt-based fractional reserve money, not by any contribution to the wealth of the nation. Such "investing" is not representative of a capitalism with a human face, which brings lasting prosperity and happiness to a country's citizens.

Note

1. A *derivative* is a very complex financial instrument understood fully only by the top bankers who create it. Futures give a buyer control over large quantities of grains, meats, metals, currencies, and so forth, for very little money (leverage). Options give still more leverage. Derivatives are something like options, giving extremely high leverage positions with prospects of extremely high profits to those who understand and know how to use them—or extremely large losses to those who don't.

Chapter 18

The Long Road to Economic Justice

Free market and financial reforms—NAFTA, GATT, etc.—are being pushed arrogantly on all nations by American leaders. But a truly free, honest, and just economy is impossible with the debt-based money systems owned by private financial interests. Their main priority is obtaining the greatest profit from whatever endeavor they are involved in, not just in terms of money, but of the physical assets money can claim. Now the commodity they most want free access to is oil, but any real assets they can lay their hands on are acceptable.

The principal structures through which the big bankers and industrialists exercise their constant pursuit of profit and power are the Federal Reserve, the International Monetary Fund, the World Bank, and associated entities. They use their resources to claim and control all commerce and wealth around the world.

What Free Market Economy?

Their idea of a "free economy" is *not* accepted in the teachings of the popes. Over a hundred years ago, Pope Leo XIII wrote: "A free economy cannot be understood in such a way that it refuses to be limited by any demand for justice and becomes an unbridled affirmation of self interest only. . . . A truly free economy cannot be had when one side is so powerful as to reduce the other to subservience" (quoted by John Paul II, *Centesimus Annus*, no. 16).

While *Centesimus Annus* says *no* to state control of the means of economic production, nevertheless it teaches that the state "has a necessary role in safeguarding the prerequisites of a free economy. . . . It is the place of the state to assure a level field for the parties involved."

138

The Human Rights Agenda

The *land lords of the world*, especially those in the United States of America, have a lot to say to other countries about respect for human rights. They have organizations to monitor the compliance of these nations. At the same time, in the areas of the market economy, the judicial and educational systems, and personal freedoms, the human rights of American citizens are violated daily. We see the "slivers" in other people's eyes but not the "beams" in our own.

The major human rights that are being violated by such structures as NAFTA or GATT include:

1. The right of every human being to a recognition of his or her human dignity as a worker and producer of wealth.

2. The right to recognition of the dignity of work as a personal exertion for the sake of procuring what is necessary for self, family, and community.

3. The right to private property that is necessary for one's personal development. In modern times this includes the right of access to knowledge and technology, which is badly violated.

4. The right to form private professional associations of employers and of workers. These are natural and inalienable rights that belong to every human being, simply because he or she is a human being. They precede his or her incorporation into political society. It is a matter of justice that the state may not prohibit these. It exists to recognize and protect them (*Centesimus Annus*, no. 7). This is a specific reaffirmation of the teaching of Pope Leo XIII.

The encyclical goes into great detail about other human rights derived from these four. But it is beyond the scope of this work to treat them in more detail here.

The operations of the so-called free market and free trade structures are proof that these basic and inalienable human rights are *not* respected.

How Free Is Our Market Economy?

The claim is made that free market forces enable consumers to have cheaper goods and enjoy a higher standard of living. Those who make such claims never point out that their goals are accomplished by paying starvation wages to the peasant producers. They justify this conduct in the name of competition. They say they need to be free to buy products of cheap labor in order to compete in the world markets. In the process, the human rights of the producers in those countries are violated.

American consumers are not the only people in this world. They do not have an unqualified right always to buy at the lowest prices, while forcing the producers, their brothers and sisters in other countries of the human family, to sell their products for whatever the monopolies choose to give them. As a poor peasant in Peru commented, "Free Market? There is nothing free about my market. I either sell for what they give me or starve."

Failure of the public authority to ensure that human rights are respected violates justice, the encyclical tells us. To give all people of the earth access to a fair share of the goods we are capable of producing, we need adequate employment, respect for human rights, the avoidance of *undue* government involvement, and sensible trade barriers to prevent threats to industry and agriculture by world monopolies. There is no right to compete solely for the sake of greater profits when the price is violating the inherent human rights of the producers to make an honest living for their families.

A stable dollar created and maintained by a debt-free money system alone would remove exposure of entrepreneurs and distributors to unnecessary risks, reduce commodity speculation by monopolies, bring lower taxation, and make it easier for true and honest investors to make a fair profit without undue profit margins between producers and consumers. It would definitely remove the unfair advantage that the debt-based system gives to the big "investors" and enable the small investors of honest money to compete in truly free markets.

Free Markets and the Land Lords of the World

Since in the debt-based money system, debt is money, the first thing that the Federal Reserve, the International Monetary Fund, and the World Bank do when a new money-making situation opens up is lend their debt-based money. Thus they create more debt. The new nation, as a debtor, thus becomes another nation under their control. It *must* do as they say in order to pay interest on the debt.

The IMF and the World Bank were created at the Bretton Woods Conference on December 27, 1945, supposedly to help the nations with financial reforms. The Federal Reserve system, which had been on the scene since 1913, was their sponsor. With their power consolidated for action in the whole world, the land lords' appetite for profits has also grown. How they have been "helping" for the past fifty years is shown by the following examples.

Examples of the Land Lords of the World in Action

Russia

After the fall of communism in Eastern Europe, the International Monetary Fund and the World Bank were quick to "help" Poland and Russia with loans. But before letting them have any money, they imposed *conditions* on these nations. They demanded financial reforms, higher taxes, privatization, and free markets. They forbade infrastructure development, industry and defense, and reasonable services to the citizens, and introduced other austerities to make sure the nations could pay the interest on these loans. They withheld the funds of the promised and publicized loans until the conditions were met precisely as demanded. Russia is still waiting. This is standard procedure whenever they lend their debt-based and -created money.

In the meantime, these austere conditions cause great economic hardships for the citizens of the Eastern European nations, and they are rebelling, although the Poles are still cooperating with the International Monetary Fund and World Bank.

President Clinton and Vice President Gore both have admitted that it was a mistake to impose the World Bank's and IMF's demands on the Russian nation. Mr. Gore told Russian prime minister Viktor Chernomyrdin on the occasion of his visit to Russia after the December 12, 1993, election: "I would say that every country that has representatives on the IMF board has been slow to recognize the hardships that are caused by some of the conditions that have been overly insisted upon in the past. . . . The world has to recognize the gravity of this situation."

Chernomyrdin responded, "We should face the truth and admit that many people voted against the hardships and mistakes of the current reform, rather than for any specific (political) platform. Naturally, any 'shock' methods must be precluded in the future."

But that moment of facing the truth didn't last very long. The next day the *London Financial Times* called Mr. Gore's remarks "badly misguided." The Swiss daily *Neue Zuricher Zeitung* called them "naïve." Lloyd Bentsen disclaimed them and the controlled U.S. media generally gave the whole incident the silent treatment.

German Count Otto von Lambsdorf, current European chairman of the Trilateral Commission, said he would push the International Monetary Fund's "shock therapy" at the commission's next meeting.

On December 30, 1994, the International Monetary Fund and World Bank responded very angrily in a joint memorandum that called for a *more rapid* shutdown of the Russian economy. They sent a delegation to Russia to make plain to its leaders that the Russian government *must* speed up reforms and full market economy, close nonviable plants, cut down social expenditures, sharply reduce central bank credit, and expand privatization, including that of land and farms.[1] Those orders are meant to enable "investors" to pick up the bargains. Those who own the nations' debts dictate economic policy and devastate whole nations. Thus the international imperialism of money is in action while we demand "democratic reforms" in those countries.

Tanzania

At the end of 1991, Tanzania's foreign debt was $6.5 billion. To pay the debt, Tanzania accepted money from the World Bank and the International Monetary Fund (IMF), conditioned as always on the restructuring of the country's economy. In their recent pastoral letter, "Good Conscience—Vision of Our Nation," the Tanzanian bishops wrote: "Though the market economy is expected to raise the income of the nation, we experience the decrease in the income of the majority and the increase in the price of consumer goods. From the outside it would seem as if our economic situation has improved. But we are witnessing more hardships for the majority of Tanzanians while a few, who apparently do not care about our national problems, are getting rich."[2]

Venezuela

In December of 1993, Sir Henry Kissinger[3] paid a visit to the president-elect of Venezuela, Rafael Cardera, and his cabinet. He told the press, "Venezuela has been a country close to my heart for a long time." What is there about Venezuela that would touch Kissinger's heart that much?

Sir Henry told the press: "I had a meeting with him [Cardera] that was quite advantageous and useful for the future of Venezuela." Kissinger made a special trip to Venezuela to tell the people how lucky they are; they have oil. They also badly need, he said, high-technology capital goods in order to become a modern industrial power. So, the United States will buy their oil, and then they can buy the technology with the proceeds.

There was one catch, however. Venezuela had a debt to the International Monetary Fund and the World Bank on which it had to make a $5 billion payment. It didn't have the funds, so the technology had to wait. Venezuela had to sell its oil to make its interest payment. Because the price of oil went down (one wonders why), it took a lot of oil to make that payment. The net result of the meeting for Venezuela: a loss of $5 billion of oil wealth, a natural resource, which it had to deliver in exchange for paper stating it now has paid $5 billion on its debt. The loan was of money created by a private banking corporation based on debt, not on anything of value.

The popes and the nations themselves, especially those of the Second and Third Worlds, see debt as the one great obstacle to true progress and development of industry and infrastructure in those nations. Debt-based money, which claims the countries' true wealth, is a form of looting their natural resources and economies. This is a major theme throughout this book.

NAFTA, GATT, and Others

A *Milwaukee Journal* editorial of September 17, 1993, quoted President Clinton, in his campaign to have the NAFTA approved by Congress, as saying, "Ours is now an era in which commerce is global and in which money, management and technology are highly mobile."

In the context of a number of realities on the world scene, that statement is simply *not* true. As any well-informed person knows, commerce rides on money and is global only to the extent that money allows it to be. The power of money controls who and what nations have access to commerce, technology, and management of their own industry and finances, and to what extent. The new developing Eastern European nations, the old Middle East nations, the Third-World developing nations, African and Ibero-American nations, and Asiatic nations can bear witness to the fact that their commerce and economies have been devastated by the conditions imposed on them by the IMF and the World Bank.

The Federal Reserve, the World Bank, and the IMF are doing exactly what Britain did in colonial times to America, only in a much more sophisticated and efficient manner and on a far wider scale. Britain prevented the colonies from developing industry. All it wanted was (1) a market for the goods of its own industry, a "free market" if you want to call it that, and (2) a source of raw materials at whatever price Britain was willing to pay.

The development of infrastructure, technology, and industries was forbidden as it is now in the undeveloped countries. Taxes have to be raised, and services for health and education limited or denied. Their military forces are subjected to limitations. These nations under IMF and World Bank domination must not be able to defend themselves from unwanted encroachments into their sovereignty as independent nations. So, despite Clinton's remarks, neither management nor technology is global or "highly mobile," except within the power base of the new aristocracy and of the controlling industrial nations. The hand of the new financial colonialism was quite visible in its reach for NAFTA.

The *Milwaukee Journal* editorial then says, "Therefore, Americans need to adapt and, if possible, *exploit* this new world. *That is exactly what NAFTA seeks to do.*" This is the truth. There is no better way to exploit the productive capacities of the people of a nation than to open the trade barriers to food and financial monopolies with their unlimited access to debt-based money and credit.

Effects of IMF Conditionalities

Conditions mandated by the IMF for the interest and principal payments on debts make it impossible for the countries involved to maintain and develop basic health infrastructures. As a result, there are outbreaks of cholera, for example, in these countries. Peru tops the list with 300,000 cases. The total for the Ibero-American nations is placed at 800,000. Official government figures show that more than 12,000 Mexicans have contracted the disease.[4]

In 1994 and 1995, financial manipulations affected Mexico's peso. The peso lost much of its value. To whom? To the big banks. Citibank alone has a $2.9 billion stake, boasting of the huge profits that accrued to it from its manipulations. President Clinton, ever loyal to the financial institutions and serving their interests, found a way to bypass Congress and promise loans and guarantees in the amount of $48 to $50 billion to bail out the banks that lost. He reminded them that Mexico has "good collateral"; it has a lot of oil.

The world's land lords are not interested in just the currencies and paper financial instruments. So Mexico got our bankers' created paper, and the United States gets Mexico's oil. The physical assets are what the land lords are after, and manipulating the currencies is only a means to that end. They have the same goal in China, which also has great oil reserves.

The policies for despoiling and impoverishing the nations are set by the three new aristocracy's organizations, the Council for International Relations, the Trilateral Commission, and the Bilderbergers. All the chief operators of the debt-based money systems belong to at least one of these. Policies are determined not by any real concern for nations' welfare, but rather with a view to obtaining possession of or controlling their natural wealth and resources. Limiting their population growth, inhibiting their ability to defend themselves militarily, and finding an excuse to impose economic sanctions or war are among the means used to achieve that goal.[5]

Obstructing Development Leads to War

Fed up with the "shock therapy" that was being administered through the IMF and the World Bank, Russia presents a very dangerous situation for the world. The real power is now in the hands of the military and has the potential for leading into the ultimate tragedy of a world war.

That could end up in "shock therapy" in reverse for the land lords of the world. Or, perhaps war is what they want. There are untold profits to be gained from war. During Lincoln's presidency, the *land lords of the world* boasted that they would see to it that "great profits will be made out of the Civil War." The people, of course, are the ones who pay with their lives as well as with the wealth they produce.

The encyclical *Centesimus Annus* reminds us that a free economy that is . . . an unbridled affirmation of unbridled self-interest only . . . has led to cruel wars in which great nations invested their energies and violated most sacred human rights and exterminated entire peoples (no. 17). It points out that an economic consequence has been an insane arms race that swallowed up the resources needed for the development of national economies. Scientific and technological [resources] were directed to the production of ever more efficient and destructive weapons. . . . We must repudiate the idea that the effort to destroy the enemy, confrontation, and war itself are factors of progress and historical advancement (no. 18).

The military and defense-industry sector of the United States is the greatest exporter of military equipment to the nations of the world. That is their concept of a free-market economy. They are constantly on the lookout for new markets for munitions and military equipment. Going back all the way to the American War for Independence and subsequently in our history, these industrialist members and banker colleagues of the land lords have not hesitated to finance and supply both sides of a war. Their only loyalty is to profits and money.

Genuinely Free Markets Contribute to the Economy

In principle, within the context of an honest debt-free money system and of justice and respect for human dignity of the citizen of every country, genuinely free commerce among all nations makes sense. It would create honest and secure jobs and promote genuine prosperity in all the nations involved, based on the productive capacities of their people. With the current debt-based money system and its agricultural monopolies, so-called free trade just enables the land lords to exploit freely.

Protectionism is pictured as the great devil standing in the path to the so-called free trade. But the fact remains that the first obligation that a nation has is to be able to feed its own citizens and let them provide themselves with essential necessities of life. With the turmoil among nations and the constant threat of sanctions by the new aristocracy, it is essential for every nation to keep its agriculture and essential industries viable to protect them from being ruined by exploitation from abroad.

Pope Paul VI's Encyclical *On the Development of Nations*

How does all we have said in this chapter find support in Pope Paul VI's *On the Development of Nations*? The response to that question is the following very condensed summary of paragraphs 10–18 of the encyclical. A complete summary (with direct quotations) is provided in Appendix I.

Pope Paul VI writes in the encyclical that one great obstacle to progress in underdeveloped countries is the tension between modern techniques and technologies, which bring with them a culture that is opposed to the traditional moral, spiritual, and religious values, which give way when the new technologies bring with them a culture devoid of such values. . . . The greatest service that is rendered to peoples in these circumstances is to teach the native population how to take advantage of natural resources and become self sufficient, rather than permit the looting of these resources through the greed of foreign investors. . . . The Church has no desire to be involved in the political affairs of any nation but offers mankind a global perspective on man and human realities and reminds it that his development cannot be restricted to economic growth alone but must foster development of each man and the whole man. . . . However, here we are concerned primarily with the economic. . . . As we reap the benefits of prior and contemporary generations, we have an obligation to future generations. We are duty bound to work at the pursuit of life's necessities so that the proper scale of values can be maintained in future generations (highlights from nos. 13–18).

The New Colonialism

The same encyclical also speaks of colonialism, initially in paragraph 7: Today the Big Seven industrial nations, especially the United States and Britain, are incessantly pushing all the rest of the nations of the world toward what they call "democracy, free-market economy, and financial reforms." They are doing that through the World Bank, the International Monetary Fund, and the Federal Reserve banks and their associated organizations. For those that do not belong to the club (the new aristocracy), this is what those terms really mean.

Democracy means we don't want any strong leader in the nation whom we can't control. We do want a disorganized people, ignorant of what is going on. These we have ways to manipulate to fit our agenda.

Free-market economy means our food monopolies and big industries want a free market, a free flow of our products, to be paid for by the products of citizens' labors at a price we are willing to pay, assuring maximum profits for our investors.

Monetary reform means we want all countries to adopt our debt-based money system. We will help a nation get started by lending it money. Then it will be in debt to our bankers, and they will tell its government how to run the country. It means, in a word, colonialism.

Notes

1. Executive Intelligence Review News Service (EIRNS), January 12, 1994. EIRNS is an international organization of highly qualified reporters outside the controlled establishment media. They report worldwide news that the controlled media do not and therefore are hated by the establishment media.

2. *Maryknoll* (May 1994). *Maryknoll* is a publication of the Maryknoll missionary priests, brothers, and sisters, who since 1911 have had missions throughout the world. Maryknollers also publish *News Notes* analyzing peace and justice issues from a faith perspective.

3. Henry Kissinger has been knighted since 1993. He now represents the interests of England and is a key person serving the agenda of the *land lords of the world*, through whose involvement he became secretary of state and advisor to an American president. A former secretary of state renouncing his American citizenship by accepting an English title?

4. EIRNS (May 20, 1993).

5. Read the whole NSSM 200 document (prepared under Henry Kissinger), which targets thirteen nations for implementation of such policies (the document was described in chapter 9). The new aristocracy thought these thirteen nations were developing so fast that some day they might present a national security threat to the big industrial nations and had to be stopped.

Chapter 19
Religion, Morality, and Education

In the history of the formation of the people of Israel into a nation, there are many episodes of suffering, oppression, and slavery. Genesis and Exodus relate the slavery and the oppressive laws in Egypt. Then came the sufferings during a forty-year sojourn in the desert and the journey to the Promised Land under the leadership of Moses. In the designs of Yahweh, they were a people destined to bring the knowledge of the true and living God to the nations. Throughout their history they received the guidance and direction necessary to fulfill that mission. Nevertheless, it was up to them to choose the direction in which they would go.

Choose life and freedom, or slavery and death. Here is what will bring you freedom. There is what will keep you forever in slavery. The way to freedom and life is keeping the commandments. The way to slavery and death is to disregard the ten commandments (adapted from Deut. 30).

So long as they observed the commandments, they remained a free people and prospered. Whenever they drifted away from them, they lost their freedom. The greatest instance of this happening was the Babylonian Captivity, during which they almost lost their identity as a nation.

The commandments were not just arbitrary rules drawn up by Moses. They were laws based on the very nature and dignity of human beings as creatures of God. The people of Israel and their leaders took pride in the fact that their nation was the recipient of these laws. Their prophets cried out in gratitude: "What great nation has laws and decrees that are as just as this whole law. . . . Observe them carefully, for thus you will give evidence of your wisdom and intelligence to the nations, who will hear all these statutes and say, This great nation is truly a wise and intelligent people" (Deut. 4:8, 6).

The Splendor of Truth

Pope John Paul II puts it very succinctly in his encyclical *The Splendor of Truth*. About the Ten Commandments, he writes:

> These norms in fact represent the unshakable foundation and solid guarantee of a just and peaceful human existence, and hence of genuine democracy, which can come into being and develop only on the basis of equality of all its members, who possess common rights and duties. When it is a matter of the moral norms prohibiting intrinsic evil, there are no privileges or exceptions for anyone. It makes no difference whether one is master of the world or the "poorest of the poor" on the face of the earth. Before the demands of morality we are all absolutely equal. . . . By protecting the inviolable personal dignity of every human being they help to preserve the human social fabric and its proper and fruitful development. . . .
>
> Even though intentions may sometimes be good, and circumstances frequently difficult, civil authorities and particular individuals never have the authority to violate the fundamental and inalienable rights of the human person. In the end only a morality which acknowledges certain norms as valid always and for everyone, with no exception, can guarantee the ethical foundation of social coexistence, both on the national and international levels. . . .
>
> Only God, the Supreme Good, constitutes the unshakable foundation and essential condition of morality, and thus of the commandments, particularly those negative commandments which always and in every case prohibit behavior and actions incompatible with the personal dignity of every man. (nos. 96–99)

Here in the United States we have achieved a level of material prosperity that is the envy of the rest of the world. Yet somehow, often after a lifetime of industrious effort, millions upon millions of our citizens are left unemployed, homeless, hungry, poorly educated, destitute, or wards of the government. The poor are getting poorer and more numerous, and the rich are getting richer and likewise more numerous, as the media continue to report to us. We are a nation in economic slavery. Those in want and even the more comfortable middle class are at the service of the land lords of the world through debt and excessive taxation. Those who are rich, the land lords themselves, are not truly free either. They are spiritual slaves of their own greed.

Could we not benefit from the example and history of the Jewish nation by recapturing for our country their formula for achieving economic freedom and a life of dignity for all our citizens? Why not return to those inspired laws that were the pride of their nation? It would not only contribute to the economic freedom of the citizens who are enslaved in poverty but actually lead our nation to unprecedented greatness.

Observing even two of those commandments, the ones enjoining honesty and fidelity to truthfulness, would change the face of the planet and bring economic justice and peace. But why stop with those two? All ten were given to help us be truly human and to govern our relationships with our fellow human beings and our Creator. The founders of our nation approached the planning of our nation's *Constitution* in the same way. They held that "religion, morality, and education are necessary to good citizenship and should forever be encouraged."

That is the exact order in which they stated those "indispensable" requisites for the new experiment of democracy. Religion was placed first, because it is the foundation of morality. Certainly we cannot legislate morality, and we cannot eliminate crime by laws alone. Only religion and a sense of responsibility to our Creator can do that.

The Northwest Ordinance

One of the most significant accomplishments of the Congress of the Confederation was passing the Northwest Ordinance on July 13, 1787. This organized the northern portion of the Ohio Valley on lines laid out originally by Thomas Jefferson. Out of this territory west of the Allegheny Mountains were formed the states of Ohio, Indiana, Illinois, Michigan, Wisconsin, and the part of Minnesota east of the Mississippi.

Section 14 of the Northwest Ordinance provides us with an understanding of the mind of that Congress concerning the fundamental principles to be followed in the government of these new states. It can therefore be assumed that this was the way they understood the provisions of the *Constitution* by which the original colonies were to be governed: "It is hereby ordained and declared by the authority aforesaid, that the following articles shall be considered as articles of compact between the original States and the people and States in the said territory, and forever remain unalterable, unless by common consent, to wit: " [Six articles follow. Article III reads as follows:]

Religion, morality, knowledge, being necessary to good government and the happiness of mankind, schools and the means of education shall

151

forever be encouraged. The utmost good faith shall forever be observed toward the Indians; their lands and properties shall never be taken from them without their consent; and in their property, rights, and liberty they shall never be invaded or disturbed unless in just and lawful wars authorized by Congress . . . but laws founded in justice and humanity shall, from time to time, be made for preventing wrongs being done to them and for preserving peace and friendship with them.

It is worth noting that the education described by the founders of our country was meant to include religion and morality as well as general knowledge. These were deemed "necessary for good government and the happiness of mankind." Religion and morality must also enter into economic issues of justice and property rights, as shown by Article III's concern for the Indians.

Separation of church and state was adopted to avoid the friction that existed between the two in lands from which the colonists emigrated. The founders understood that both church and state each had their proper areas of service. They believed that there should be honest cooperation, with the state encouraging religion and the church promoting good citizenship. For the state to divorce itself from religion completely is contrary to the intention of the founding fathers.

Today, instead of encouraging religion, the state has been doing just the opposite. It impedes it in various ways and imposes irreligion on our educational system, judicial system, and public life in general. The state has injected itself into an area in which it has no competence, that of morality, and is thereby interfering with the church's work and mission. The state has more than enough to do to provide for the economic welfare, protecting "the life, liberty, and the pursuit of happiness" of its citizens. It should leave the religions free to do their work without discrimination or favoritism. They are better qualified for teaching morality, even with their differences.

Life, Liberty, and the Pursuit of Happiness

President Clinton, like all our nation's presidents, has taken the oath of office to uphold and defend the *Constitution*. This includes Article XIV, Section 1, which states: "Nor shall any State deprive any person of life, liberty, or property, without due process of law or deny to any person within its jurisdiction the equal protection of the laws."

The science of biology is witness to the fact that even a single newly conceived cell is a human being, with all the characteristics of a distinctive individual, already programmed in its genes. Neither human nature nor personhood exists in the abstract. There is no such thing as human nature in general. It is always in a particular human being. The fetus has a right to the same protection from the state as every other person. Removing all restrictions to abortion, impeding parental involvement and obligatory counseling, and opening the door wide to experimentation on unborn children are inconsistent with Mr. Clinton's oath of office. The *Constitution* forbids depriving any person of the right to life without due process of law and provides for equal protection of the law for all.

The president's assertion that he is not pro-abortion but for "choice" is neither honest nor responsible. Every person already has the power to choose, and too many women choose abortion, mostly because of ignorance of its intrinsically evil nature as well as of its consequences for themselves. But every person with the power to choose also has the responsibility for the choices he or she makes before conception.

No True Democracy without Education for Citizenship

As regards education, the third necessity listed by the founding fathers, the state has not proved itself any more competent than the church. In our country, as well as in most countries of the world, the church has always shown concern for good education and has initiated most of the great universities. It can be counted on to prepare people to be good citizens. Giving children a religious foundation for moral life is the cheapest and most effective means for reducing crime and the economic and social costs of maintaining prisons.

Education is also conducive to a sound and prosperous economy in other ways. There cannot be a sound economy without honesty and respect for other people's right to a life worthy of human dignity, and for people's property. An educational system whose main goal is to prepare each generation for a life motivated by self-interest, personal gain, profit, and greed fails to prepare our youth for honest and fully responsible citizenship.

Intentionally rooting out religion from education, which the founders of our nation considered "necessary," for good government, and substituting secularism, forcing it upon all our children through a public school monopoly, little wonder that so many of our judges and legislators formed by that system find themselves incapable of providing us with justice and just laws. They reflect their education.

By tax discrimination against religious schools and removing religion completely from the formation of our youth, our society has come to the point of not knowing how to prevent or reduce its heavy crime rate. Without religion, it is unable to find a solution for the ever increasing teenage pregnancy rates, the violence in our big cities and suburbs, riots, the AIDS epidemic, or the moral irresponsibility and violence that starts with the greatest child abuse of all, not permitting them to be born. In spite of the fact that we are spending almost five times more on education than we did only twenty-five years ago, we have failed to form our young people to be good citizens. Missing is the ingredient our founders considered "necessary."

To reverse that discrimination, the least we can do is give the churches the same freedom to maintain their schools with their own tax dollars that the people who use public schools have to maintain them with their taxes. Why the double taxation of people exercising their primary right as parents to teach their children in schools that include religion in forming responsible citizens?

The sooner that we overcome our foolish opposition to religion and morality in education, the closer we will be to the ideals of our founding fathers, who considered them necessary for good government. Other nations have taken such steps. So can we. Let the true American spirit of fair play prevail.

Chapter 20
Is There a Solution?

These Are the Problems:

1. *Unemployment,*
2. *Federal budget deficits,*
3. *The national debt,*
4. *Deteriorating infrastructures and environment,*
5. *Poverty, injustice, and associated social evils,*
6. *Inflation and the erosion of the value of money,*
7. *Economic depressions,*
8. *Third World underdevelopment and poverty,*
9. *Wealth concentrated into the hands of the few, and*
10. *Confiscatory taxation.*

There are many proposals for solutions to these problems by eminent economists. Dr. Martin A. Larson presents an excellent and factual review of just about all the recognized economists and theoreticians. The confusion among them and their stubborn adherence to their own theories are great. None of the solutions based on the premise of a fractional reserve debt-based money system is capable of solving any of the problems mentioned, in spite of the best intentions of their proponents.

As shown in all the foregoing chapters, money is the lifeblood of an exchange economy. All trade, all economic activity in a nation that has developed beyond the barter stage, moves on money. The quality and character of the money system used are both crucial and critical.

The problems of ***deficits and debt*** cannot be solved within a debt-based money system because it causes them. The very existence of debt-based money depends on debt. If debt is eliminated, the system is destroyed. The same holds true of ***excessive taxation***. Taxes can't really be cut within such a system because taxes are the system's only support.

The problems of *infrastructures, industry, technology, health care*, and so on cannot be solved by the use of fractional reserve money, because while development creates value, fractional reserve money robs the economy of value they create. The solution to these problems requires money that is based on value in a debt-free money system.

The solution for the problem of *unemployment* depends on solving the problems of development spoken of above. The potential is unlimited. The condition of our infrastructures alone requires more labor than is available. The solution to the problems of *poverty and injustice* is tied to that of full employment at adequate wages and to a stable dollar with a value that is not being constantly chipped away by inflation, which is caused by the use of fractional reserves. *Cutting taxes*, which a debt-based money structure cannot and dare not do, will also contribute immensely to the elimination of poverty and welfare problems.

Inflation and depressions won't be eliminated by a private debt-based Federal Reserve banking system because it doesn't want to eliminate them. Inflation and depression cycles provide the system with the mechanism for achieving great profits—the reason the system was established.

Likewise the ever-expanding economic *gap between the rich and the poor* throughout the world cannot be closed by the debt-based imperialism of money that causes it. Nor can there be *development in the Third World nations* when access to technologies and development of industry, social services, and infrastructures are forbidden them by the institutions of the International Monetary Fund and World Bank.

All of the financial history of the world supports the above statements. More than enough has been presented here to enable the reader to come to the same conclusions.

The international bankers themselves, who certainly understand all aspects of money, agree with this assessment in an unwitting editorial in the *London Times* in response to Lincoln's debt-free money (noted in chapter 11). **The editorial is quoted here again** for the sake of the continuity of the development of this very important chapter on a comprehensive solution to the economic and social problems noted:

If that mischievous financial policy, which had its origin in the North American Republic during the late war in that country, should become indurated down to a fixture, then that government will furnish its own money without cost. It will pay off debts and

*be without debt. It will have all the money necessary to carry on
its commerce. It will become prosperous beyond precedent in the
history of the civilized governments of the world. The brains and
wealth of all countries will go to North America. That government
must be destroyed or it will destroy every monarchy on the globe.*

"Prosperous beyond precedent in the history of the civilized governments of the world" are the bankers' own words.

An Honest, Uncomplicated Money System Is a Necessity

The bankers mentioned above did not call Lincoln's greenbacks "fiat money," as some economists do. They knew better. Actually, all money is fiat money. *Fiat* is the Latin word for "let it be so." Somebody has to be in a position to say the *fiat*, that is, to determine what is going to be used for money.

In 1100 in England, King Henry I said, "Let these wooden tallies be money," and the tallies served as valid and honest money until 1694, though the money lenders threatened to get rid of them much earlier.

Kubla Khan, the great Mongol emperor, said, "Let this bark of the mulberry tree specially treated by the emperor be money." And so it was. First issued in 1260, it can still be found in some museums.

The government banks of Venice and Genoa said, "Let these bills of credit, or these bank notes be money," and they served the city states for 623 years without panics or depressions. The Chinese did this much earlier.

Then came Baron Meyer Amschel Rothschild. He told his five sons to go to the European nations and persuade them that gold should be used for money. That was his *fiat*. Rothschild is quoted extensively as having said, "Permit me to issue and control the money of a nation, and I care not who makes its laws." Gold was then used as money, or to control its issue (along with silver at times) until 1933.

The question comes down to this: "Who is going to say the *fiat* for our nation's money?" Whoever determines and controls the nation's money becomes the actual sovereign power.

Fake *Fiat* Money

In the end, neither wampum, nor the early colonies' bills of credit and bank notes, nor Lincoln's greenbacks, nor even gold survived. The new aristocracy, through its Federal Reserve banks, said, "Let our Federal Reserve Notes be the money of the realm." Federal Reserve notes are based *not* on wealth or production but on government debt. They are fake *fiat* money because they are neither created by nor do they have their value maintained by a sovereign government. The citizens deserve better than that.

Analyzing the factors at work in any system, including the complicated debt-based Federal Reserve notes, we can arrive at the requirements for a simple and honest money system; we learn what to include and what to avoid in order to produce an honest money system that will serve the needs of our country adequately and fairly.

Requirements for an Honest Money System

Requirement No. 1. An honest money system must create money that represents value or wealth based on natural resources and/or productive labor or services. The supply of money based on value inevitably leads the nation to more production, greater prosperity, and a higher standard of living; that is, to more value. Supplying money that has no relationship to value leads to inflation.

Requirement No. 2. Government debt and all other debt as a base for the creation of the nation's money must be rejected. Government borrowing from a private banking institution is a surrender of the nation's sovereignty to perpetual government debt.

Requirement No. 3. To implement an honest and just money system, Congress, and Congress alone, representing the whole nation and not private interests, has the authority to say the *fiat*, that is, to determine what is to be our nation's money, to issue it, and to control its value. Congress has been delegated by the people to be their legitimate and sovereign government, not the new aristocracy. Congress is responsible to the people who elect it for what it says *fiat* to, for creating the nation's money and regulating its value. The colonial states gave up their sovereignty and power to create money and regulate its value to Congress, not to any private central banking system. They did it in the interests of unity and for the well-being of the whole nation, not to enrich any private monopoly. For Congress to give away that sovereign power to private bankers was an act of treason, clear betrayal of their trust and their country.

Requirement No. 4. Whatever Congress chooses for its *fiat* must *not* be a commodity, like gold or any other scarce material, which can be monopolized by any private individual or group of people. Monopoly ownership or control of the commodity used as a basis for money would again deliver the sovereignty of the nation and creation of money to private interests.

This fact concerning the use of specie was not well understood by the framers of our *Constitution*, or, more likely, the wording for Article I, Section 8, Clause 5, reflects a compromise or concession to the powerful financial interests. They saw the use of specie as an opportunity to regain full control of the money of the new nation. This is not a guess but a reasonable conclusion based on the fact that this is what they later actually did under the leadership of Alexander Hamilton with his "implied powers" expedient. There can never be such a thing as an implied power of legislators to give away a nation's sovereignty.

Thomas Jefferson in general also supported the redemption of money by gold or other specie. He saw that, in practice, issuing paper money would provide a temptation for Congress to overspend and then issue too much money, causing inflation. *That would happen if Congress failed in its duty to maintain a balanced relationship between the volume of money and production of value.* Jefferson agreed that *if* the relationship between the issue of Treasury notes and production of value were strictly controlled, paper money alone, without gold or any other specie, could serve as money. And that control is our next essential for honest money.

Requirement No. 5. The supply of money must be controlled by the government *professionally* through a branch of its treasury department, acting for Congress in such a way that there is an equilibrium between the wealth of the nation and money, its symbol. This must be done by preventing counterfeiting and by the government's twin powers of creating the nation's money and removing it from circulation through taxation. To say that Congress cannot be directed to issue and control the nation's money in a responsible and professional manner is tantamount to saying that the people of the United States are incapable of providing and electing a Congress that can manage the issue of the country's money honestly.

Requirement No. 6. The money issued by the government must always be full legal tender accepted by the government in payment of all taxes, debts, and obligations, *without restrictions.*

Requirement No. 7. Credit, which is a claim on wealth to be produced in the future, cannot be issued except by the community through its government.

Requirement No. 8. The use of fractional reserves for creating and loaning money must be permanently rejected.

Requirement No. 9. Banking, to keep its original purpose, must be a service to the nation, *not* an industry for profit. There is no practical way of changing our banking system from an industry to a national service short of revoking the Federal Reserve Act and all its subsequent amendments. The Act by its very nature makes all banking an industry and promotes it as such. As a service, banking deserves to be adequately rewarded and fully respected.

A Practical and Scientific Plan Is at Hand

Two distinguished surgeons with a great deal of business and organizational experience, Dr. Charles S. Norburn and Dr. Russell L. Norburn of Asheville, North Carolina, devoted their retirement years to a thorough and scientific study of the U.S. money system and its effects on the nation's economy. They devised a simple plan to change from a dishonest debt-based money system to an honest one *meeting all the above requirements*. They describe the plan in a book entitled *A New Monetary System*, which is now out of print. I update, expand, and explain their plan in chapter 21.

Lessons from the Federal Reserve

Not everything the Federal Reserve did has been bad. We have learned much from its operations. For example, we can see the importance of central banking, which brought a certain amount of order into the very confused banking situation of the early part of the twentieth century. It has also provided us with a template for many efficient procedures that work effectively to achieve the purposes for which the system was designed, namely, the profit objectives of its owners, the banks of the nation. We can apply these lessons in establishing an honest, debt-free banking system.

Above all, the operation of the Federal Reserve system of banking since December 1913 has proved beyond all doubt that those with the power to create the money of a nation derive all the benefits. Repeal of the Federal Reserve Act will open the way for those benefits to go to the new and rightful owners, the government and citizens.

We have also seen that the use of *fiat* money in the form of Federal Reserve notes (paper money without specie) works very well, just as it has for hundreds of years.

Most of all, we learned from the system's architect, Paul Warburg, the absolute need for education and molding of public opinion for the success of our venture.

The total vision of the benefits that an honest debt-free money system can give the nation and its citizens is described in the final chapter.

Chapter 21

Monetary Reform—a Major Change in Our Money System[1]

Chart No. 1 below provides the framework for the numerous sections of the bill proposed here. Studying the chart enables the reader to understand the basic structure, which is fleshed out in the chapter.

Chart No. 1:

The Structure of the Proposed United States Treasury Banking System

1. The **President** (and the **Congress** of the United States) appoints
2. The **Secretary of the Treasury** and **Board of Governors** to implement and administer the Provisions of the Act of Congress establishing the Banking System through
3. A **Central Office** with

4. **Professional Staffs and Departments** needed for the administration and operation of	5. **Professional Staffs** to gather and process data needed to set policies for supplying money through

6. Twelve **United States Treasury Regional Banks** that create the money through loans and grants processed by various departments in accordance with the policies of the Board of Governors and regulations of the Secretary of the Treasury for

7. a) departments of the federal government;
   b) states and local government units;
   c) commercial banks for private lending; and
   d) other institutions as may be provided by law.

No Alternative

The objective of this bill is to repeal the Federal Reserve Act of 1913. There is no effective alternative to taking that step. Bills and memoranda are constantly being presented to Congress for reform of the Federal Reserve or calling for reports or accounting. They have proven fruitless. Even the very powerful Sovereignty Resolution (described in chapter 16) must fail so long as the competing sovereign money power, the Federal Reserve Banking system and its debt-based money system, remain on the scene. There can be only one sovereign power in the nation; any competing power must be disposed of. Otherwise, the money creating power will always prevail over Congress, as it has done in the past. Fortunately, Congress has one important "trump card": the power to repeal the Federal Reserve Act. With this bill Congress will be playing that card.

Another Important Alert

Even with the adoption of this bill to repeal the Federal Reserve Act of 1913, the struggle will not be over. But one crucial battle will have been won. Congress and the nation will still have to face the fact that we are dealing with international bankers who hold the powers that debt-based money gives them throughout the whole world. They really *are* the land lords of the world. Their words—"The Nation that engages in the mischief of creating its own debt-free money must be destroyed"—are no idle threat. They mean exactly what they say, and they will do their utmost to carry out their threat.

However, the United States is strong in many ways. We can steel our wills and face that problem, firmly resolved to contribute to the well-being of *all* nations by eliminating debt-based money and banking systems and replacing them with honest debt-free systems.

Exactly how to go about meeting the challenges of the international bankers, who will try to discredit and destroy any nation that tries to create its own debt-free money, we must leave to trustworthy people committed to such a system and to a fully knowledgeable diplomacy. The author is confident that a nation committed to honesty, justice, and genuine brotherhood will prevail if its citizens prove their mettle with perseverance and love.

The first objective should be to undo what was done at Bretton Woods in 1945. The International Monetary Fund and the World Bank were established there, supposedly to help developing nations. They turned out instead to be the tools the land lords of the world use to throw nations into debt and prevent development. They must be removed from the world scene, along with the debts. At present, 178 nations are members of those two institutions. If, through the initiatives of the United States, their many debts are cancelled, it would not only greatly help those nations, but they would elicit their cooperation in leading the world out of the morass of debt and poverty. Then all nations could "start from square one" to establish debt-free financial structures.

A World Development Bank as called for by Pope Paul VI in his encyclical *On the Development of Peoples* (quoted in Appendix I), could be established to provide needed credit of debt-free money for true development of precisely those areas which the present IMF and World Bank conditionalities forbid: education, health, infrastructures, industry, and access to modern technology. This could all happen once we mature enough to get beyond our juvenile preoccupation with profits and self-interest, understand the real meaning of love, and reach for the goals of international cooperation and brotherhood proposed for us so passionately by Popes Paul VI and John Paul II.

We must begin in our own nation by adopting the Norburn Plan.

The Norburn Plan

Of all the many proposals offered on how to accomplish the changeover from a debt-based to a debt-free money system, none meets all the requirements for such a system better than the Norburn Plan. It is scientific, logical, and well elaborated.

One of the best features of the plan is that it follows the pattern of efficient organization under which the private Federal Reserve system now operates its debt-based money system. This will make the change to the new and honest debt-free system the Norburn Plan proposes much easier. In fact, this new debt-free system will be simpler and will not need many of the procedures now used by the Federal Reserve. Their plan is really Thomas Jefferson's plan in its essentials.

The original text of the bill proposed by the Norburn brothers is used below freely, without quotation marks, because it would be cumbersome in a text I have so heavily adapted. I fully and gratefully acknowledge that the plan presented here is essentially their plan.

The changes I have made are intended to make the plan more understandable by ordinary citizens. It is extremely important to remember that no such major change as that proposed by the Norburn

164

brothers can be implemented without intelligent and sustained support from ordinary citizens. To give that support, they need to understand what is involved in bringing it about.

No step given here may be omitted in the following bill without danger of leaving a loophole for the current owners of the nation's money system to regain control of it once this bill restores it to Congress. They *will* most certainly try to regain control. History shows us that.

The Proposed Bill, with Commentary (*In italics*)

Step 1:   A Congressman Introduces the Bill
A bill to vest in the Congress of the United States of America the sole, absolute, and unconditional power and duty to issue the nation's money and regulate the value thereof, pursuant to Article I, Section 8, Clause 5 of the *Constitution of the United States of America.*

The bill as presented is not something new but a confirmation of a power any sovereign nation already has by virtue of its nature as a sovereign nation. The United States Constitution *reaffirms that sovereignty.*

Section A. Be it enacted by the Senate and House of Representatives of the United States of America in Congress assembled, that, pursuant to section 30 of the Federal Reserve Act of December 23, 1913, wherein Congress expressly reserved to itself the power to repeal said Act, the Congress does hereby Repeal The Federal Reserve Act of December 23, 1913, and all amendments and laws dealing with it and with banking and/or in any way conflicting with this new law now enacted. This ends the term of office of every Federal Reserve official. (A simple majority vote in both houses of Congress and the President's signature is all that is required.)

Thus, as soon as there is a majority of knowledgeable legislators, and equally knowledgeable citizens to support them, the bill will be passed. The president's signature is also required. The repeal of the Federal Reserve Act will then be accomplished, and a new and honest debt-free money system can be implemented based on the provisions that follow.

Section B. The outgoing officers are hereby directed and required to surrender to the Secretary of the Treasury, acting for Congress, the Federal Reserve buildings and other property of every nature, and Federal Reserve records in their usual and present condition.

Because of the operations of the Federal Reserve banking (with its controlled depressions and inflationary periods) and taxes, American citizens have paid for this property many times over. Reclaiming it will not deprive any individual or group of individuals of what honestly belongs to it or is its due.

Section C. In compliance with the method of liquidation as laid down in the Federal Reserve Act of December 23, 1913, the Secretary of the Treasury is directed to take charge of the Federal Reserve surplus, which is a matching fund, and with this pay the Federal Reserve member banks for their stock. Following this, the Secretary of the Treasury shall take possession of the stock in the name of the United States government.

If for any legal reason the commercial banks are to be paid before the surplus is taken, the Secretary of the Treasury is hereby authorized to make such payments from any available fund. Any property belonging to the commercial banks shall be returned. It is deemed that the so-called reserve of the Federal Reserve is not property in this sense, but shall be taken over as part of the Federal Reserve banks. There is no use for fractional or any other reserve in the new money system provided by the bill.

This method for an honest liquidation of the Federal Reserve system was provided for in the act itself. Since the stock the commercial banks purchased belongs to them, this liquidation is returning their original investment.

Section D. Clause 1. As hereinafter provided, all government bonds and other securities thus recovered from the Federal Reserve banks shall be tabulated and then burned, thus reducing the federal debt. The new system is not based on such instruments.

Clause 2. All notes and other evidence of debt owed to Federal Reserve banks shall be collected by the Secretary of the Treasury. The bank credits issued to the government and currency printed for the Federal Reserve banks shall be canceled. These are not needed in the new system.

This provision concerns only government bonds and other debt instruments paid for by fractional reserve money created through Federal

Reserve system procedures. These bonds are now in possession of the
Federal Reserve banks drawing interest and adding approximately
$300 billion to the deficit every year. The interest is paid by citizens'
taxes. The procedure to be followed in the implementation of this section
will be given later in the text of this bill.

The bonds purchased by private citizens as savings with money
earned honestly will of course be honored and treated fairly. Destroying
the government bonds and securities specified in this section (those in
possession of the Federal Reserve banks) will eliminate much of the
national debt, and eliminating the annual interest due on these bonds
will significantly reduce the deficit. That alone would have balanced
the budget and left a little surplus in 1995.

Section E. The name of this system is hereby changed to **the United
States Treasury Banking System** and each of the twelve regional
banks shall be called **United States Treasury Regional Bank of** (*its
respective city*).

These name changes will describe the new system accurately.

Section F. Clause 1. The Secretary of the Treasury shall implement
the provisions of this Act of Congress, acting directly under the House
Committee on Currency and Banking; shall reorganize the twelve Regional United States Treasury Banks; and shall form an organization to
operate the United States Treasury Banking System, with competent
civil service employees, retaining those from the old system's clerical and
service force who 1) wish to continue, 2) who can qualify, and 3) who will
pledge support to the new order of national debt-free money.

Clause 2. The United States Treasury Banking System shall be a national central bank consisting of the twelve Regional United States Treasury Banks and their branches, and every privately owned commercial
bank in the United States. Its control shall extend to every money-lend-
ing institution in the nation.

Clause 3. The headquarters of this system shall be located in the nation's capital.

Clause 4. The governing body of the system shall consist of a central
board of three governors, appointed by the president with the advice,
consent, and approval of the lower house of Congress. One of these positions shall become vacant every two years. Thus, the first governor appointed shall serve only two years, and the second four years. All terms
thereafter are appointed to be six years. Any board member, as well as

any other official of the bank, the Secretary of the Treasury included, may be removed at any time by a two-thirds vote of no confidence by the lower house. These three governors, under the Secretary of the Treasury and under the control of Congress, shall operate the system consistent with the provisions of this Act. The system shall be kept entirely free from lobbyists and all other self-seekers.

Clause 5. Any executive of the United States, including the president of the United States, acting in any way to circumvent the United States Treasury Banking System created by Congress by the enactment of this act, shall, upon sufficient evidence of his or her actions, be impeached by Congress.

Clause 6. Hereafter, the only currency issued shall be the United States Treasury Note. These notes shall bear a distinguishing mark of the new system. They shall be in denominations of $1, $5, $10, $20, $50, and $100, and shall replace all Federal Reserve notes dollar for dollar as they come into any commercial bank. For larger amounts, credit vouchers from the United States Treasury regional banks shall be used. The commercial banks will utilize the credit by the use of checks, as at present, as provided later in this act. Coins shall continue to be minted in the same face value as at present.

Clause 7. Money will be passed into circulation by supplying it to three types of institutions:

> The United States government;
> State and local governments; and
> Privately owned commercial banks.

Clause 8. The first principle for furnishing money for *government services* that benefit all the people shall be that this money shall be issued free of any charge to the government entity providing the services. To maintain the proper balance between the value offered and the volume of money in the economy, the money issued must eventually be returned, either for services received or through taxation.

The government thus will never incur a debt for government services, but will always issue sufficient money to pay for the services it offers. The extent to which it will need to recover the money through taxation, will depend on how much those receiving the services will be paying for them and the profits the United States Treasury derives from its operation of the banking system. Section Q provides for uniform interest rates throughout the nation. Differentials in interest rates will be established not on the basis of different states but on the risks involved in various types of loans. Section Q attends to the elimination of political interference with the professional operation of the United States Treasury Banking System in accord with the provisions of this Act.

Clause 9. The second principle for furnishing money to state and local government bodies: The United States Treasury regional banks will issue money in return for state or local bonds carrying a minimum interest charge, just sufficient to cover administration costs. This will provide governmental units with funds needed for various infrastructure capital improvements and yet assure the United States Treasury of a return of the money, to keep the volume of money in balance, prevent inflation, and maintain the value of a stable currency.

Clause 10. The third principle concerns privately owned banks. They serve primarily the private sector, not the people as a whole. They will, however, serve the nation's economy by providing the credit that is so important for a prosperous economy. These banks will borrow all the money they need at an interest rate lower than the current discount rate charged by the Federal Reserve and will lend it at an interest rate low enough to provide easy credit yet high enough to leave the banks a small but adequate margin of profit in order to maintain them as service institutions. These loans must be properly secured, strictly accounted for, and returned with interest as provided for hereinafter.

Money in repayment of the loans returned to the United States Treasury regional banks, with the small interest charge, in the aggregate could conceivably be quite large, and will reduce the need for taxation to zero, given a strong economy. The major change here is that the United States Treasury regional banks are the source of the commercial banks' money. Instead of borrowing from privately owned Federal Reserve banks, which create money and an ever-increasing debt for the government, which has to be repaid with interest by the taxpayers, the government will be creating its own and the nation's money, paying it into circulation for government service and by loaning it as described above (collecting a small interest where applicable), and thus lowering the tax payers' burden. Beyond that significant difference, there will be few changes in the operations of the community commercial banks.

The qualifications of any prospective candidates for the governing board spoken of in Clause 4 are critical. They must be men or women whose honesty and integrity are beyond reproach and who are totally committed to an honest money system in the hands of a sovereign nation. They must relinquish whatever ties they may have had to the debt-based money system of the Federal Reserve. Congress will have the responsibility to assure that these qualifications are fully met. The provision that any official, including the secretary, may be removed by a two-thirds' vote of no confidence by the lower house is an excellent and a wise one. At present, the president appoints the chairman of the Federal Reserve Board, but that is a meaningless gesture because the candidate must first be someone committed to the private Federal Reserve system. After appointment, the chairman is totally independent and "reports to no president," as Federal Reserve chairman Paul Volcker told President Reagan.

Section G. The Secretary of the Treasury is hereby authorized to use out of surplus funds already appropriated such sums of money as may be necessary to carry out the purposes of this act until the new system can be put into effect. Thereafter, the management of the United States Treasury regional banks shall be so adjusted as to be not only self-supporting, from interest paid on its loans, but to produce revenue for the Treasury.

The surplus funds mentioned can be from the Treasury's own operating budget or any other funds appropriated by Congress, whose responsibility it is to implement the provisions of this act. It is understood, of course, that the operation of the system by Congress will not be an operation for profit, as industry is meant to be, but as a service to the citizens of the country mandated by the Constitution. *Nevertheless, it is possible that more revenue will come to the Treasury from interest payments than is presently received from taxation. In that event no taxation will be needed to regulate the money volume and maintain the economic equilibrium necessary for a stable dollar and economic prosperity without either inflation or depressions.*

Section H. The United States Treasury regional banks, under this new management, shall forthwith resume their present function of issuing money and credit, and with these serve the nation, as provided below.

Section I.
Clause 1. The United States Treasury regional banks, taken over from the Federal Reserve system, will already have in full operation most of the departments required for the new system. These may be easily adapted and others established by the board of governors and the Secretary of the Treasury as required for conducting the functions of the new banking systems in a professional manner.

New departments each United States Treasury regional bank will need immediately to fulfill the functions of the new money system:
1. *Special Drawing Rights (S.D.R.) Department* to issue credit at interest to commercial banks.

2. *Department of United States Currency* to receive coin and currency from the Bureau of Engraving and Printing and supply them to the commercial banks.

3. *United States Treasury Federal Tax Department* to receive the federal taxes and turn them over to the General Fund Disbursing Department, where they are to balance out, within a practical margin, with the expenditures of U.S. government agencies.

In paying out, the government adds to the money supply. Taking in taxes decreases the volume of money in circulation, keeping the money supply in balance and thus maintaining the value of the dollar and avoiding inflation while providing for a progressive economy with full employment for the citizens.

Clause 2. The central office of a typical U.S. Treasury regional bank will house the regional bank's officials and assistants; and their staff of accountants, statisticians, computer experts, and other personnel needed for operations. This office is to be connected with every other department by current computer technology, which provides it with access to records of every transaction. This will permit either the details or the sum total of every type of operation, such as loans made, loans collected, money withdrawn from circulation and canceled, and money remaining in circulation, as well as other pertinent information, to be available instantly to every bank in the system.

The officials in this central office will receive orders from the governors' office in Washington, transmit them to the proper divisions of their bank, and bear final responsibility for their proper execution. They also direct the accounting and the gathering and analyzing of data from the entire economy and transmit these reports to the main United States Treasury office in Washington for consideration in decisions made by the governors.

Section J. Refer to earlier section f, clause 8:
Clause 1. Each week the Secretary of the Treasury shall prepare a list of the United States government monetary requirements for the coming week. This will include payment of the salaries and wages required in the operation of all the departments of the federal government and of all government programs that affect the people of the nation as a whole, as approved and appropriated for by Congress.

Clause 2. This weekly requisition shall not include self-balancing or self-supported programs, such as Social Security, which are funded by their own special taxes and not by the general taxing power of government. *Eventually* the request should also exclude general programs affecting the needs of particular groups of citizens, such as housing, agriculture, and health care. These needs can be served by the private sector, with the assistance of financing as provided in subsequent sections of this act, far more efficiently and economically than by government bureaucrats.

An honest money system with adequate employment and credit will enable all able-bodied citizens to take care of their own needs with dignity and without the intrusion of government. People who are not able-bodied or who are victims of circumstances can best be served by state or local governments, with nothing more than funding at the federal level.

The principle of subsidiarity requires that good government allow its citizens to take care of their needs at the lowest level that they can. Government from the top deprives people of freedom, dignity, and self-respect. Eventually such government invades all areas of human life and assumes total control through unelected bureaucracies, which continue to grow and consume all the wealth the citizens are able to produce. That is fascism.

Section J. Continued:

Clause 3. These monetary requirements will then be provided for by credit being issued to whatever department needs the money. This will be done at the central office of the Treasury Department, following policy and instructions of the board of governors, by credit entries on its books. A voucher showing the credit issued and checkbooks to use in paying its obligations will be furnished to the department making the request for funds.

As the checks are presented at the commercial banks throughout the nation for cashing or for credit on their local bank's books, the money will increase the money supply of the nation. As the checks are returned to the United States Treasury regional banks for clearance, they will be charged to the accounts of the departments that issued them, canceled, and returned to the respective departments concerned.

This procedure is similar to the way the Federal Reserve system now creates money, with some very important differences. These are:

1. The Federal Reserve system as a private institution must have a government bond before it creates money for the government. This adds to the national debt and obliges the government to pay additional interest and thus collect more taxes.

Under the new system, when the United States Treasury clears the checks and cancels the credit previously issued, there is money in the economy that is free of any government debt or interest obligation requiring more taxes from the citizens.

2. What the Federal Reserve does suits its plans as an industry "for profit," with no control by Congress. It never reveals those plans or

172

lets the government in on them. Whatever the United States Treasury does under this new system is done as a service to the nation and is under the control of Congress.

Section K. Confer Section F, Clause 9:

Clause 1. *The state or local government unit* that needs to borrow money for government, social needs, or infrastructure, in accordance with the general policy of Congress to assure fairness to all sections of the country, will be able to obtain a loan by meeting these requirements:

a. The Unit's voters must approve tax-supported interest-bearing bonds at a low and lenient rate set by Congress to minimize the burden of local taxation and to allow progress in the Unit's economy and early retirement of the bonds.

b. The state or local government unit is forbidden to sell the bonds to, or in any way borrow the money from, any private individuals or financial institution, except the United States Treasury.

c. The government unit will apply to a regional bank for the loan, submitting the interest-bearing bonds as security.

Clause 2. The United States Treasury Regional Bank's division for state and local loans will issue the credit on its ledgers to the government unit requesting it and will send the unit a credit voucher showing the credit, along with a supply of checks. The checks are to be imprinted with the name of this division and, in a subheading, with the name of the unit receiving the credit.

Clause 3. The unit that receives the credit will use these checks to pay its bills for its purposes. When accepted at any commercial bank and deposited to the accounts of contractors and suppliers, these funds enter the nation's economy and increase the money supply. The commercial bank or banks where these checks are deposited or cashed will send them to the United States Treasury Bank Check Clearance Pool for clearance. There each commercial bank concerned will receive credit for them. This will increase its credit in its Clearance Pool account. At the same time, the account of the government unit that issued the checks will be charged the amount of the checks. The checks will be stamped paid and returned to the government unit as its evidence that it has used that much of its credit and paid its bills.

The original indebtedness of the government unit to the United States Treasury Department remains, along with the unit's bond, which that department will retain until the government unit retires the loan

173

by payment of the principal and interest, at which time the bonds will be returned to the unit.

Clause 4. For the payment of its bonded indebtedness to the United States Treasury Regional Bank, the state or local government unit will collect taxes and send partial or full payment by check drawn on any commercial bank where it does its banking to the United States Treasury Regional Bank's department from which it received its loan.

Clause 5. At the Treasury department that issued the loan, the amount of payment on the *principal* will be deducted from the original credit entry made when the loan was granted. This will remove that much money from the money supply of the nation, which was increased and put into circulation when the loan was granted. The *interest payment* on the loan is sent to the general fund department. This too is money being taken out of circulation by the unit's local taxes, but this amount has not been created by a loan. So it is not used to offset a loan but is being returned to the general fund to reduce its expenditures and need for taxation, thus lowering the tax burden for the citizens. Records of all transactions are to be sent to the control office, where the money supply is monitored.

The checks for principal and interest payments are sent to the check Clearance Pool for clearance. There, the accounts of the commercial banks upon which the checks were drawn are debited, and the checks are stamped paid and returned to the government body that wrote them.

Section L. Refer to Section F, Clause 10: The *true* personal ownership of all privately owned financial institutions shall be recorded by the officers of such institutions in the office of the United States Treasury and in the office in which the institution does business. This information shall be at all times available to the general public.

This section requires that true owners be identified and the information open to the public. This is not true of the present Federal Reserve system, which has consistently resisted all efforts to open the records of both its activities and its true and complete ownership not only to the public but even to government requests. Technically, the Federal Reserve system is owned by the commercial banks. But who owns the top twenty-five megabanks where most of the speculative mischief takes place is their secret. Nor is the ownership of all the other commercial banks generally available to the public.

Section M.
Clause 1. All commercial banks shall be national banks. The banks not now of this nature shall be converted immediately. All shall be under the

direct supervision and control of the Secretary of the Treasury, operating under policies consistent with the provisions of this act as set by Congress. They will remain privately owned and all their current divisions that are already in operation and running smoothly will continue.

Clause 2. The United States Treasury Regional Banks shall create and lend money to the commercial banks at a *low rate of interest*, for reloan, dollar for dollar, to the commercial banks' customers at a *higher rate of interest*. The interest rate differential shall accrue to the commercial bank; the basic low rate to the United States Treasury. This differential shall be set by Congress for the entire nation, in order to forestall speculative transfers from state to state.

Clause 3. Each United States Treasury Regional bank shall set up on its ledgers at the Drawing Rights Division and assign to each commercial bank in its district a drawing right (the right to borrow money).

The amount of each commercial bank's drawing rights at the United States Treasury Regional Bank shall be determined in accordance with the need for expansion or contraction of the money supply as established by the board of governors and the approved needs of the commercial bank. This shall be determined professionally by the Treasury Department, not by politics. Congress shall be finally responsible that such professional approach be taken.

Clause 4. Each commercial bank receiving its Drawing Right will get a certificate of authorization from its Regional United States Treasury Bank, giving the limits for its borrowing and a supply of blank checks that the commercial bank will use in exercising its drawing right. The blank checks will have on their face the heading "(regional Treasury Bank's name) Drawing Rights" and a subheading identifying the local commercial bank by name, location, region and computer number.

Clause 5. The commercial bank will receive the full amount to be drawn; there will be no discounting. No interest will be charged the bank until its drawing right is dated when the loan to the customer is granted. Simple interest will be payable at the expiration of the loan. Loans to the bank customers will follow the same rule in regard to interest payments.

Clause 6. The money supplied by the Regional United States Treasury Banks through this division shall be the only money either borrowed or loaned by the commercial banks. There shall be no loans of the bank's money or the customers' money. Fractional reserve banking is absolutely forbidden. Likewise, the private creation and issue of bank credit in any form is absolutely forbidden.

Clause 7. The commercial bank's services shall consist of being custodian of its customers' money, clearing their checks, making loans, and collecting loans. It will make charges for these services. It will not pay interest on the customers' funds because it will not be using them in a profit-making business thereby exposing them to loss.

Clause 8. All banks shall be examined at irregular intervals by rotating civil service bank examiners and accountants.

Commentary on Section M: This section will change the whole concept of banking from an industry primarily for profit to banking as a service institution, operating at a profit with well-paid officers and staff, but primarily as a service to the citizens of the nation.

The twelve thousand commercial banks throughout the small communities of our country will welcome the change to an honest and stable money system once they understand it and its advantages. They are having a difficult time under the Federal Reserve system, especially during depressions. During 1992 the 25 Megabanks we have mentioned made record profits; that same year, 440 of the banks the average citizen deals with failed. Depressions, caused by the powers that know how to profit from them, bankrupt smaller community banks.

The customers' deposits shall be neither borrowed nor loaned. This will assure the customers that their money is safe. The stable value of the dollar that the United States Treasury Banks will maintain will assure the customers that the money they keep on deposit will maintain its buying power. This alone will more than offset not receiving interest on deposits. Investment will be done or not done by the customers themselves, as they see fit, with the degree of risk they choose to take. The Federal Insurance Corporation, which was unable to handle bank losses without the tax payers' help, will not be needed under the new debt-free monetary system.

An Introductory Note for Sections N and O

The provisions in these sections are essentially the same as those followed today by the debt-based fractional Federal Reserve system. Simpler steps are specified by this act of Congress in order to close every foreseeable loophole that could give current or future financiers an opening to regain their debt-based fractional reserve operation of creating the nation's money. Citizens must be constantly on the alert in protecting government creation of money, free from government debt and fractional reserves.

Section N. Making Loans in the Debt-Free Banking System
Clause 1. In order to keep the relationship between the United States Treasury Banks and the private commercial banks simple, it is hereby ordered and required that in each commercial bank there shall be established a loan department, if the bank does not already have one.

Clause 2. The sole and exclusive function of this department shall be borrowing money from the Regional United States Treasury Banks through the use of the Special Drawing Rights for their respective regions, and lending that same money to the commercial bank's customers, following the procedures given below.

Clause 3. The loan department of a commercial bank shall be distinct from every other department and shall not collect the loans or perform any other banking operation. This is to maintain the identity of its unique relationship with the United States Treasury in furnishing the money created by the United States Treasury Banks. It is understood that smaller community commercial banks may need to share personnel with more than one department.

Clause 4. The loan department's equipment shall be furniture, ledgers, computers, loan records, and Drawing Rights checks—no money, money claims, or vault. Its sole stock in trade shall be its Special Drawing Rights at the U.S. Treasury Regional Bank and the blank checks with the regional bank's name on them and its own name in subheading.

Section O-1. The Procedures for making loans at commercial banks shall be as follows:
Step 1. Loans applied for and granted at the loan department of the commercial bank are to be made following U.S. Treasury Bank regulations, at simple interest. Renewals shall be new loans.

Step 2. The customer gives the bank's loan division a note or mortgage covering the amount of the loan as agreed upon.

Step 3. The customer receives from the loan department the commercial bank's check drawn on its Drawing Right Account at the Regional U.S. Treasury Bank for the full amount of the loan.

Step 4. The customer presents the check at the bank's customer window and receives the money: cash or a deposit to customer's checking account.

Step 5. Both the customer's note or mortgage and the check from the commercial bank shall be stamped with the date issued and the date due. Each instrument will note the principal loaned; interest due the

177

Regional United States Treasury Bank, interest due the commercial bank, and the total.

Step 6. When the loan department's check on the commercial bank's Drawing Right is received at the Regional United States Treasury for clearance, the commercial bank named on the check will automatically receive a credit to its account in the check Clearance Pool, raising its total credit there. This credit is the new money at its point of insertion into the money supply of the nation. Its creation at this point is triggered by the loan for which the commercial bank had no funds in its check Clearance Pool prior to the loan.

The Federal Reserve banks do exactly the same thing today. They create the money for the government by taking the bond the government "sells" them for funds they create by entry of a credit for deposit to the government's treasury account at the respective banks.

Step 7. The commercial bank receives its loan from the Regional United States Treasury Bank in the credit to its account at the Clearance Pool.

Step 8. The check is then sent to the commercial bank's Drawing Right department at the Regional United States Treasury Bank. There the department enters the amount of the checks as a credit to the total money supply and a debit to the commercial bank's drawing right account, showing that the commercial bank has borrowed the money and will be repaying it.

Step 9. The commercial bank's check shall then be stamped "Paid" and kept at the special drawing rights department as evidence of the credit created for the commercial bank. When the bank pays its loan on the due date, the canceled check is returned to it, completing the whole transaction. The money supply will be debited and the commercial bank's account will be credited by that amount. The money created by the loan will have done its work and this transaction will serve to keep the money volume in balance.

Section O-2. Customers will repay loans at the commercial bank as follows:

The customer at due date shall repay the loan and interest at the commercial bank's collection department. To renew the loan, the customer shall arrange for a new loan at the bank's loan division, following the same procedures required for the initial loan.

Section P-1. The procedure for repaying the commercial bank's loan to the Regional United States Treasury is as follows:

178

Step 1. At the same time that the customer's note or mortgage is due and paid, the commercial bank shall repay the principal and the interest to the Regional U.S. Treasury Bank's special drawing rights department.

Step 2. The commercial bank's own check in payment of the principal will raise the bank's special drawing rights account by that amount, offsetting the debit to that account made when the amount was borrowed. This credit in the commercial bank's SDR account will also result in the regional bank's debiting the money supply. (This was credited when the SDR account of the commercial bank was debited.) By payment of the loan, the money has been taken out of circulation; that is, the loan created the money, and the payment of the loan removes the money. This step serves to keep money supply in balance.

Step 3a. The interest that is paid on the loan also removes money from circulation. But this money was not created by a loan; it had to be earned by the bank's customer and the commercial bank's services. So it must be treated in a different way when it is received at the Regional United States Treasury Bank.

The interest due the Treasury from the commercial bank goes to the government's general fund. As this interest took money out of circulation, it will now enable the government to require less in tax money to maintain the volume of money in balance—both interest received and tax revenue do the same job. It is conceivable that the interest revenue received from the loaning operation of the new banking system could exceed current income tax revenue and make the income tax unnecessary. This would greatly enhance the funding needed for the nation's infrastructures or other worthy programs, at whatever level necessary to keep the money supply in balance and the value of money stable.

Step 3b. The interest from the customer due the commercial bank is credited at the Regional United States Treasury Bank to the commercial bank's check Clearance Pool account. The bank's check is then returned to the commercial bank.

In our present debt-based money system, interest also is money that has to be earned by the citizens and removes money from circulation, but none of it goes to the government. It all goes to the private owners of the banking system.

Section P-2. If a customer's loan is not paid, the following procedures apply:

Clause 1. If the customer's loan is to be renewed, it shall be in the form of an application for a new loan, as specified in Section O-2. In that case, the commercial bank shall also apply for and receive a new loan, but shall pay both principal and interest to the SDR department of the United States Treasury Regional Bank, even though the customer did not pay. The commercial bank will receive proper credits as provided for in Section P-1. Procedures for new loans (Section O) shall be observed.

Clause 2. If the commercial bank stays within the United States Treasury's guidelines concerning securing its loans to customers to prevent losses, the commercial bank shall be held harmless in the event of a default on a loan. That loss will be the responsibility of the Regional United States Treasury Bank.

Clause 3. As stipulated in a previous section, the difference between the rate of interest the Regional United States Treasury Banks charge the commercial banks and the interest the commercial banks charge their customers shall be enough to pay for good services and no more.

Section Q. Interest rates for the use of United States Treasury money shall be uniform throughout the nation (and eventually throughout the world). This is intended to discourage shifting funds from state to state and nation to nation for quick, manipulative profit that contributes nothing of value to the community. These rates shall be set by the United States Treasury operating the system professionally for Congress; rates can be different for each and every type of loan.

Section R. To obtain currency and coin, the commercial bank shall send its request and cashier's check to the Regional United States Treasury Bank's currency department. The commercial bank's check shall then be debited to its account at the check Clearance pool and credited to the Regional United States Treasury Bank's currency department, which shall send the currency and coin requested to the •commercial bank. The credit shall then be forwarded to the Bureau of Engraving and Printing account at the check Clearance Pool, which will enable it to replenish its supply of currency and coin by the amount.

Section S. Loans outstanding as of the date of the passage of this act shall receive special treatment as follows:
Clause 1. The loans outstanding as of the date of the repeal of the Federal Reserve Act are hereby declared as valid debts owed by the borrowers to the banks.

Clause 2. The money for outstanding loans is hereby recognized as money created by the fractional reserve debt-based banking rules when the loans were made; it is therefore not all honest money earned by the bank loaning it.

Clause 3. Nevertheless, the money so created is now in circulation in the form of Federal Reserve notes and dollars credits and has increased the nation's money supply. As the loans are repaid, this money will be removed from circulation. This shall no longer be done by Federal Reserve banks, which do not exist as of the date of the passage of this Act, but by the new Regional United States Treasury Banks. The money will then again be paid or loaned into circulation as determined by the United States Treasury board of governors to maintain a balance in the volume of money in the nation's economy.

Clause 4. As these loans are repaid to the commercial banks, the commercial banks shall send both principal and interest to the special drawing rights department of the Regional United States Treasury Bank. There the total amount shall be debited to the money supply and credited 50 percent to the commercial bank's account at the check Clearance pool and 50 percent to the general fund of the United States Treasury. This shall be considered a just and favorable settlement for the commercial banks and a reimbursement to the nation for the use of a debt and fractional-reserve money system, as well as in lieu of income taxes (from which the Federal Reserve banks excused themselves).

Clause 5. From the date of the passage of this Act, all new loans and repayments of them shall follow the procedures in Sections O and P. *Renewal of old outstanding loans* shall be treated as new loans and follow Section O, with the first repayment via new loan to be sent to the special Drawing Rights department and be subject to the settlement specified in clause 4.

Clause 6. The stipulation that the commercial banks' own funds shall not be available for loans is to be strictly observed; it is repeated here to emphasize that the enhancement of the bank's account at the Clearing Pool in the settlement for the old outstanding loans shall *not* entitle the bank to use those funds for loans. The only money available for loans by the commercial banks shall be the money borrowed from the Regional United States Treasury Banks. The banks, as well as individuals, shall be free to use their own funds for other investments, assuming the risks that go with them, but exclusive of any kind of lending business.

Section T.
Clause 1. Neither the United States Treasury nor any other department or agency of the United States government, or of any state or local governments, shall advance money, credit, or guarantee to any private corporation or individuals, except through the commercial banks, as provided in this act, Section M and the following.

Clause 2. The United States Treasury Banking System shall be the sole source of money to the United States government and its agencies, and to all other state and local government units, as provided in Sections J and K.

Clause 3. The commercial banks shall be the sole suppliers to private corporations and individuals of money and credit created by the United States Treasury Banking System.

Clause 4. Depositors' money may be loaned by such financial institutions as savings and loan associations, credit unions, and investment banks, under conditions established by the United States Treasury board of governors, for purposes for which they are chartered. These institutions shall strictly abide by the regulations governing the safety and risks involved in each type of operation, shall provide their own insurance through private corporations, and shall provide the public with full information concerning the risks as well as the advantages to be derived from these investments.

Clause 5. Any attempt to furnish money for lending from any private source except in the manner provided for in the above clause of this section, or any attempt to subvert the purposes of this act and return the creation of money to a private organization or individual, shall be deemed an act of counterfeiting, for which Congress shall provide punishment as established by the *Constitution*, Article I, Section 8, Clause 6.

Section U.
Clause 1. The Regional States Treasury Banks shall clear their own checks, just as Federal Reserve banks cleared theirs under the Federal Act that is hereby being repealed. They shall collect on checks for all out-of-town commercial banks and shall record all aggregate local clearing by shifting, in the regional bank check Clearance Pool, funds from one bank's account to that of other banks, as needed.

Clause 2. The commercial banks shall provide this clearing service for their customers through the United States Treasury Regional Banks, at the customers' expense, it being a service to their advantage.

Section V.
Clause 1. The commercial banks shall receive their customers' deposits, for which the bank will pay no interest; but instead they shall make a service charge for providing security and the convenience of a checking account.

The commercial banks in the new United States Treasury banking system do not use the depositors' money for investment and speculative

purposes, as the banks belonging to the Federal Reserve system do to-
day, exposing the depositors to risk of loss or to the necessity of a bailout
by the taxpayers. Therefore it would not be fair to expect the commercial
banks to pay interest on those deposits. The prospect of depositors pay-
ing for banking services and not receiving interest is more than compen-
sated by the real and permanent benefits they will derive from an honest
debt-free money system. If the commercial banks wanted to include
these services and also pay a little interest there is nothing in this Act
to prevent that so long as their ordinary interest income is adequate.

Section W.
Clause 1. The Congress of the United States of America, pursuant to the
provisions of the *Constitution*, Article I, Section 8, Clauses 5 and 6, and
of this act, shall provide such penalties as will adequately and effectively
protect its power to create the money of the nation and regulate its value
through the United States Treasury Banking System as provided in this
act from any encroachment.

Clause 2. Specifically, upon complaint initiated by the United States
Treasury's bank examiners, or by any member of Congress, involving
noncompliance with any provision of this act by any banking institution
chartered to provide banking services within the United States of
America, or by an employee thereof, the United States Secretary of the
Treasury, upon conviction, shall dismiss such employee from any further
employment within the United States Treasury Banking System, in addition to any penalties determined by Congress. In the event that the
banking institution itself is found guilty of the noncompliance through
its board of directors and refuses to comply, the United States Secretary
of the Treasury shall revoke its charter to do business, in addition to
other penalties determined by Congress as the gravity of its noncompliance may require.

Clause 3. Any attempt to furnish money for lending from a private source
except in the manner provided for in Section U or any attempt to obstruct
or in any way to impede the United States Secretary of the Treasury
from implementing this act; or any attempt to subvert otherwise the
purposes of this act and to return the creation of money to a private
organization or individual shall be deemed an act of counterfeiting for
which Congress shall provide punishment as established by the *Constitu-*
tion of the United States, Article I, Section 8, Clause 6.

Section X.
Clause 1. The board of governors of the United States Treasury Banking
System shall be accountable to Congress for the honest and professional

implementation of this act. It shall use state-of-the-art technology to gather and evaluate economic data and the reliability of various indices and shall use the services of the best accounting professionals to determine within an acceptable tolerance how much money should be in circulation in relation to the true value that is being produced, the productive capacity of the economy, the unfilled needs for employment, and to ensure adequate incomes that will enable especially the lower third of the population to purchase the products and services made available to satisfy their basic needs.

Clause 2. After ascertaining the relationships spoken of in Clause 1 of this Section, it shall be the duty of the board of governors of the United States Treasury Banking System to determine how much money is being withdrawn from the volume in circulation for the conduct of government and for other expenditures appropriated by Congress, how much is not retrieved by the interest received by the United States Treasury, and how much needs to be withdrawn through taxation in order to maintain a stable dollar; and at the same time to provide for a prosperous economy without placing unnecessary tax burdens on the citizens. It shall then provide Congress with guidance for the proper tax-and-appropriation policies. It shall perform these duties utilizing the best professional services available.

Clause 3. It shall be the duty of Congress to respect the professionalism of the United States Treasury Department and to avoid all political interference with its professional operations.

The provision in this clause is essential to prevent political interference with the United States Secretary of Treasury carrying out financial policy as established professionally by the board of directors, which could cause inflation through an excessive issue of money.

Clause 4. It shall be the duty of Congress to establish for the citizens of our country a United States Monetary Institute. This will have two major responsibilities: First, the training of qualified civil-service personnel to handle the finances of the nation, as well as foreign exchange, in accordance with the Unites States Treasury Banking System as provided in this act; second, the education of the citizens, keeping them alert to the constant threats, schemes, and deceitful propaganda of the financial powers.

Section Y.
Clause 1. This act shall *not* be repealed. Repealing it would be tantamount to repealing Article I, Section 8, Clause 5 of the *Constitution,*

which this act seeks to implement, reaffirming the nation's sovereign power over the creation of money and maintaining its value.

Clause 2. Any effort in Congress to repeal or weaken this act or promote a constitutional convention shall be considered prima-facie evidence of bribery, and the offender shall be expelled by a majority vote of the legislative body to which he or she belongs, and shall be indicted by a grand jury and tried for that crime.

It shall be the duty of Congress to be vigilant to this and any other threat to the permanence of the United States Treasury Banking System as instituted by this act and to alert their fellow American citizens to the dangers, counting on their support in opposing such threats.

Clause 3. This act may be amended only for the purposes of improving the efficiency, services, or organization of the operation of the United States Treasury Banking System by the majority vote of both houses of Congress.

Clause 4. Any decisions found necessary for a prompt and smooth changeover from the Federal Reserve banking system to the new United States Treasury Banking System not covered by the preceding sections of this act shall be decided by the board of governors in consultation with the Secretary of the Treasury, whose responsibility it is to implement the provisions of this act.

Section Z.
Clause 1. It is anticipated that the passage of this act will cause an enormous temporary shock to the financial markets.

For years the Federal Reserve system, the International Monetary Fund, and the World Bank have been engaged in looting and devastating the economies of many nations. The financial markets are now operating in an artificial stratosphere in which structures such as derivatives lay claims to some $40 trillion of earned wealth, which no nation's economy can deliver. In such an extremely speculative environment, all these financial institutions are all destined for a disastrous fall. So let them fall now while the fall can still be managed. It will be a healing experience for many nations, enabling them to start building a solid future for themselves with honest earned investments and debt-free money created by their own sovereign governments.

Clause 2a. It is not the mind of the new United States Treasury Banking System, the Secretary of the Treasury, or of Congress to see any injustice done. Therefore, the board of governors with the Secretary of the Treasury and the United States Treasury Banking System shall make every effort possible within the provisions of this act to see that no genuine investors of earned income shall suffer financial harm in the changeover. This does not include speculative income created by borrowing or manipulation that was subject to the risks in the Federal Reserve financial system.

The purpose of this clause is to protect the genuine investor of earned income in any business from harm as far as possible.

Clause 2b. Commercial banks, deprived by this act of their "for profit" status, will certainly see the price of their stocks drop. The Secretary of the Treasury with the board of governors and Congress shall deal fairly with the stockholders who invested earned income in these stocks. They shall provide for reimbursement of the original value of those investments, exclusive of speculative or stock-split gains, but allowing a reasonable dollar amount added to the original investment to compensate for the loss of the purchasing power of the dollar during the time their money was invested. This shall be deemed a generous settlement completely entrusted to the discretion of the board of governors of the United States Treasury Banking System and not subject to any litigation.

Clause 2c. Bank holding companies shall be liquidated and the banks strictly forbidden to compete with their customers in any way. Banking services as provided for in this act, strictly controlled trusteeship, and credit cards at a proper rate of interest approved by Congress shall be the banks' only functions.

Clause 2d. Those United States government bonds representing the national debt of $5 trillion that are in the possession of the regional Federal Reserve banks as of the passage of this act shall be returned to the government and shall be destroyed, as stated in Section D. The need for the United States Treasury to sell government bonds or other debt instruments is eliminated by the institution of this new money system under the provisions of this act. The bond markets, of course, will reflect this.

United States government bonds in the possession of retirement or other trust funds, or investment funds shall be exchanged either for cash from the United States Treasury Banking System or for other short-term United States government bonds carrying a lower interest rate, no greater than the maximum interest that the United States Treasury Banking System charges for the loans it provides under Sections L and M, initially at the option of the owners of these bonds. Eventually they shall be retired for cash, depending on the ability of the economy to absorb the additional money, as determined by a board of governors with the responsibility for maintaining the stable value for the dollar.

Clause 4. Following the period of implementation and adjustment, the United States Congress, the Secretary of the Treasury, and the board of governors of the United States Treasury Banking System shall be receptive and open to further development of services to private associations, like the savings and loan associations, credit unions, investment banks, mortgage companies, licensed brokerage firms, all regulated by law and financed by private earned income financing and strictly regulated and monitored by the United States Treasury Banking System in accordance with varying degrees of risks involved in each type of financial operation and its speculative character.

Under no circumstances shall any of these financial associations be permitted to conduct a lending operation based on any type of government debt or guarantee, or on any type of fractional reserve or margin. It is possible that for the more conservative associations the United States Treasury Banking System could arrange to supply money in keeping with the sections in this act dealing with loans. In dealing with these financial matters, Congress and the board of governors shall be constantly vigilant that no situation develop that could allow the so-called big investors of this or any other nation to regain the power of creating and managing the nation's money and consequently its economy.

Chart 2 below summarizes the characteristics and differences between the two systems:

Chart No. 2

Comparing Structures and Characteristics of Present and Proposed Banking Systems

Present (Federal Reserve Banking System)	Proposed (United States Treasury Banking System
Central banking system made up of	Central banking system made up of
Twelve regional Federal Reserve banks	Twelve regional United States Treasury System banks
Owned by commercial banks (investors)	Owned by the people of the United States
Serving as a "banker's bank," intended for its owners' profit objectives	Serving the nation's needs for conduct of government services, commerce, infrastructures, and employment through its commercial banks

Creates banking as an industry, but one that produces no value	Restores banking to its original purpose as a service
Creates money and debt for the government by loans	Creates the nation's money by loans to commercial banks and communities and by grants
Receives bonds from the United States Treasury in return for Federal Reserve bank credits	There is no need to issue bonds and go into debt
The government obligates itself to pay interest on the bonds and to collect taxes to do so	There is no interest to pay. Instead, the government collects modest interest on its loans, providing revenue that further decreases the need for taxes
Commercial banks loan money they do not have, creating it on the basis of fractional reserves	Commercial banks do not lend anything but money loaned to them at interest rates lower than they now pay. No fractional reserves are allowed
Creates money as claims on value without creating value, in effect looting value from the nation's economy	Creates money for value received or value to be created, in effect adding to the value of the nation's economy
Allows the big banks to create money for buy outs, derivatives, and other speculative ventures, further looting the economy	Does not provide money for speculation, only for actual or future production of goods and services
High interest charged on loans claims money that was never created when the loans were made. This further depletes the economy while creating profits only for the banking industry	Very low interest also takes money out of the economy, but this accrues to the Treasury and can be replaced by new money created for goods and services, again adding to the prosperity of all
Depositors' money is used in the conduct of business and is only as safe as the individual banking enterprise	Depositors' money is never used for loans; it is kept safe for depositors as a service

Depositors receive a small interest payment, which never equals the loss in value of the dollar through inflation	Depositors receive no interest, but the stable value of money more than offsets the loss of interest
Governed by an independent Federal Reserve board of governors	Administered by the Secretary of the Treasury and a board of governors fully accountable to Congress
The appointment of members to the board of governors by the president is made from candidates acceptable to the owners of the debt-based fractional reserve banking system	The appointment of members to the board of governors is made by the president, subject to the approval and possible dismissal by Congress
Creates more government debt because its whole existence depends on debt	Is debt-free and will eventually rid the nation of government debt
Control of the money supply is for the profit and speculative objectives of its owners. It continues to erode the value of the dollar by adding to the government debt	Control of the volume of money is for the purpose of keeping it in balance with the goods and the services produced and maintaining a stable value for the dollar

Except for the very significant differences, noted in the act, most of the procedures for the operation of the new system will follow the procedures of the Federal Reserve system, which have been perfected over eighty years.

Some consequences of the differences shown above are these:

1. No government debt will be incurred when money is created by loans and credits and government expenditures in the United States Treasury banking system. The Federal Reserve debt-based system, on the other hand, has quadrupled the national debt (from $1.142 trillion in 1982 to more than $5 trillion in 1997) and has it increasing by $1.2 billion a day.
2. United States Treasury–created money will be backed by the productive capacity of the citizens and will create wealth for the nation. Federal Reserve–created money is backed by government debt, which removes wealth from the people and places it in the hands of the owners of the debt.

3. Interest on money created by the United States Treasury banking system will go to the United States Treasury, lowering the need for taxes, or to furnish funds for major infrastructure improvements, or to provide funding to community commercial banks so they can maintain their services to their communities. Interest on the Federal Reserve banking system's money, on the other hand, goes to increase the big banks' profits, removes money from the economy, gives nothing in return, and increases the need for taxes.

4. The United States treasury banking system will be accountable to Congress for regulating the value of the dollar to keep its value stable. The Federal Reserve banking system is not accountable to anyone.

5. The United States Treasury banking system plan is honest and based on production and real assets. The Federal Reserve banking system, based on government debt and fractional reserves, is inherently dishonest.

6. The United States Treasury banking system's objective is to narrow the gap between the rich and the poor. The Federal Reserve system by its very nature as a fractional reserve system keeps on widening that gap.

Note

1. This chapter contains a great amount of detail. It is assumed that the reader has read all the preceding chapters, and will devote the time required to read—and re-read—this chapter for full comprehension.

Chapter 22
Political Reform

A Challenge

It is for us the living . . . to be dedicated here to the UNFINISHED work which they who fought here have thus far so nobly advanced . . . that government of the people, by the people, for the people shall not perish from the earth.

—Abraham Lincoln

These words were spoken by our greatest president, Abraham Lincoln, on November 19, 1863. They challenge us to pick up the unfinished work advanced by those who gave their lives during the Civil War to continue the work of providing the nation with a more truly representative government of, by, and for the people. Lincoln was not completely successful in achieving that objective; the financial powers proved too powerful and prevailed in stopping him, ultimately with an assassin's bullet. It appears that we have moved further away from the unfinished task instead of advancing it.

Government by the People and for the People?

There are 435 representatives and 100 senators, 535 in all. When they bow to the pressure from the president and the thousands of lobbyists working for special interests worldwide, can we say they are representing the citizens? Nobody seems to know exactly how many lobbyists there are; not all are registered. Estimates range all the way up to eighty thousand. Whatever their number, they greatly outnumber the legislators, whom they influence to make laws serving the interests of their employers. Hardly government by and for the people!

Not all legislators succumb to lobbyists and pressure from the president. Nevertheless, it is evident from the legislation that is passed, that dies in committees, or that is rejected on the floor of the legislative bodies, that for the majority of legislators reelection is their main concern, not the common good of the people.

Perhaps the greatest assault on *"government of the people, by the people, for the people"* comes from the government bureaucracies, created but not adequately controlled by Congress. They are not elected by the people, yet it is through them that the land lords of the world exercise the most power over the citizens. By their regulations, often confusing and contradictory, they deprive the citizens of elementary rights and justice; there is no recourse from their decisions, regardless of what the *Constitution* says. And one of our Supreme Court justices was bold enough to state that the *Constitution* means what the justices want it to mean. So, by whom and for whom are we governed?

The Norburn brothers have this to say about the political dictatorship that blocks monetary reform: "The right to issue money is a matter of total power. In practical terms, all else is secondary. The financiers who control the Federal Reserve and the great commercial banks haven't the slightest idea of giving up their racket. They will never relent. . . . They will spend billions in propaganda; fight; stop at nothing to retain their favored position. . . . None of them have any real concern for our country, save to plunder it. These men are, however, not the ones to call to account. Our own elected officials . . . and we who have submitted to this misrule, must bear the responsibility for its correction" (chapter 6).

Thus the brothers first plan genuine political reforms that will provide a truly representative government. However, their plan departs so dramatically from what we have now that I do not believe it is achievable without prior monetary reforms; it is essential first to remove the financial powers opposed to meaningful political reform.

The monetary reforms are more readily achievable within our current political environment, in which Congress has already reserved to itself the power to repeal the Federal Reserve Act. All the citizens need to do is to elect a Congress that will be committed to repealing the act. That is a formidable challenge in itself. But it is achievable with sufficient prior education and a new political party. Then the road to full political reform will be open.

During the twenty-four years since the Norburn book was written, the land lords of the world have extended their rule throughout the world. The Norburns wrote an extensive and well-documented account, but for us the examples given are dated. Assuming that people already know a good deal about current abuses of trust, we'll turn our attention here to a positive approach to correct a system that fails to provide a "government of the people, by the people, for the people."

Political Reform

First, we take a look at how the people in office got there. How much say did we have in selecting the candidates to be our representatives? Candidates for office are usually selected by a political party. We could define a political party as a group of citizens organized for the purpose of winning public office, directing the policies of the government, and enjoying the spoils.

The leadership of a political party consists of two principle elements: first those of great wealth who have an interest in the outcome of the elections; and second, the national political bosses, who expect the party to produce the desired outcome for its financial supporters. Office holders and others seeking office cluster around these bosses and must make peace with them in order to gain support from the party. That is called "party discipline."

The membership of the party consists of those who are willing to support the party by their dues and services. They trust the promises of the party. They see the country (and themselves) benefitting from their membership.

Some belong because of a genuine and sincere patriotism and a desire to help their country. They assume that the leadership of the party is honest and place their hopes in the party's promises.

Others seek the prestige and power that go with their party holding office. They may enjoy the prospect of a well-salaried position if their candidate wins, or hope to gain wealth through influence of the office, or desire to help their friends through their position in office. Even the very rich, with no need for any more wealth, may see a particular party as the road to power and a name in history, or to protecting their own class and increasing its wealth. The list of reasons could be as numerous as the people joining the political party.

At the bottom of all the business deals and promises made within the political system, prior to elections is the overriding need for money to finance the campaigns for high office. Campaigns and elections now cost billions of dollars. Indeed, the 1994 Republican Party victory alone is reported to have cost a quarter-billion dollars, just a minor mid-term election. Great amounts are needed just for the nominations, so political bosses cater to the wealthy and to special interests who can be counted on to provide money. When elected, office holders must take care of these benefactors first, almost always at the expense of the people, who thought they were electing a government to represent them.

John H. Bear, Ph.D., and associate professor of journalism at the University of Iowa, made this statement and asked the question that follows it:

> The skillful disbursement of $500 million through saturation advertising and public relations techniques, campaign organization, and "good faith" patronage commitments will assure White House occupancy for any man in a presidential campaign—regardless of his personal qualifications. Does the democratic process contain the seed of its own destruction?

Aspiring presidential candidate Phil Gramm, asked for the answer, said, "I have the best friend anyone can have in politics, money."

Bear also asks if we have ever wondered why a president at the outset of his administration, against all precedent, would announce that he would rely on the Federal Reserve exclusively for monetary policies and economic regulations, and would recognize the complete independence of the Federal Reserve to carry out these programs.

That was in 1970. In 1992, President Clinton made the same kind of an announcement, carried in the daily press throughout the country.

Specifics for Political Reform

The Norburn brothers suggested specific changes to our political system. Their major objective is to remove structures that keep the government from being a government of, by, and for the people. Their proposal entails the following provisions:

1. The people of each congressional district and each state must be free to choose their own representatives and senators without interference or the influence of interests from outside their districts or states. Therefore, no money, lobbying, or assistance to a campaign from the outside will be permitted. This includes, for example, speeches by any current member of Congress, governor from another state, or anyone from the presidential office.
2. A political party, with a well-defined platform that takes a clear stand on one or two major issues and objectives, shall be responsible for the candidates it provides from within each district and state,

for the national ballot. These candidates shall be from among citizens at the grass-roots level who share the views represented by the party.

This provision will save both the candidates and the voters from the confusion that results because of the large number of topics and the ambiguities that are presented by the various parties, often overlapping each other. When a given party is successful in the election, it will need time to implement the one or two major planks of its platform. Then it can take up other issues. If it doesn't resolve these to the satisfaction of the majority of the citizens, the party can be ousted in the new elections that will follow shortly.

3. Every two years each political party shall have a well-advertised district or state caucus. The purpose of this caucus shall be to discuss thoroughly and select *their own district priorities as well as one or two specific pieces of national legislation that are a major concern in the district, as well as what issues of national interest need attention from Congress.* This shall all be done with loyalty to the basic philosophy and major objectives of the party. When consensus has been arrived at, the caucus shall elect by secret ballot one person from within the residents of the district who is in sympathy with the declared position to represent the district at the national convention.

We can see that this is representative democracy in action. Each congressional district is a sealed unit representing that segment of citizens, not financial or lobbyists' interests from outside its boundaries. The state is a sealed unit in the election of senators. The same procedure can be adapted to local elections.

4. A national convention of each party shall be held soon after the caucuses are held, once every two years. This shall be a very simple and quiet working convention for the sole purpose of writing the party platform for the forthcoming election. The platform shall be written in simple, clear, and specific language so that every candidate and every voter may know exactly what is meant. The proposed handling of just a few important issues should be gone into thoroughly, so that the voters can distinguish at once the differences between or among the parties. Platforms prepared this way by representatives from the district and states will reflect what is for the best interests of the country instead of serving the special interests and lobbies that now control the legislative processes. These conventions shall be held close to each other, so that the public will be able to compare them easily.

5. Following the national conventions, the federal government shall require all newspapers to carry the full text of each party's platform in the next two Sunday editions. This shall be deemed a patriotic duty of the press and a service to the country. Each party's platform shall be binding on all the party's candidates, elected officials, or their appointees. In their oath of office, they shall be required to subscribe to the provisions of the platform.
6. The logical time for candidates of any party to register and announce their candidacy is after the platforms have been published. Allowing two weeks for this should be ample.
7. A candidate may use his or her own money, up to a modest limit, and donations from constituents to explain and promote the platform of the party he or she represents, not to exceed $1,000 from any one individual. No donations from any corporate body or PAC will be permitted.

   A strict accounting of all of the candidates transactions and expenditures shall be required, and before the primary elections, the local press shall report these records without charge. No funds shall be spent after such disclosure. The total amount a candidate may spend shall be limited by law. These conditions allow candidates to surface on the basis of qualifications rather than fund-raising. Failure to meet any of these requirements shall disqualify the candidate.
8. Federal primary elections shall be held at federal expense, nationwide, on the same day. The candidate receiving a majority of the vote in his or her district or state shall be declared the nominee of the party having the platform he or she has pledged to honor. In the event that no candidate receives a majority, a run-off election will be held promptly between the two top candidates with no further campaigning. The one of these two receiving the highest number of votes shall be declared the nominee. Nominees, upon confirmation, shall take an oath that, if elected, they will follow the party's platform.

The National General Election

1. The campaign now shall be for the party's platform and not for any candidate. Each party will already have its candidates selected.
2. The federal government shall bear the total cost of the campaign. It shall be a modest but adequate amount, the same for each party.

196

No candidate shall be allowed to spend his or her own—or anybody else's—money. A strict accounting and required penalties shall support this requirement.

3. Leaders of all parties shall have equal time and space for coverage in the media, *not* to endorse candidates but to discuss the issues of the day and to explain the party platforms.

4. Political opinion polls shall be forbidden by law so as not to interfere with the elective process.

5. National ballots or machines shall carry only the names of the parties, not the names of any candidates. The election shall be held the same day in all states. No partial results shall be announced while the voting is still going on in some sections of the nation. Only after *all* the votes are counted shall the victorious party in each district and state be announced.

The Election of the President and Vice President

To eliminate the billion-dollar political spectacle and media "hoopla" with which we are entertained every four years in electing a president and vice president, we need to go back to the thinking and ideals of the founders of our nation.

Article II (Sections 2 and 3) of the *Constitution* reflects some of their thinking. These sections direct the appointment of electors, who presumably would be the best qualified citizens available, ones with no financial interest at stake but only the best interests of the nation at heart.

These men were to elect the president and vice president. It was that system that gave us presidents and vice presidents like George Washington, John Adams, Thomas Jefferson, and James Madison. With the advent of active political parties and the growing power of the financial interests strongly engaged in the political process, the electors provision has become a meaningless gesture and has no value whatever as far as contributing to the ideal of government by, of, and for the people is concerned.

True political reform would eliminate the so-called anachronism of the electoral college but keep the principle of making the choice of president and vice president truly representative of the people. This is what the reform details presented here propose to do, as elaborated by the Norburn brothers.

6. The newly elected congressional representatives so carefully chosen by their respective districts every two years form the closest bond with the people. It is assumed they are the majority party.
7. The selection of president and vice president shall be placed directly in the hands of the members of the House of Representatives just elected. The speaker of the House shall have no vote except in the case of ties. In such an event, the Speaker shall cast the deciding vote.
8. The first order of business of the newly elected House of Representatives shall be the selection of the president and vice president. All persons nominated shall come from the political party having the majority in the House and must subscribe to the party's platform.
9. **The procedure:**
9a. Each member of the House must submit in writing two names of people he or she deems best qualified to be president, at least one from outside his or her state. All balloting shall be secret on the floor of the House, but all ballots shall be signed and later made public. The speaker of the House shall tabulate the results, break any tie by his or her own vote, and shall announce the names of the five receiving the most votes.
9b. The second ballot would eliminate the lowest of these five; the third ballot the lowest of the remaining four; the fourth ballot the lowest of the remaining three. This would leave two candidates. *The fifth ballot would determine which of these two will be president and which vice president.*
10. The term of office of the president and the vice president shall be two years—until the next election of the next House of Representatives. After being elected, the president and vice president shall be sworn in and take office immediately. This would eliminate what we call a lame-duck presidency, with the opportunity that this presents for abuse of the remaining period of a presidency.
11. If in two years the same political party elects a majority of the representatives, at their first meeting they shall vote whether or not to confirm the president and vice president for another two-year term. If the vote for either is negative, a new election shall be made for that vacant office. If the vote is in the affirmative, the incumbent shall continue in office. The term of office for both presidency and vice presidency shall be limited to three terms (six years).
12. In the case of death, recall, or retirement of the president, the vice president shall succeed as president. The House shall then lay aside all other business and shall elect a new vice president.

Judiciary Reforms

This properly comes under the heading of political reform inasmuch as the whole process of presidential appointments to the Supreme Court has been disgracefully politicized.

1. The term of Supreme Court justices shall be reduced to eight years; a justice may serve no more than two terms.
2. Congress shall be able to override the ruling of any court, just as it can override a presidential veto, by a two-thirds majority.

Other Reforms

1. Congress shall have the authority to recall any and all elected or appointed officials by a two-thirds vote of no-confidence by the House of Representatives.
2. Retirement at age seventy shall be mandatory for all federal officials, elected or appointed.
3. Representatives shall be well-compensated but also forbidden to accept other compensation.
4. Senators, who have not been mentioned specifically in speaking of these reforms, should have their term of office on a par with that of the members of the House; they too could be elected in each state following the same directives as for the district representatives.

Consequences of These Political Reforms

These political reforms would bring government back to the ideals of the founders of our nation, a government of, by, and for the people. Starting at the congressional district level, the reforms presented offer true representation of the people of the district by eliminating all financial and personal influence from outside of the district. By limiting the contributions and expenditures for the campaigns, the reforms broaden the prospects of more qualified candidates entering the race for political office. Further, excluding special interests at the district level and obliging the local candidates to concentrate on issues important to the local district and the nation, and on loyalty to the party platform, will enable the representatives to be better legislators and not to succumb to the influence of lobbyists.

The proposed reforms provide for fair and well-ordered political campaigns, involving the media in preparing the people to vote intelligently and responsibly on the issues rather than engaging in delving into the personal lives of the candidates and what they did five, ten, twenty years ago. Good people can make mistakes and bad people can change. What is important is who and what the candidates are now and how qualified for office they are now.

These political reforms greatly simplify the political process of representative government and will save billions of dollars' worth of meaningless campaigning and wasted time. They will help bring honesty and integrity into government and avoid the interference of the big financial and other special interests in the conduct of government. Elected officials will not need to waste their time or money on campaigning for reelection. Having done their job well and loyalty to the party platform will be the only requirements for reelection.

With the executive and legislative branches of the government in the hands of a majority party, there will be unity and cohesion. Meaningful legislation prepared from input at the grassroots level at the national convention and embodied in the party's platform will be passed.

With these monetary and political reforms implemented, the United States will be a model democracy. Other nations will no longer submit to "shadow democracies" imposed on them by the International Monetary Fund and World Bank and other members of the new aristocracy.

A New Majority Political Party

In the light of our financial and political history, there is no possibility whatsoever that either major political party will pass either the monetary or the political reforms presented in the last two chapters. Both the Democratic and the Republican Parties are so completely dominated by the land lords of the world that it is impossible for them to institute anything more than cosmetic changes, ones that do not touch the privileged positions of their masters. They will continue to haggle over balancing the budget like they have been doing for the past several months as of January 1996, because as mentioned here before, it is impossible to balance the budget or amortize the national debt under the debt-based money system without destroying the social and infrastructure programs of the nation and the money system itself. No one can serve two masters as they are trying to do.

A new political party is urgently needed, completely free from all ties to the financial interests following the debt-based money system and fractional reserves. There are many good legislators in the present major parties who could qualify for membership in the new party and be better able to serve their country without being subjected to the dictates of financial or other special interests.

The Minimum Requirements for Membership in the New Political Party

Members of this new party must take pride in being invited to take part in a *true aristocracy* of citizens, who, by Thomas Jefferson's definition, aim to be best qualified by virtue and talents to assume the responsibility of democratic government for the nation.

They must be totally convinced and committed to the proposition that only through a well-organized new majority political party can the necessary agenda for monetary and political reforms be effectively implemented.

Finally, they must accept and be loyal to the party platform.

The Present Potential for a New Political Party

During the 1992 presidential campaign, 22 percent of the voters were dissatisfied with the candidates from both of the major parties. And many people didn't vote at all. There are many state legislatures that have passed resolutions and memoranda calling upon Congress either to repeal the Federal Reserve Act or to audit or control this independent, private, banking monopoly. Among the states passing such resolutions are Arizona, Arkansas, Idaho, Washington, Oregon, Indiana, Alabama, Texas. They would be happy to support a new political party with monetary reform on its platform.

On the educational front, Ludwig von Mises Institute at Auburn University (Auburn, Alabama) provides training for thousands of economists and is strongly supportive of a repeal of the Federal Reserve Act of 1913 and of monetary reform. In addition, the Schiller Institute, with American headquarters in Washington, D.C., deserves special mention. Its philosophical basis is even more sound that than of the Von Mises Institute and it is influential throughout the whole world. Its twin is the *Executive Intelligence Review*, an outstanding international news source with headquarters in Washington, D.C., and European headquarters in Germany and Denmark (with fifteen other international bureaus). The Liberty Lobby and the Spotlight provide a strong voice for monetary reform, which includes repeal of the Federal Reserve Act as well as an alternative news source. Lyndon La Rouche and Associates espouse sound philosophical principles and many sound economic objectives. The practical solutions they propose are obscured for the average citizen by excessive wordiness and critical abrasiveness.

There are many other smaller educational entities. They all limit their effectiveness in the public arena by being unnecessarily abrasive and critical of their opponents. Naturally none of the above-mentioned media will receive a kind word from the establishment-controlled news media or the land lords of the world, because in varying degrees they represent a threat to them. There are some positions in all of the above organizations with which the author does not fully agree, but the emphasis here is on support for the things they all do agree on. They are significant and present a basis for cooperation and the unity without which none of their goals can be achieved.

On the political front, the United We Stand America organization founded by Ross Perot has over four million paid members and could provide a good beginning for a new political party. It has many good objectives, sincerity, and honesty, but is weak philosophically and a disaster in its economics. If the whole organization moved in accordance with the goals for monetary and political reform presented here, it could provide powerful leadership and push for the educational effort needed for a genuinely new political party.

There are some eight hundred other organizations, individuals, incipient political parties, and influential periodicals in the country promoting Jeffersonian populist ideals and reporting developments throughout the world.

There *is* potential for a new political party, but at present efforts are dispersed in many different directions. The example of the original thirteen colonies should inspire and encourage them to coalesce and form one powerful united front. The colonies gave up their sovereignty and power to create money for the sake of the unity that was necessary to become one nation. The sooner we accept the challenge of cooperation called for by Pope John Paul II and others, the better for all concerned and for the world.

Late 1996 Presidential Primaries Update

The vote totals being called in to VNS (Voter News Service), a corporation owned by CNN, ABC, CBS, NBC, and AP wire services, leaves the way wide open for computer fraud and vote scams and does not bode well for honest elections.

Chapter 23
How Monetary and Political Reforms Can Be Achieved

Strategic Essentials

If citizens take the time to plan carefully what is essential to success and commit themselves to the task out of the motive of genuine love for their country and for the poor of the world, they are capable of instituting reforms. If Paul Warburg, who masterminded the Federal Reserve Act and its passage in Congress in 1913, could achieve the bankers' goals in the face of great opposition and from evidently selfish motives, it should be easier for honest citizens with a cause that already has great support to reach unselfish objectives. We can follow Warburg's successful strategy:

> The articles published by me from 1908 to 1910 . . . constitute a series of persistent efforts to arouse public opinion to a recognition of the fact that banking reform in the United States, in order to be successful, would necessitate . . . radical change (Warburg 1:39)

It was clear to him beyond all doubt that, unless public opinion all over the United States could be educated and mobilized, any sound banking reform was doomed to fail (ibid., 66). It will help to take special note of what he said:

1. It took a series of *persistent efforts* to *educate and arouse the public*.
2. Reform necessitates *radical change*.

The "persistent efforts" were not just those of Warburg himself, but of the new aristocracy headed by the bankers—*well organized, united, and mobilized*. Their goal was to impose their political will upon Congress; their ultimate objective was personal gain. They have continued to be persistent in those respects for the past eighty-four years and will continue to be in the future. Citizens must do no less in order to achieve meaningful reforms.

Public opinion is crucial; it determines the outcome. As Abraham Lincoln said, "Public opinion is everything. With it, nothing can fail; without it, nothing can succeed." The problem we face is not so much opposition as ignorance, confusion, false perceptions of how the present debt-based systems work, a lack of unity, and a lack of a clear sense of direction for reform. We are also at a disadvantage when it comes to the media. So far the major networks have denied access to reform efforts. Therefore we must find other ways of reaching the public and creating the desired public opinion.

Warburg's plan required *that people be made aware of the need to accept radical change* in order for reform to be achieved. For us the change to honest, debt-free money and banking would also be a radical one. While we accept the concept of a central bank, our goal is to change who owns it and by whom the money is created.

Warburg often comments that any reform is doomed to fail unless the public is educated and mobilized. It is a most important point. After three years of intensive education and propaganda, neither he nor the bankers succeeded completely in swinging public opinion their way. They had to resort to intrigue, deceit, bribery, and manipulation of legislators to achieve the passage of the Federal Reserve Act. Current reform efforts, too, must acknowledge the importance of education and public opinion, but efforts at reform must be strictly honest.

We need leaders to help us to coalesce, to become more knowledgeable, leaders with the honesty, integrity, and fearlessness willing to face up to the moneyed interests and call for an honest money system.

The land lords of the world know that they can always count on human weaknesses, ignorance, lack of firm convictions and commitment, and lack of perseverance. Their many past experiences in dealing with ordinary citizens tell them they will always win in the end if they only pursue their goal without relenting.

We can learn from them and, as people who really love our country, rise to the challenge with shrewdness and perseverance equal to theirs in order to pursue an unselfish goal. We have to admit our weaknesses. We need mutual support from one another. And we also need the divine help that will always be there when we seek justice.

We have responsibilities as members of society, families, and citizens of our country. No government can do that for us, and no land lords of the world will. In our past history, leaders attempted to change social and economic structures that were destructive of the welfare of our nation, yet their success was short-lived. Why? They did not have the involvement and support of a fully knowledgeable citizenry at the grass-roots level. Without that support leaders alone are unable to withstand the pressures and power of the moneyed interests.

Political action cannot be dispensed with either. By political action the power to create the money of the nation and its sovereignty were lost. But they can be regained the same way they were lost—through the political process. The necessary political action to do so has been described in chapter 22.

The Formula for Success

The formula for success in any endeavor has been expressed succinctly by a new Notre Dame coach who was given the task of restoring the Fighting Irish to their winning ways. The three indispensable requirements he called for were *trust, love, and commitment*. That formula will work for anybody if followed faithfully.

The first part of that formula is *trust*. We need to trust (1) in our own ability, once we have adequate knowledge; (2) that we can secure the cooperation of our fellow citizens; and (3) that God will support our efforts to change unjust economic structures, as well as ourselves, if we ask.

Second, love for our country and its people, especially the poor, and for God, is the only motivation strong enough for real commitment, the third component of the formula for success. Love casts out fear that prevents commitment. There are many people, including legislators, who have the necessary knowledge but lack the courage to make the commitment. They are afraid to use their knowledge and to help educate their constituents and initiate the significant reforms that are needed. They know from past experiences what the so-called elite will do to them when they come up for reelection. *Courage* has been defined as the ability to do the things we are afraid to do. The courage that is needed for a commitment to reform means facing fears that are promoted widely by the media when the privileges of their owners are endangered.

The Time for Action Is Now

The opportune time for action is now. The mood of the people and candidates during the past election and now is for change.

Both the legislators and the new aristocracy are frightened by the national deficits and debt and the pressures for health-care and welfare reform. They don't know what to do without asking for more taxes, which they know are already too high and would be counterproductive for the economy.

There is no solution to their dilemma within the present debt-based money and banking systems, nor within their two present political parties, most of whose members are committed to those systems and will not change them for fear of not getting reelected.

There is only one alternative left. That is for the grass-roots citizenry to respond to the mood and the need for change by becoming true aristocrats and forming a new majority political party that will institute the monetary and political reforms necessary.

An Example of Citizen Involvement

Paula Gonzalez, a Sister of Charity based on the campus of the College of Mount St. Joseph, near Cincinnati, Ohio, is a model and an inspiration of citizen involvement. All her activity, travels, and workshops throughout the United States, her lectures and writings, deal with ecology. She is not only thoroughly knowledgeable on that subject, but she has a broad comprehension of all the other problems that we are facing on this earth.

Gonzalez says, "We need all the wisdom we can gather right now on this planet if we are going to get out of the mess we are in. We live on a finite planet, in trouble ecologically, politically, socially, economically and definitely spiritually." She points out that we *have* both the knowledge and the tools to change the direction in which we are going, if only we have the *will*, both personal and political, to use them.

Getting Started

While the need for political and economic reforms is widely recognized, especially around election times, various means used to assess the interests of our citizens consistently indicate a very low level of interest in politics by the average citizen. Yet in a representative democracy that is where the action is. One reason for such apathy, like in other areas, is a lack of sufficient knowledge of the issues involved; much "political" discussion is no more than rehashing the personalities and promises of the candidates.

207

So a book such as this one, which gives a definite focus to the kind of substantive changes and reforms that are needed and establishes an intellectual basis for them, requires much more than a cursory reading. It calls for action proceeding from a thorough understanding and conviction of the validity of the reasoning, logic, and principles involved.

From Awareness to Action

The following suggestions have been highly effective in putting ideas into action. They are clearly needed for a massive educational effort.

- Expand your reading, personal study, and understanding.
- Associate with someone else to discuss the issues.
- Seek out or form a study group.
- Join or found a base community, such as those in Brazil and other South American countries, for the purpose of study and action.
- Form action cells, a highly effective tool for the formation of dedicated participants.
- Learn to use the media and communication technologies.

Chapter 24

Consequences and Expectations—a Vision of Life with a Debt-Free Money System

An enumeration of the immediate and near-term consequences of the monetary reform as presented in the act to repeal the Federal Reserve Act of 1913 follows. The points are based on a logical evaluation of the cause-and-effect relationships and the experiences of history in the area of the economic life of nations.

The expectations aspect is bound up with the consequences and forms an integral part with each item. It provides a realistic and practical vision for a nation's economic life with a debt-free money system. This vision is likewise supported by the testimony of the experts and authorities in money matters, the international bankers and financiers.

- The first and immediate consequences will be alarm within the new aristocracy, especially the financial segment of it. If there was alarm back in 1862 when Abraham Lincoln issued debt-free money, followed by a campaign in the media and politics to reinstate the financiers' power, this time we can expect a much stronger reaction. They have been practicing "shock therapy" on nations of the world. This will be a shock to them but really a loving shock that will bring genuine healing both to them and the nation.

- To persevere as citizens, we must be secure in our knowledge and not waver or permit ourselves to be swayed by all the *inevitable propaganda*, lobbying, accusations, labeling, name calling, deceit, distortions, bribery, promises, and so on. We must not allow the history of the 1860s to repeat itself.[1]

- The second consequence will also be earth shaking. The mountains of debt will be leveled. Our national debt will immediately start decreasing. Eventually the national debt will be completely amortized as more bonds are retired and the money channeled into productive enterprises. The national debt will be paid off completely by the retirement of all bonds held by the banking system, insurance companies, corporations, and other institutions, according to a timetable in order not to distort the balance of money volume in the economy.

- The congressional budget will always be in balance.
- With no budget deficit and no further borrowing from a private banking system, and with the United States Treasury receiving interest revenue from its operations instead of paying it out to a private money-creating system, the income tax can be greatly reduced.
- Industry will find that funds released from investments in government bonds will gradually begin to flow into it. That, together with credit available from the United States Treasury Banking System at lower interest rates, will enable industry to finance improved and more efficient production.
- Revenues derived by the United States Treasury from the operation of the United States Treasury Banking System will be greatly increased as the demand for credit is generated by the increased economic activity.
- Much lower taxes and lower interest costs will serve to encourage industry and entepreneurial activity and make them more profitable. These two major creators of jobs will also be enabled to give labor better wages and true investors a better return, as well as making internal financing more available.
- Unemployment will decrease as more and more jobs are created by revitalized industry and entrepreneurs.
- Still more employment will result from rebuilding infrastructures financed by the United States Treasury banking system.
- Service industries will experience the multiplier effects of the healthy productive economy and will be more prosperous, also making a contribution to the solution of unemployment problems.
- Infrastructure needs throughout the nation gradually will be filled as labor is available.
- Poverty and welfare will disappear as more and more people become self-supporting through adequate employment income, lower taxes, and a stable dollar. Full employment at fair wages, sustained with the help of infrastructure maintenance, will provide buying power for the forty million Americans who are now at or near poverty levels, or unemployed, and have many unmet needs. This huge pent-up demand for the products of industry made effective with the purchasing of these forty million, and sixty million middle-class citizens, will keep industry and private entrepreneurs busy indefinitely.

- The gap between the rich and poor, recognized by the media as continually spreading, will begin to close. The rich will not be despoiled of wealth truly earned, yet the poor will have a fair field in which to move out of poverty.
- A greatly reduced need for taxes at the federal level could eventually eliminate the need for the Internal Revenue Service. Its functions could easily be absorbed by the United States Treasury banking system and served by the nation's commercial banks, providing them with an additional source of income at the level of communities throughout the nation. The federal income tax Sixteenth Amendment was adopted to accompany the Federal Reserve Act of 1913 for the specific purpose of enabling the government to guarantee the payment of interest on the government debt, which was planned to grow, even at cost of war. With the adoption of the United States Treasury banking system and the repeal of the Federal Reserve Act, that professed need for the IRS will no longer exist.
- Banking will no longer be an industry for profit, but a highly respected service to wealth-producing industries and the community, which will earn for it just and adequate rewards.
- Commercial banks, divorced from the system of creating debt-based money by the use of fractional reserves, will not have funds for speculative activities such as derivative operations or for the purchase of bonds that tie up funds that should be available to the nation. These banks will be the service institutions that banks were meant to be, completely safe and honest institutions serving their communities using only debt-free United States Treasury banking system money. They will be free from the risks of failure inherent in speculative activities. Honesty and competence of the local personnel will be the only variables required for a completely successful operation and services of the commercial banks.
- Personal savings will be more meaningful and attractive than ever with a stable dollar maintained by the board of governors of the United States Treasury banking system. People will not need to fear the dollar losing its purchasing power in future years. Through such personal savings and other investments, people will be able to assume responsibility for their own health and retirement needs, leaving the government concerned only for the few who are not capable of doing so on their own. The stable dollar will be the result of the United States Treasury's keeping a balance between the volume of money and the production of value.
- Inflation and depression cycles created by the debt-based money banking system operators throughout the world will be eliminated

entirely, first in United States and eventually in other nations as they too reform their monetary systems.

- The stable dollar will make continual pay raises and cost-of-living increases unnecessary.
- Savings will, of course, temporarily remove that many dollars from the volume of money in circulation. The Treasury will remedy that easily by replacing money removed from the economy with new money, which will be doing its job in the economy while savings are waiting to be used when needed. Thus people desiring to save need not feel guilty that their savings are lying idle in the bank. They will not be earning interest but will be keeping their value, which is far better than receiving a nominal interest and losing many times that much through inflation and taxes.
- Investing of surplus earned dollars in private productive industry and entrepreneurial enterprises will offer the hope of increasing true wealth and savings, while accepting the risks of the ventures. These true investors of earned money will no longer have to compete with the big speculators who use huge sums of easily borrowed money created by a fractional reserve system.
- States and communities will be able to issue bonds at very low interest rates to fund infrastructures and improvements. These bonds will be issued to the United States Treasury only, in accordance with the provisions of the Monetary Reform Act establishing the United States Treasury banking system. Infrastructures at the national level will be funded for construction by private industry, involving no interest charges.
- Research and development, technology, and replacing outdated structures will be strengthened by the influx of new money as the various government bonds are gradually retired.
- Lower taxes and credit costs will make it easier for investors of earned funds in industry to make an honest and fair profit.
- All working citizens will be able to support their families in reasonable comfort without the need for both parents to work. Parents being able to spend more time with their children will be a step toward solving the juvenile problems in our society.
- Much of the hopelessness, violence, and drug culture in our society and in the world will disappear with gainful employment, and with this vision of a more certain and dependable economic future and development will come justice and peace.
- Not all problems will be solved by material prosperity. The spiritual poverty in our nation is even greater than the material. But the basic structural causes of institutionalized poverty and injustice in

the world that have been with us for centuries will be eliminated. This will allow greater freedom and more time for the citizens to develop their cultural and spiritual lives.

- The Statue of Liberty will regain its original meaning as *huddled masses* find compassion and welcome at our shores with our nation in need of immigrants rather than rejecting them. Our problems with illegal immigration will likewise ease when other nations follow our example and begin to solve many of their own problems.

The year 1994 marked the third centennial of the creation of a debt-based money and banking systems. Let this year mark the beginning of a new era in the economic and financial histories of the world's nations, an era of true independence and freedom from the economic slavery to which the nations are being subjected by the land lords of the world.

However, let us beware. History shows that the land lords of the world will try to destroy a reform government. Maintaining victory will have a price. The colonists won a great victory on the battlefield in the war for independence and then lost that hard-won victory to the financial interests because they relaxed and let down their guard too soon. We must be the true aristocracy, defined by Jefferson as convinced and dedicated citizens always on the alert to the dangers of losing our victory.

The lesson we learn from the experience of the colonists is not to act prematurely. We must not jump into halfway measures like nationalizing the Federal Reserve banks or agitating for the government to control them. History shows us those measures won't work; the bankers always find ways to get back in control and consolidate their power. Witness what happened when Mexico "nationalized" its banking system. In no time the banks were back with a vengeance.

Or the same powers can just change their address and occupy the offices of the government to make the citizens believe they are national, like the London Exchequer. We have to be ready to do the job completely and not waste our time with halfway measures. The plan in chapter 21 is for a complete changeover to debt-free money and banking.

Do the Land Lords of the World Have a Vision?

You bet your life they do! They have had it for a long time and are now very close to achieving it. It has been in a long secret gestation period, promoted and nurtured by the Bilderbergers, Trilateralists, and Council on Foreign Relations, all the big moneyed interests, all the land lords of the world. Now they feel so sure of success and unstoppable that they no longer hesitate to make it public. In fact, they have to do that if their media are going to do the propaganda for them. The media are their principal creators of public opinion, and they have already been at it at an increasing pace for the last twenty years.

What Is Their Vision?

On June 1, 1994, the United Nations Development Program released its Human Development Report, which confirms what we already know about the land lords' vision from reports of the planning that went on in their Bilderberg and Trilateralist secret meetings for at least the past five years. Their vision is for one world—a new world. They want to get rid of the sovereignty of all nations, one way or another, and put them all under one government, the UN, completely run by the land lords of the world. In other words, they want to create a world dictatorship.

That one world naturally will be created according to their own materialistic and secular image. That has been the great vision they actively have been engaged in planning and now feel close to realizing. The other specifics of the vision the Human Development Report gives are these:
- A *world court* with power to "call the nations on the carpet" if the UN does not approve of what they are doing.
- A *world police*.
- A *world bank*. A nation's central bank can control only one nation. To have all those central banks in sovereign nations around the world will not serve. There has to be a central bank for the whole world in their vision. There already is a World Bank, along with the International Monetary Fund, but to be able to control the economies of all areas of the one world, the central world bank must be the *sole* power.
- A *world treasury* and a *world income tax*.
- A *world military*. The military forces of all developing nations must be dismantled.
- A *world trade and production organization*. NAFTA and GATT are a first step. They will tell you what and where you can produce or what and where you can buy something to eat or the clothes to wear or anything else that their "free market" policies require.

- A *population and development committee*. The first step was the Cairo 1994 conference followed by the one at Beijing. The goal here is to cut down the population, using contraception, abortion, condoms, and so forth.
- An *economic security council*. The purpose of this will be to see that citizens follow regulations using the "bread and butter" approach. Economic welfare will be tied to keeping regulations.
- Not mentioned in the Human Development Report is outcome-based education, but that too is the tool that will help them achieve their vision of the one world. The outcomes will help form their kind of society: secular, hedonistic, insisting on rights, forgetting responsibilities, rejecting absolute values.

These Are the Visions Before You

It is hard to believe that the foregoing are not just fantasies of the land lords of the world. But those are their own statements in the report, seriously made, and the plans are being implemented, though not as quickly as they planned because they are being strongly opposed by nations that treasure their ethnic values, traditions, and sovereignty.

The United Nations

The concepts of one world and United Nations are not evil in themselves. They are good and highly desirable. But true unity and cooperation can only come as a consequence of love in action. Maneuvering nations into debt, forcing "reforms" into debt-based financial systems and so-called "free markets" to be monopolized by the industrial and agricultural land lords, privatizing their resources into the hands of the land lords, dispensing military hardware to create more debt and war, in short, practicing new colonialism, are *not exactly* acts of love. They are not ways to forge unity and a true one world, but only fascism, dictatorship, and more war.

Acts of love on the international level called for by the encyclicals of both Pope Paul VI and Pope John Paul II are assistance and cooperation with the undeveloped Third World nations in the development of their own systems of education, infrastructure, social services, government, and industry, sharing our technologies, helping them to establish their own debt-free financial reforms and respecting their

215

sovereignties. That is all precisely what IMF and the World Bank are forcing those countries to eliminate to be able to pay interest on their debts.

The hour is late. If we citizens choose to stay asleep and then awaken only partially, the media will gently lull us back to sleep or keep us entertained with sports and scandals, as foreseen by editor Phillip Freneau two hundred years ago (chapter 13). When eventually we wake up, it easily could be too late.

Note

1. The reader is invited to review chapter 11, in which the whole story and reason for the international bankers' alarm is given.

Epilogue

The story I have presented in this book is just the tip of the iceberg. What is happening in the world today is beyond the power of words to describe. The devastation of nations and of the human dignity and lives of billions of people striving to maintain some semblance of it are without precedent in the history of the world.

The "imperialism of money" has touched every nation on earth and has already destroyed the livelihood of countless people. It continues to move incessantly and unrelentingly toward its goals of genocide and total domination under the guise and mantle of the United Nations. It is engaged in a war for the minds and souls of humankind.

People have been lulled into complacency by being entertained with sports, casinos, and other trivia, just as ancient Rome kept its citizens quiet and subdued by supplying them with circuses and bread. The pressure is on to make citizens ever more dependent wards of an all-powerful state.

In the meantime, through its control of the media and politics, the "imperialism of money" keeps people in ignorance while quietly taking away their basic rights and freedom. The founders of our nation treasured freedom and shook off the chains of slavery at great cost. But while the people who followed them relaxed their guard and succumbed to ignorance, unaware in sufficient numbers of what was happening, the imperialism of money reared its head again. It did not die in the battles of the American Revolution. It continued to grow ever more bold until it has reached its present position of power. Now it holds almost all humankind in debt and economic slavery.

But it will do us no good to bemoan the past. I wanted rather to bring hope and encouragement, to hold up a vision of what the future can be. Our monetary and political systems will be changed; they cannot go on this way. Whether the change will be by bullets made by our arms industries or by ballots and the love within our hearts is our choice.

This book provides structures that will enable nations to make revolutionary changes in the way they conduct their economic and political affairs in the next millennium. But of itself it will not change anything unless many human hearts are changed. That can be done only by people themselves, with God's grace. For nearly two millennia, the message has been before us: "Avoid greed in all its forms" (Lk. 12:15). . . . "Love one another" (1 Jn. 4:7–21). But so far humanity's love has not been strong enough to prevail over the destructive emotion of greed.

Love must be energized, especially in people who aspire to leadership roles. Without genuine love for God and humanity, people will always fear the risks that go along with commitment and never commit themselves to any worthwhile reform. Love is a *gift* (1 Cor. 13), which must be asked for to be energized by it.

At the beginning of this book, I quoted Robert T. Kennedy speaking of sending forth "a tiny ripple of hope, which multiplied millions of times would build a current that can sweep down the mightiest wall of oppression and resistance." Now, at the book's end, we have come to recognize that we need a spark from the fire of love to kindle a fire in the hearts of millions of people in order to consume the greed and injustice that stand in the way of hope. The hour is late. We do not wish to play on people's fears, but rather to appeal for the love that can conquer all things.

"Someday, when we have mastered the winds, the waves, the tides and gravity, we shall harness for God the energies of love.
Then for the second time in the history of the world, man will have discovered fire." (Teilhard de Chardin). May that day usher in a new century!

Appendix A
Pope Paul VI Encyclical on Development of Peoples—a Summary

Summary of Key Points Made in the Encyclical

The problem "of hunger, misery, endemic diseases and ignorance" and giving the peoples of underdeveloped nations a "wider share in the benefits of civilization" calls for their "*development*."

"Peoples who have recently gained national independence experience the need . . . to seek their own internal social and economic growth so that they may be able to take care of their own people. Those nations want "to take their rightful place with other nations."

While the colonial powers left some benefits that persist, the people were often used to further the colonial powers' "own interests, power, and glory," and "their departure has sometimes left a precarious economy." This caused great hardships, especially for the farmers, accounting for social conflicts and civil wars that "have taken on world dimensions." In the meantime, "a restricted group enjoys a refined civilization."

In this situation of tensions between the old and the new, the people's "moral, spiritual, and religious supports of the past often give way without securing in return any guarantee of a place in the new world. . . . The resulting dangers are . . . violent popular reactions, agitation towards insurrection, and a drifting towards totalitarian ideologies."

The early missionaries "were among the pioneers in material progress as well as in cultural development. . . . However, local and individual undertakings are no longer enough. The present situation of the world demands concerted action based on clear vision of all economic, social, cultural, and spiritual aspects." The unity and cooperation of all people of good will are necessary for such development in all nations.

The Christian Vision of Development

The encyclical's vision is shared by other religions and all people of good will. "Development cannot be limited to mere economic growth." The human must not be separated from the economic, "nor development from the civilization in which it exists." The individual person, endowed with intelligence, free will, and unique talents and qualities, is ultimately responsible for his or her own growth and development as a child of God. In this the person is either helped or impeded by the environment of education and those with whom he or she lives. Impeding personal development are "less than human conditions."

As members of a community, we all have a responsibility for community development. We have received from the past, we benefit from the work of others in the present, "and we cannot refuse to interest ourselves in those who will come after us."

"Both for nations and for individual men, avarice is the most evident form of moral underdevelopment. . . . The acquiring of temporal goods can lead to greed, to the insatiable desire for more, and can make increased power a tempting objective. Increased possession is not the ultimate goal of nations nor of individuals."

The values that will permit authentic development are love, friendship, prayer, and contemplation. Our hearts are too small for the love that we need to have, and they must be "stretched" by prayer.

The Action to Be Undertaken

The encyclical is not just presenting us with some basic principles for the development of peoples, but is calling for "concerted action." It leaves the specific actions to leaders, legislators, and citizens motivated by genuine love and the desire to contribute to the common good.

It speaks of unjust and evil economic structures spawned by avarice and greed and identifies the principal ones as *liberal capitalism and the international imperialism of money*. It condemns them, and says, "It is the responsibility of public authorities to look for a solution . . . to such problems . . . with the active participation of individuals and social groups."

Some basic principles that must govern actions include these:
- "The world is made to furnish each individual with the means of livelihood and the instruments for growth and progress."

- "All other rights whatsoever, including those of property and of free commerce, are to be subordinated to this principle. . . . Private property does not constitute for anyone an absolute and unconditioned right."
- "It is unacceptable that citizens with abundant incomes from the resources and activity of their country should transfer a considerable part of this income purely for their own advantage, without care for the manifest wrong they inflict on their country by doing this."

Together with research, the ability of many to take calculated risks and show boldness in enterprises has made an "irreplaceable contribution" to the development of peoples. There is no quarrel with a *just* form of capitalism invested in such development.

The unfortunate thing is not industrialism as such but the *abuses* centered in greed that provided the occasion for "the international imperialism of money."

The International Imperialism of Money

Pope Pius XI had pointed out the root cause of poverty and oppression in his encyclical *Quadragesimo Anno* as the "international imperialism of money." Paul VI explains that the new industrialism, while good in itself, provided the occasion for certain "pernicious economic concepts" to grow up along with it. They include these premises:

- Profit is the chief spur to economic progress.
- Free competition is the guiding norm of economics.
- Private ownership of the means of production is an absolute right, with no limits or concomitant social obligations.

These three constitute "unbridled liberalism" in economics, which paved the way for "international imperialism of money." All three of those concepts persist to this day and are rebutted as false and inadequate in the encyclical.

It is urgent to remove these oppressive structures from society because the gap between progress of some and regression of others is growing. However, we must be patient and not succumb to the temptation of violence or armed revolution.

"We want to be clearly understood: . . . Development demands bold transformations, innovations that go deep. Urgent reforms should be undertaken without delay. It is for each one to take his share in them with generosity, particularly those whose education, position and opportunities afford them wide scope for action."

The encyclical emphasizes education and support for the family, correct demographics, organization, respect for human dignity, and assistance programs as the proper area of involvement through which to achieve reform. In all of those areas we must "maintain the correct orientation to human dignity, freedom, and man's final end. Above all, we need to be aware of the dangers and temptations of materialism." Part II of the encyclical is an earnest plea for solidarity and cooperation among nations. It supports the concepts of a unified world based on the principles of community and universal charity. It speaks of the great need of nations to build and upgrade their infrastructures, the problems of money and the ever-present need for credit, and suggests a world fund. It calls for international dialogue and cooperation in the areas of trade.

Pope Paul VI, in his speech to the representatives of the United Nations in New York, held out a beautiful vision of what a world authority could accomplish for humanity. He did not identify himself with the United Nations or with the World Bank or the International Monetary Fund, which had been in existence for over twenty years before his call for a world fund. Evidently he knew that these were not doing the job for which they were ostensibly created.

Today Pope Paul would be disappointed to find that the United Nations has degenerated into a political tool manipulated by a few self-serving nations and ideologies, autocratically and arrogantly imposing economic sanctions that devastate whole nations and oppress poor peoples. The World Bank and International Monetary Fund, instead of serving the development of nations, forbid the building of infrastructure, industrialization, and social progress, and impose debt and "conditionalities" for the payment of interest. Missing are the essentials for true cooperation and development: love and community.

In his 1967 encyclical, Paul VI said: "The world is sick. Its illness consists less in the unproductive monopolization of resources by a small number of men than in the lack of brotherhood among individuals and peoples." Our world is much sicker now.

Finally, the encyclical renews its pleas for cooperation and solidarity, even as Pope John Paul does in *Centesimus Annus*. The call is not only to action but also to prayer. "The prayer of all ought to rise with fervor to the almighty. . . . This prayer should be matched with resolute commitment of each individual."

Pope Paul VI closes by saying that "development is the new name for peace," because it removes the principal causes of war.

Appendix B

Confidential Circular from Number 3 Wall Street, July 5, 1863

To Friends and Clients

1. Any number of persons, not less than five, may organize a national banking corporation.

2. Except in cities having 6,000 inhabitants or less, a national bank cannot have less than $1,000,000 capital.

3. They are private corporations organized for private gain and select their own officers and employees.

4. They are not subject to the control of the state laws, except as congress may from time to time provide.

5. They can receive deposits and loan them for their own benefit.

6. They can buy and sell bonds, and discount paper and do general banking business.

7. To start a national bank on the scale of $1,000,000 will require the purchase of that amount (par value) of U.S. government bonds.

8. U.S. government bonds can now be purchased at 50% discount, so that a bank of $1,000,000 capital can be started at this time with only $500,000.

9. These bonds must be deposited with the U.S. Treasury at Washington as security for the national bank currency, that on making of the deposit will be furnished by the government to the bank.

10. The U.S. government will pay 6% interest on the bonds, in gold, the interest being paid semi-annually. It will be seen that at the present price of bonds, the interest paid by the government itself, will itself amount to 12% in gold, on all the money invested.

11. The U.S. government, under the provisions of the national banking act, on having the bonds aforesaid deposited with its Treasurer, will on the strength of such security, furnish national currency to the bank depositing the bonds, at an annual interest of only one percent per annum. Thus the deposit of $1,000,000 will secure the issue of $900,000 in currency.

12. This currency is printed by the U.S. government in a form so like the greenback money, that many people do not detect the difference,

although the currency is but a promise of the bank to pay—that is, it is the bank's demand note, and must be signed by the bank's president before it can be used.

13. The demand for money is so great that this currency can readily be loaned to people across the counter of the bank at a discount at the rate of 10% at 30 days' to 60 days' time, making it about 12% interest on the currency.

14. The interest on the bonds, plus the interest on the currency which the bonds secure, plus incidentals of the business ought to make the gross earnings of the bank amount to from 28 to $33\frac{1}{3}$ percent. The amount of the dividends that may be declared will depend largely upon the salaries of the officers that the banks vote themselves, and the character and rental charges of the premises occupied by the bank as a place of business. In case it is thought best that the showing of profits should not appear too large, the common plan of having the directors buy the bank buildings and then raising the rent and salary of the president and cashier may be adopted.

15. National banks are privileged to either increase or contract their circulation at will, and of course, can grant or withhold loans as they see fit. As the banks have a national organization, and can easily act together in withholding loans or extending them, it follows that they can by united action in refusing to make loans, cause a stringency in the money market and in a single week or even a single day cause a decline in all the products of the country. The tremendous possibilities of speculation involved in this control of money of a country like the United States will be at once understood by all bankers.

16. National banks pay no taxes on their bonds, nor on their capital, nor on their deposits. This exemption from taxation is based on the theory that the capital of these banks is invested in U.S. securities, and is a remarkable permission of the law.

17. The secretary may deposit the public money with any bank at will, and in any amount. In the suit of Mr. Branch against the United States, reported in the 12th volume of the U.S. Court of Claims, reports on page 287, it was decided that such "government deposits are rightly mingled with other funds of the bank, and are loaned or otherwise employed in the ordinary business of the bank, and the bank becomes debtor of the United States as it does to other depositors." Requesting that you will regard this as strictly confidential, and soliciting any favors in our line that you may have to extend we are.

Most Respectfully Yours,
Ikleheimer, Morton, & Vandergould

A Commentary on the Above Circular

The message the circular carries to prospective bankers is quite clear. Let's look again at certain points.

Point 3 tells the whole story. Most people, even today, believe that our money system and banking are government functions, that the Federal Reserve banks are really government institutions. Ask your congressman or senator, or even a Federal Reserve bank official employed and paid by a bank check, not by a government check. They will tell you that the Federal Reserve is a government agency. This is nothing but pure ignorance. All the maneuvering by the big bankers, from Alexander Hamilton to Paul Warburg to the present, has been for private central control of banks and money creation and for total independence and freedom from any interference by the government. There was never any intention that the banks be government institutions or agencies; they are "private corporations organized for private gain."

Under **Point 7** par value has been highlighted. Face value is evidently meant, as is clear from *Point 8*. The government goes into debt to the banks, selling the bonds at half price, which entitles them to interest on the *full* face value of the bonds. Interest is to be paid by the tax payers.

In **Point 9** we learn that the government offers to "babysit" the bonds for the bank. It calls these bonds *security* for the currency it will print for the banks to use in making more loans to people, making another 10 percent on short-term loans (*Point 13*) or to buy still more bonds with, if they wish. What a game! One can almost smell the corruption and bribery among the congressmen who turned over to private corporations the government's sovereign power to create money and then even print it for them.

Point 15 reminds the banks how to create depressions and inflations, a cycle it assumes they already know, providing them "with tremendous possibilities of speculation" and profits from the sufferings of the people. To the land lords of the world, people don't count, only money and profits do.

Point 16. The bankers are exempt from taxation—"a remarkable permission of the law." All they need is legality. Morality is not their concern.

Point 17. Most people think that the money they deposit in a bank is theirs, available any time they want. Honest and stable money is indeed that. But the money we (or a government entity) deposit becomes the bank's stock in trade, part of its business. All the bank gives the depositor is an acknowledgment of its own liability to the depositor. If the bank can't meet that liability, the depositor loses the deposited money.

The Federal Deposit Insurance Corporation (FDIC)

To the question about point 17, does not the FDIC insure the depositors against losses, note that in 1933 the FDIC was created to insure the deposits of individuals up to $100,000 and of banks up to $1,000,000.[1] Both the FDIC and the FSLIC were creations of the Federal Reserve banking system, not of the government. The FSLIC ran out of money by 1989 with liabilities of $100 billion in excess of assets and closed operations, passing its obligations to the FDIC.

On December 31, 1990, the FDIC paid out $4.244 billion to the failed Capital Bank and Trust Co. of Boston, the biggest single payout. During 1990, 108 banks had failed, with an additional 440 expected to fail by the end of 1992. As of July 1992, the FDIC was in the red to the tune of approximately $500 billion, the amount Congress was called upon to borrow from the Federal Reserve, adding to the national debt and to the interest the taxpayers are expected to pay. The Resolution Trust Corporation (RTC) was formed to take over and dissolve the failed banking institutions. By July 1992 it had dissolved 452 of them and placed another 66 under conservatorship. As the assets of these banks are sold and administration expenses deducted, major depositors considered "essential" to the system are reimbursed. In the meantime, government estimates suggest it will take another $500 billion to complete the bailout, not counting any current or future bank failures.

As of December 1995, there are requests before Congress for additional funding, which Congress does not seem to have any problem with. Meanwhile, Congress is debating which social services to eliminate in order to balance the budget, not even mentioning the banking debacle to the public.

This is just one way in which citizens are misinformed and manipulated while the land lords of the world follow the plan laid out by the Confidential Circular toward achieving ever greater profits and financial control of the nations.

Note

1. The Federal Savings and Loan Insurance Corporation (FSLIC) serves the same function for savings and loan associations.

Analytical Index to Facilitate and Enhance Study of the Text

233

To order on your credit card call toll free
U.S./Canada 1-800-882-3273 or
ORDER WITH THIS COUPON

VANTAGE PRESS, INC.
516 West 34th Street, N.Y., N.Y. 10001

Please send me _____ copies of

LAND LORDS OF THE WORLD
Justice and Prosperity vs. Injustice and Poverty
At $17.95/copy plus $2.50 postage & handling
(Please make checks payable in U.S. dollars.)

Name _____

Address_____

City _____ State_____ Zip _____

❏ Check Enclosed   ❏ Visa   ❏ MasterCard
❏ Amer. Ex. ❏ Optima   Exp. Date _____

Card # _____

Signature_____

N.Y. State residents please add sales tax.